权利、权力与权威

——人类社会三权逻辑关系探析

Right, power and authority:
analysis on 3-factor relationship of human societies

宋 波

By Song Bo
Translated by: Guo Ping

本书由美国亚洲文化出版社（Asian Culture Press）在博尔德出版

1942 Broadway, Suite 314c,

Boulder, CO 80302,

United States

封面设计：王林

排版设计：王林

翻　　译：郭平

Published in the United States of America

First paperback edition December 2022

本书2022年12月在美国第一次出版

To protect people's rights (freedom), political power came into being in human society. In gaming between right and political power, authority (authoritarian) can play the role of checks and balances and restraints on right (power), and true authoritativeness (generally accepted by social members) promotes the formation of a good and harmonious order in human society.

为了保护人们的权利（自由），人类社会衍生出政治权力。在权利与政治权力的博弈过程中，权威（威权）可以起到制衡约束权利（权力）的作用，真正的权威（被社会成员普遍信服）则促使人类社会形成良好和谐的秩序。

Table of Contents

I. About Right

目　录

一、权利篇

III. About Authority
(I) Authority in Human Society

三、权威篇
(一) 人类社会的权威

权利篇
About Right

Baby's Cry

The moment a baby is born, he or she instantly has a right --- "to cry" --- which all people believe is its right that cannot be deprived, disregarding this innocent while loud cry has disturbed the peace of others or not. Hence, the doctor or midwife will pat with hand on the soles of the feet of a baby when it is born without crying to force them to make a sound. As we are all afraid that a human baby who has just come into this world cannot "cry", which situation implies that it may have certain disease or die.

A baby is truly separated from its mother and becomes "free and independent" after the umbilical cord is cut. Simply it has no choice but to cry as it's unable to speak. It cries just because he is hungry, or wants to sleep, or is ill, or feels unfit... And no matter what, the parents will try their best to satisfy its needs. In the parents'

婴孩的啼哭

一个婴孩，从呱呱坠地之时，他（她）便有了一种权利——"啼哭"，不管这个稚嫩、响亮的哭声有没有搅扰到他人的安宁，世人都认为这是他（她）的权利，不可剥夺。以至于当一个婴孩一出生不会哭的时候，医生或是接生人要用手拍打他（她）的脚底板，迫使他们发出声音，因为我们都害怕，刚刚来到这个世界的同类不会"啼哭"，因为如果那样，将预示着他们可能带着某种疾病或是夭折。

剪断脐带后，他（她）真正与母体脱离了，"自由了，独立了"，只是因为还不会语言，只能哭，有时是饿了，有时是想要睡觉了，或是生病了，不舒服了…不管如何，婴孩的爸爸妈妈都会尽力去满足。在爸爸妈妈的眼里婴孩的每一个声音，都说明他们在传递某些信息，他们的所有诉求，都是合理的，

eyes, every sound from the baby is conveying certain message, and, all its demands --- breast milk, interesting colorful balloons ... --- are reasonable. The parents would like to give it everything that can make it calm, excited or laugh unreservedly.

A baby who doesn't cry is sure to make its parents sad. Without the "right" to cry, it means that the baby has no way to express its demands, and the parents will anguish for this too. Doesn't anyone anguish in a life without "rights"? The "rights" here refers to the right to cry for hunger, pain... and the right to smile or laugh for happiness...

A baby's "right" to cry has no boundaries. Its requirements are way too simple. It will not disturb the adults' happiness and peace, let alone to harm anyone. Instead, it will make people who see it feel happy and forget their worries and sadness.

A baby is to cry, and, to cry is a "right" exclusively for baby.

母亲的乳汁，有趣的彩色气球，总之能让他们平静、兴奋、大笑的所有东西，爸爸妈妈都想毫无保留的给他们。

如果一个婴孩不会哭，那他（她）的父母一定会非常伤心难过，没有啼哭的"权利"，意味着婴孩没有办法表达他们的诉求，大人们也会因此而痛苦，没有"权利"的人生又有谁不痛苦呢？这里的"权利"就是饿了，痛了，我要哭…开心了，我要笑…

婴孩啼哭的"权利"是没有边界的，他们的要求太过简单，也不搅扰成人世界的幸福和安宁，更不会伤害到谁，反倒会让看到他们的人们感到开心和愉悦，忘记烦恼忧愁。

婴孩要啼哭，啼哭是婴孩特有的"权利"，有人会反对吗，

Does anyone object to it? No one will object except for a handful of people like the ancient Egyptian pharaohs [1] in the Moses era. Almost all humans agree that a baby can cry at will, and this is the most original "right" of everyone on earth that is irrefutable --- the freedom to do what they want.

A status is depicted in "Leviathan" --- it's impossible for peer-to-peer war to happen in the babies' world [2], and, a baby's rights have no boundaries. Almost all it demands shall be satisfied as it has no power and chance to destroy this world at all. The motive and reason for satisfying a baby "without hesitation" is quite simple, it's because of life --- human life. Everyone has the right and freedom to survive. And a baby's life in infancy needs to

除了摩西时代古埃及法老王之类的极少数人，不会再有人反对。几乎所有的人类，都同意婴孩可以尽情的哭，那么这便是生活在这个世界上的每一个人毫无争议的一份最原始的"权利"——可以按照自己意愿去做的自由。

《利维坦》当中描述的一种状态——每一个人对每一个人的战争，在婴孩世界中是不可能会出现的，并且婴孩身上的权利也没有边界，几乎他们所有的诉求都应得到满足，因为他们丝毫没有破坏这个世界的力量和可能性。"无所顾忌"的满足婴孩的动机和理由很简单，是因为生命，人类的生命，每个人都有活着的权利和自由。而婴孩时期的生命是需要他人悉心照料的，那时的他们只有哭闹索取才能够在这个世界上

---

[1] *Bible*, National Committee of Three-Self Patriotic Movement of the Protestant Churches in China (National TSPM), China Christian Council (CCC), 2009 edition, (Exodus 1:22) p.53.

《圣经》，中国基督教三自爱国运动委员会、中国基督教协会 2009 年版，(出 1: 22) 第 53 页。

[2] *Leviathan* by Hobbes [Britain], translated by Zhang Yan and Zhao Wendao, Hu'nan Literature and Art Publishing House, 2011 edition, p.72.

[英] 霍布斯:《利维坦》，张妍、赵闻道译，湖南文艺出版社 2011 年版，第 72 页。

be taken good care of by others. Only by crying and asking for something can a baby in infancy survive in this world. All these are the rights it deserves to sustain life --- rights without boundaries.

What if boundaries are set for a baby's rights? It'll cry when hungry. Can its small mouth be muffled lest wake people around? Can a baby be prevented from sleeping in its parents' bed because its excrement soiled clean bed sheets? The answer of anyone who is normal will definitely be "No" as it is a kid yet and there are its "most basic rights". So, for the continuation of life, in no cases shall boundaries be set for the rights of a baby in infancy.

Runaway "Little Horse"

As a baby grows gradually, especially when it starts to walk on the ground by itself, its parents find that it has become naughty and unmanageable. It tries to

存活下来，为了维系生命这些都是他们应有的权利——没有边界的权利。

如果给婴孩的权利设置边界，可不可以呢？他们饿了，要哭，为了不吵醒身边的人们，可以捂上他们的小嘴巴吗？他们的排泄物弄脏了干净的床单，可以因此而不让他们睡在大人的床上吗？正常的人们，都会有肯定的回答——不行，他们还是小孩，这是他们"最基本的权利"。所以，无论如何，为了生命的延续，襁褓之中婴孩身上的权利，是不应有边界的。

脱缰的"小马"

随着婴孩的慢慢成长，特别是开始下地走路的时候，父母发现孩子们变得淘气和难以管理了，家里无论什么东西，他们都要设法弄出声响，或是

make a noise with whatever in its house, or to put them into mouth to know the taste. But some stuff is not eatable at all, and some stuff will harm it. So, in such case, the parents must first check through the places wherever the kid goes to make sure that there are no dangerous or valuable articles before allowing the kid to be there. Yet, unexpected situations still happen to the parents.

Not seen for just a little while, it has walked along the tea table to the sill, standing on its little tiptoe, with a cup the parent put on the sill before getting within the reach of its little hand, which is its mom's favorite craft ceramic cup. Its dad, having seen this, rushed up with a lunge and promptly grabbed the cup. Only by doing so has a property loss and the mom's mood swing been avoided.

When the mom was cooking and the dad was answering the phone and no one was paying attention to the kid, it quietly

放在嘴里试图尝出味道，有些东西根本就不能吃，有些东西会伤害到他们。所以这个时候，凡是小孩所到之处，爸爸妈妈必先巡视一番，确定没有危险和贵重物品，才能让孩子出现在那里。但仍然有让爸爸妈妈预料不到的状况发生。

一会儿没看到的功夫，他（她）沿着茶几，走到窗台边，踮起小脚，小手已经够到了，爸爸妈妈事先放在窗台上的水杯，那是妈妈最喜欢的工艺陶瓷杯，爸爸看到了一个箭步冲上去，迅雷不及他们掩耳，快速夺下水杯，才避免了财物损失和妈妈的心情波动。

妈妈在做饭，爸爸在接电话，没人注意他们的时候，他们又悄悄地挪向窗台，这次不是走过去的，是爬过去的，并

moved to the sill again. It didn't walk but crawled there, and even climbed onto a chair by the sill, with one little hand holding the window, its little body leaning against the sill, and the other little hand attempting to open the window like its parents do. Its mom, hearing the sound of opening window in the kitchen next door, ran to the kid as flying and took it down from the window immediately. She got so nervous that her heart almost jumped out of her body as their house is 5-storey high from the ground...

In such case, the kid is like a runaway little horse, running around. There are many very dangerous places but it doesn't know at all. There is much stuff that can make people sick after being eaten but it tries to swallow them again and again. For its safety and health, its parents need to put a "rein" on it to confine the range of its activities forcibly, and timely seize articles that are harmful to it. . . "Boundaries"

且还爬上了窗台边的一把椅子，那个椅子紧依着窗台，他（她）一只小手扶着窗户，小身子靠着窗台，另一只手开始学着大人去打开窗户，妈妈在隔壁厨房听到了窗户打开的声音，飞一样的跑到小孩身边，不容分说，立刻抱下，那可是5层高的楼房，妈妈的心脏都快跳出来了。

这个时候的小孩，就像是一匹脱了缰绳的小马，四处乱窜，好多地方很危险，他们却浑然不知，很多东西吃下去可以让人生病，他们却一遍又一遍的试图把它们吞下去。为了他们的安全和健康，爸爸妈妈需要给他们套上"缰绳"，要强行控制他们的活动范围，及时夺下对他们有害的物品…小孩们可以自由去做的状态，也第一次出现了"边界"——不可以随心所欲，这便是人类社会当中最

arise for the status that a kid can do stuffs freely for the first time --- it can no longer do what it wants --- This is the most original boundary of rights in human society, simply the boundary of rights at this stage is mainly set by its relatives and the direct purpose is to protect the kid's safety and health.

"Smokeless" Battlefield

In a community or village, when the kids start to learn to walk, their parents will usually take them out for fun. Hence, the kids begin to contact each other and communicate in their own ways. Although at this stage real communication does not take place among kids but among their parents in most cases, they will excitedly draw attention from pals with weird sounds or actions shortly after their parents introduce them to each other and teach them how to greet pals. Afterwards, they will gradually become friends-like "enemies". For any tasty food or

原始的权利边界，只不过这时的权利边界，主要是由身边的亲人设定的，并且直接目的就是为了保护小孩的安全和健康。

没有"硝烟"的战场

在一个社区或是村落，小孩们开始学习走路的时候，大人们通常都会带着他们外出玩耍，于是小孩和小孩之间开始接触，并且用他们特有的方式进行交流。虽然这时小孩们的交流还算不上是真正的交流，大多是带他们的大人们在交流，然后彼此介绍他们认识，教给他们如何给小朋友打招呼，很快他们就会很兴奋地开始用奇怪的声音或动作，引起小伙伴的注意。再接下来，慢慢的他们就成为朋友式的"敌人"，凡是好吃的，好玩的，他们都会争抢或是冲着自己的大人哭闹索要，丝毫不会顾及身边人的

anything fun, they will scramble, or cry and ask their own parents for it, not thinking of the feelings and situations of the people around them at all. No matter whose these stuffs are, if no parents to mediate, "wars" will usually occur among them in grabbing stuffs or toys. And most of such "wars" can be resolved due to the presence of their parents. The parents will adopt the interpersonal communication rules they are already familiar with to delimit a "boundary" for their own kids. For example, 'This toy is Peter's. You have to be obedient. Mom will buy one for you.' says the parent of one kid; and, the other kid's parents will say the same way, 'He is undoubtedly your good pal, let him play for a while, and he will let you play his toys too.' The kids will, when obedient to their parents, be praised. The parents are rather willing to let them learn to master these "boundaries" to get along with other pals. Because these aim to protect each other's

感受和处境。不论这些物品是谁的，如果没有大人出来调停，他们之间通常都会因为抢东西或玩具而出现"战争"，这时的"战争"因为有大人在，大都会被及时化解掉。大人们会用自己已经熟悉的人际交往法则去给自己的小孩划出"边界"。比如，'这是东东的玩具，你要听话，不能闹，妈妈会给你买'对方大人也会说'明明是你的好伙伴，你让他玩一会儿，他的玩具也会让你玩的'当孩子们听从大人们的话后，都会得到称赞，大人们很愿意让他们学会掌握这些"边界"来和其他小朋友相处，因为这些是为了在利益之争中维护好自己和对方的最大利益，避免因为玩具或食物，而造成"战争"的扩大化，使大人们也处于尴尬的"敌对"状态，一个新奇的玩具导致两个小孩打架，一个被抓破了脸以后，大人们再去处理，远不如在孩子们的"战争"还没有爆发时，就给他们设定"边界"——某时某地不可以自由去做的"权利边界"，这样给大人和小孩们带来的后果就要好

maximum interest in clashes of interest lest "wars" for toys or food exacerbate, which will in turn cause embarrassing "hostility" between the parents of both sides. It is far more worse for the parents to treat it after one kid's face is scratched in fight between two kids for a novel toy than to set "boundaries" for their kids before the "war" breaks out between them --- "boundaries of rights" that they are not allowed to behave freely somewhere sometime, which will lead to much better result to the parents and the kids of both sides. The world among kids is no different from a battlefield, where "smokeless" wars may occur anytime. Because one only knows to "satisfy himself/herself' at first, which is a human nature; whereas right is the twin of mankind's natural attribute of "only to satisfy self", which may not and should not be completely deprived.

很多。孩童们之间的世界无异于一个战场，随时都会上演没有"硝烟"的战争，因为人类的本性最初只知道"满足自己"，权利就是人类"只知满足自己"这一自然属性的孪生物，不可能，也不应该完全被剥夺。

Learn to Live "Peacefully"

As the kids gradually get to know how to play with other kids, their parents will not follow them like they did when they were very little, but let the kids stay together themselves and deal with clashes and problems among them on their own. In previous clashes, kids already knew what the consequences would be if they did something at will. So, in contacting with other pals, they begin to think of others and pay attention to the feelings and attitudes of other kids.

They try to compromise and negotiate, "Let's exchange our toys to play, ok?" most kids no longer make unrestrained requests. In order maximize their fun getting along with each other, and not to lose their pals, they begin to know how to restrain themselves and get the joy and trust of their pals so as to satisfy their own needs. Like

学会"和平"相处

随着孩子们慢慢知道该怎样和其他小朋友玩耍，大人们就不像他们小的时候那么跟着他们了，而是让孩子们自己在一起，独自处理彼此之间的矛盾和问题。在以往的冲突中，孩子们已经知道如果放任自己的行为，会出现什么样的后果，所以在与其他小伙伴的接触过程中，他们开始顾及别人，注意其他小朋友的感受和态度。

他们会试着去妥协和协商，"我们换着玩吧，好吗"，大多数孩子都不再一味地放纵自己的要求，为了能在彼此的交往中得到最大的乐趣，为了不失去小伙伴，他们懂得了自己约束自己，并以此取得小伙伴的喜悦和信任，从而满足自己的需求，就像大人们一样，小孩子也不想孤单，没有朋友。最

adults, kids also don't want to be alone and have no friends. Most importantly, in getting along with their pals, they gradually get to know how to use self-discipline in exchange for "harmony" in getting along with each other so that the interests of themselves and other kids can both be protected.

The "self-discipline" mentioned here refers to the experience they gained from their parents as well as their own personal experience. The boundaries of rights their parents once set for them have now become their codes of conduct, or to say they get to know the functions and benefits of boundaries of rights. From obeying the boundaries and surrendering rights passively, to disciplining themselves actively and exercising their rights cautiously --- they get to know that they can't do what they want anywhere anytime. The reason they do so is initially to exchange for greater interest --- to get pals to play with, more toys

重要的是，在和小朋友的交往过程中，他们逐渐学会了如何用自我约束来换取"和平"的相处，使自己和其他小朋友的利益都能得到维护。

这里的自我约束，便是他们从大人们那里，还有自己切身经历中得来的经验。大人们曾经给他们设定的权利边界，现在已经成为他们的行为准则，或者说他们知道了权利边界的作用和好处。由被动的服从边界，交出权利，变为自己主动进行自我约束，谨慎小心的去行使权利——他们明白了不是任何时候，任何地方，自己都可以自由去做想做的事情。他们这样做最初只是为了换取更大的利益——有小朋友一起玩，有更多的玩具和好吃的食物…但不可否认的是，为了"满足自己的更大利益"，很小的孩子就可以学会如何与别人"和平"相处。

and tasty food. . . Undeniably, however, in order to "satisfy their own greater interest", even very little kid can learn how to "peacefully" get along with others.

School --- the "Fetters" of Right

Although kids' rights have been restrained in being with their parents and playing with pals --- such restraint is perhaps due to the prohibition of parental discipline, or to "satisfy their own greater interest." But such boundary of rights formed due to external or internal factors has a far less powerful impact on kids than the restraint of rights imposed by schools and kindergartens on kids.

Because every morning they have to get up very early and have breakfast, and then go to school.

Unlike in their "infancy", they could sleep as long as they want, and eat whenever they want. The most uncomfortable thing for kids is that they are generally not

校园——权利的 "桎梏"

尽管在爸爸妈妈身边，在和小朋友们一起玩耍的过程中，小孩子们的权利已经有所收敛——这种收敛或许是因为父母的管教禁止，或许是为了"满足自己的更大利益"。但这种由于外部或内在因素而形成的权利边界，对于小孩子们的影响，都远比不上学校、幼儿园对于孩子们的权利约束来的强烈。

因为每天早晨他们必须早早地从睡梦中起来，然后吃饭，然后去学校。

在他们的"襁褓时代"，他们是可以想睡到什么时候就睡到什么时候，想什么时候吃就什么时候吃的。最让孩子们感到难受的是，到了学校或是幼儿

allowed to talk and move freely like they do at home when they are at school or kindergarten. With the increasingly onerous learning tasks and the teachers' discipline, they gradually get to know what discipline is, what punishment is, what is right and what is wrong before a teacher. This is the reason why kids are generally unwilling to go to school at the beginning --- their rights will be subject to so much restraint if they go to school that the schoolyard is simply "fetters" of rights to them compared to the restraint of rights from their parents or pals.

Entering the schooling period, teachers and parents will instill in kids a consciousness again and again --- be obedient, follow what the parents say, follow what the teachers say, don't be naughty, and obey various school disciplines. The kids know from their childhood experiences that the main purpose of the parents' such requirements are for their good and the things their parents don't

园，通常情况下是不允许他们像家里一样乱说乱动的，对于孩子们来说这才是最难受的事情。带着日益繁重的学习任务和老师们的管教，他们也慢慢明白什么是纪律，什么是惩罚，在老师面前什么是对的，什么是错的。这就是一开始孩子们普遍不愿意去学校的原因——他们的权利，会因为去学校而受到太多太多的约束，以至于和他们在父母那里或是小伙伴那里的权利约束比较起来，校园简直就是一个权利的"桎梏"。

进入学校时代，老师和家长都会一遍一遍地给孩子们灌输一种意识，要听话，听爸爸妈妈的话，听老师的话，不能淘气，要遵守学校里的各种纪律。孩子们也从小时候的经历中知道，大人们这样要求主要目的还是为了自己好，爸爸妈妈不让做的，都是对自己有害的事情。在学校听老师话，遵守纪律，好好学习，是为了学到知识本领，将来能有好的工作，好的前途，

allow them to do are all harmful to them. To follow what the teachers say, to obey the disciplines, and to study hard at school is to learn knowledge and skills so as to have a good job, a promising future and a happy life.

Such kind of cognition leads most kids to surmount the rights requirements brought by their nature, disciplining themselves, not violating the boundaries of rights set by their parents and teachers. But there are also some kids who choose to passively restrain themselves because they are afraid of punishment for violating the rules of their parents and teachers. Simply this type of kids may seek chance to claim their rights anytime. The main manifestation for this is that they will do things without prior permission as long as such things are not expressly prohibited by their parents and teachers. To them, free expansion of rights is normal while restraint is just exceptional. But most kids

能生活的幸福。

这样的认知导致绝大部分孩子，会克服本性带来的权利要求，进行自我约束，不去违反父母和老师给自己设置的权利边界。但也有一部分孩子，是由于惧怕违反父母和老师的规则而带来的惩罚，而选择被动约束自己。只不过这类孩子，随时有可能找机会去舒张自己的权利要求，主要表现为只要是父母和老师没有明确禁止的事情，他们就会不经允许地去做，对于他们来说权利的自由扩张是常态，受约束只是例外情况。而绝大部分孩子，都在自我约束自己的权利，对于他们出现了上面的情况时，他们通常都会征求父母或是老师的意见，询问'我这样可以吗？'，未经允许，他们不会擅自放纵自己的权利要求。除了上面两种类型，还会有极少数孩子，始

are restraining their rights by themselves. When they encounter the above situation, they will usually solicit the opinions of their parents or teachers and ask, 'May I do this? ', and they will not make unrestrained requirements of rights without permission. In addition to the above two types of kids, there are also a few kids who are always unwilling to get any of their rights restrained. They usually behave very rebelliously. At home, they have a tense relationship with their parents; at school, they contradict with teachers, violate school disciplines, and even interfere with and affect the regular order of the schools. The reason for such situation is that such types of kids are unwilling to get their rights restrained. But it is possible for them to be punished by the schools for improper behaviors, or to break off relations with their parents to run away from home.

Compared with the kids who are unwilling to be restrained, the first two types of kids can easily

终不愿让自己的权利受到一点约束，他们通常表现的很叛逆。在家里和父母关系紧张，到学校会冲撞老师，违反学校纪律，以至于干扰影响学校的正常秩序。出现这种情况的原因是，这种孩子不愿让自己的权利受到约束，但他们却面临着会因言行过火被校方处分，或与父母决裂，离家出走的可能性。

相比不肯受约束的孩子，前两种类型的孩子们，都可以较轻松地学会如何在学校或是家

learn how to enjoy freedom in the "fetters" of school or family --- as long as they follow what their parents say, there will be tasty food, favorite toys and love from the parents; as long as they follow what their teachers say, complete homework on time, and get good grades in exams, they will win praise and recognition from the teachers as well as the envious glances from the classmates, and their parents will be proud of them as well. All these will make these kids accustomed to restrain their rights so as to get more benefits, and "freely" enjoy various funs in life in the "fetters" of school or family.

Whether to Surrender "Rights"?

Whether with their parents or before their school teachers, kids will have a feeling that their rights have boundaries. Some food cannot eat too much, and some toys cannot own as they want.

庭的"桎梏"当中,享受自由——只要听父母的话,就会有好吃的,会有喜欢的玩具,还有父母的宠爱;只要听老师的话,按时完成作业任务,考出好的成绩,就能得到老师的表扬和肯定,赢得同学们羡慕的目光,父母也会以此为荣。这些都使这些孩子们,习惯用约束自己的权利,让自己得到更多的益处,让自己在学校或是家庭这样的"桎梏"当中,"自由的"去享受各种各样的生活乐趣。

要不要交出"权利"

无论是在父母身边,还是在学校老师那里,孩子们都会有一种感觉,那就是自己的权利是有边界的。有些食物不可以多吃,有些玩具不能想要就有,要遵守课堂纪律,完成学习任

They have to obey class discipline and complete learning tasks. The area where they cannot do what they want is the very boundary of rights that their parents and teachers have delimited for them, and things beyond which cannot do freely. This implies that kids need to surrender some of their rights (freedom). They could have eaten chocolates and candies for three meals per day, they could have slept as long as they wanted in the morning, they could have talked in class, and they could have quarreled and clashed with classmates at will. . . Most kids understand, however, that they can get more benefits after boundaries are set by their parents and teachers. So, usually they will actively give up freedom (rights) outside the boundaries of rights and let their parents and teachers arrange something that they have the freedom to choose. That is, the kids surrender such freedoms (rights) that they could have done as they wish to their

务。不能随心所欲的那个领域，便是父母、老师给自己划定的权利边界，超出权利边界的事情是不可以自由去做的，这样就意味着孩子们需要交出原本属于自己的一部分权利（自由）。原本他们可以一日三餐不断地食用巧克力和糖块，原本他们可以早上想睡到什么时候就睡到什么时候，可以在课堂上说话，随心所欲地和同学争吵冲突…但大多数孩子明白，父母和老师给这些事情设置边界以后，他们可以藉此得到更多的好处，所以他们通常都会主动放弃权利边界之外的自由（权利），让父母和老师去安排原本属于自己自由选择的事务。也就是说，孩子们把这些原本可以按照自己意愿去做的自由（权利），交给了自己的父母和老师。交出这些权利的目的，是为了得到更多的利益——为了还能吃到巧克力和糖果，为了学到知识，拿到好成绩…，他们必须交出这部分权利。

parents and teachers. The purpose of surrendering such rights is to get more benefits --- in order to get more chocolates and candies to eat, to learn knowledge and to get good grades . . . , they have to surrender such rights.

But some kids are unwilling to surrender such rights. They will always protect their freedom, constantly fighting against external pressure, quarreling with parents, confronting teachers, and clashing with classmates. . . They think all these are what they can do freely, and there is nothing that they can't do in their eyes. In their opinion, life is supposed to be like this --- free and unrestrained. In the adults' world, most people also agree that it is a human nature to uphold freedom. It's not impossible for peer-to-peer wars to happen. If all are unwilling to surrender their rights, wars will be on the verge. Unlike in the infancy, even if for a student --- a very little student, if he/she is unwilling to surrender his/her inherent rights, he/she may

但有一些孩子他们不愿意交出这些权利，他们会始终保护自己的自由，不断地同外部压力争斗，和父母争吵，和老师对抗，和同学们冲突…他们认为这些都是他们可以自由去做的事情，在他们眼中没有什么是不可以去做的。在他们看来，人的生命原本就应该是这样——自由自在，无拘无束。在成人世界里，大多数人也都赞同，人的本性就是崇尚自由，每一个人对每一个人的战争，不是没有可能性，如果每个人都不愿交出自己的权利，战争就会一触即发。不同于人的婴孩时代，即便是一个学生，一个很小的学生，如果他（她）不愿交出他们与生俱来的权利，他们就可能会有很强的破坏力和杀伤力（放火、投毒、伤害、杀害…），从而给人类社会带来灾难。在人们的

be awfully destructive and lethal (arson, poisoning, hurting, killing, murder...) , consequently causing disasters to human society. The above problems emerge as early as in school days. Generally, students who are willing to surrender rights are easy to manage; while students who are unwilling to surrender rights will remain the same as nothing had happened after their parents and teachers try their best to indoctrinate them.

Because, as mentioned above, human rights are inherent. From the perspective of life, one's freedoms (rights) are inherently legitimate.

"Rebelliousness"

Some kids who refuse to surrender their rights and refuse to obey their parents and teachers' disciplines are usually regarded as "rebellious". In most people's opinion, it's correct and natural for kids to follow what their parents say and obey the teachers'

学生时代，上述问题就已经显露，愿意交出权利的学生，通常比较容易去管理，不愿交出权利的学生，家长和老师费尽心思去教化，却仍然无济于事。

因为如前面所述，人的权利与生俱来。从生命的角度来看，一个人的自由（权利）有着先天的正当性。

"叛逆"

一些拒不交出权利，拒不服从家长和老师管教的孩子，通常被人们认为是"叛逆"的。大多数人都觉得听父母的话，服从老师的教导，对于孩子们来说，是正确而自然的事情。

inculcations.

The human nature of pursuing freedom, however, determines that all freedoms (rights), including baby's cry, are "inherently" legitimate. Because such freedoms (rights) are all for satisfying one's needs: some for physical needs, and some for psychological and spiritual needs. From this perspective, for free cry of baby, satisfaction of all of mankind's physical and psychological needs as well all of mankind's needs that derive from mankind's natural attribute (human nature), human freedom (rights) shall not be put on any fetters. All human freedoms are legitimate to certain extent as they satisfy human nature. We can also say so: the kind of "rebelliousness" of those kids who refuse to surrender their rights and refuse to obey disciplines, instead, better preserves mankind's most original features of desiring life, pursuing freedom and rights. It's not because these kids are rebellious and disobedient, but

但人类崇尚自由的本性，决定了包括婴孩啼哭在内的所有自由（权利），都具有"先天的"正当性。因为这些自由（权利）都是为了满足人的需求，有些是为了生理需求，有些则是为了心理和精神的需求。从这个角度看去，为了婴孩自由的啼哭，为了满足人类所有的生理和心理需求，为了满足源自人类自然属性（人性）的所有需求，不应该给人类的自由（权利）套上任何枷锁，人类所有的自由都会因为满足了人性而具有一定的正当性。也可以这样说，拒不交出权利，拒不服从管教的孩子们身上的那种"叛逆"，反而更好的保留了人类渴望生命，崇尚自由，追求权利的最原始特性。不是这些孩子叛逆，不听话，而是他们不明白为什么要交出原本属于自己的自由（权利），他们身上仍然保留着人类对自由的原始需求，就像婴孩一样，他们想要自由的"啼哭"。他们表现出的"叛逆"，反倒是一种生命的热情，一种不愿屈服妥协的精神。因此，这些孩

because they don't understand why they have to surrender their own freedom (rights). They still retain the original human need for freedom. Like babies, they want to "cry" freely. The "rebelliousness" they showed is, instead, a passion for life, as well as a spirit of unwillingness to yield or compromise. So, the "rebelliousness" of such kids, in terms of satisfaction of human nature, is almost normal and reasonable. Also, their "rebelliousness" presents the true side of human nature.

In most people's eyes, "rebellious" kids are usually regarded as ignorant. At home, they don't follow what their parents say, not being grateful but just asking for something; at school, they don't respect teacher, violating disciplines recklessly, often clashing with classmates, being intolerant and immodest. Being violent, drinking alcohol excessively, etc. happen on them one after another. Classroom is

子们的"叛逆",从满足人性的角度来看,是近似正常而有理由去做的,并且他们的"叛逆",也展示了人性真实的一面。

"叛逆"的孩子在大多数人的眼中,通常被认为是不懂事的。在家里不听父母的话,一味索取,不知感恩回报;在学校,目无师长,肆意违反纪律,经常和同学们发生矛盾冲突,不知忍让谦卑,暴力、酗酒等现象会一样一样地在他们身上出现。教室根本不是他们能长久待下去的地方,老师的说教,也不是他们能够长时间忍受的事情。于是,户外街头、网吧、酒吧这些可以让他们觉得"自

not where they can stay for long at all; and teachers' indoctrination is not what they can stand for long too. Thus, outdoor streets, Internet cafes and bars, where they can feel "free", become their frequent destinations. In such places, they will confront youths more "rebellious" than them. They will learn how to make themselves stronger and not get bullied by others. So fist and violence will gradually become their powerful weapons to make life go on.

Their parents can do nothing with them except worrying about their personal safety. The parents cannot change the traits and personality of their rebellious kids. And, schools and teachers' discipline imposed on such "rebellious" teenagers has little effect. Usually, a "rebellious" student will be expelled by the school upon a serious clash or mistake and they have to go into the society much earlier. Letting such "rebellious" student continue to stay in school will only disrupt

由"的地方，就成了他们经常的去处。在这些地方，他们又会遇到比他们更"叛逆"的青年，他们会学会如何让自己更加强悍，不被别人欺负，拳头和暴力慢慢成为他们继续生活的有力武器。

爸爸妈妈已经拿他们没有办法，除了担心他们的人身安危，其他的什么也做不了，父母们无法改变叛逆的孩子身上的特质和性格。学校和老师们在对这些"叛逆"的少年施加管教之后，往往也收效甚微，通常是一次严重的冲突或错误之后，学校会开除这名"叛逆"的学生，让他们早早的走向社会。继续让"叛逆"的他们留在校园，只会破坏校园里的秩序，让更多的学生们变得"叛逆"。因为这些孩子们身上，折射出的是人类崇尚自由的本性，

the school order and cause more students to become "rebellious". Because what such kids reflect is the human nature of pursuing freedom, which is extremely attractive to all people, especially minors. It's the essential attribute of human rights to do what they want freely. No one wants their rights to be restrained and bound by the outside regardless of what consequences such rights will result in. Most students choose to surrender their rights actively because they think that this will bring greater benefits to their future. Once they find that they will be freer if they refuse to surrender their rights like the "rebellious" kids do, they will rush to follow suit and no longer obey school and family rules, letting the teachers and parents feel very troublesome. So, it's a common practice for schools to keep "rebellious" teenagers away from obedient kids.

In terms of human nature, however, the "rebellious" kids

对每一个人，特别是未成年人来说，都具有极大的诱惑力。可以自由的去做自己想做的事情，这是人类权利的本质属性，先不管这份权利会带来什么样的后果，没有人会愿意自己的权利受到外在的约束和捆绑，多数学生们选择主动交出权利，是因为他们觉得这样会给自己的将来带来更大利益。一旦他们发现，像"叛逆"的孩子那样，拒不交出权利会更加自由，他们就会争相效仿，不再主动遵守学校规章和家庭规矩，让老师和家长头疼。因此让"叛逆"的少年远离听话的孩子们，是学校的通常做法。

但正如上面所述，"叛逆"的孩子们，由于丝毫不隐瞒自

will, as mentioned above, appear more real and not hypocritical, since they never conceal their desires and claims. Their thoughts and practices are what most kids want to do but choose to give up forcibly or voluntarily. Once the "rebellious" teenagers succeed in doing such things and their desires are satisfied, such "rebellious" teenagers will become the "heroes" in their peers' eyes or "school kings" that no one dares to offend.

"Rebels" Not to Yield But to "Deform"

There is a documentary TV program in China with very high audience rating --- "X-change" [1]. It mainly tells stories that some "rebellious" teenagers leaving pampered urban environment for remote and poor rural areas with difficult living conditions

己的欲望和要求，从人性角度来看，会显得更真实，不虚伪。他们的想法和做法，是绝大数孩子们想做，却被迫或主动选择放弃的东西，一旦"叛逆"的少年做成这些事情，满足了自己的愿望，"叛逆"少年就会变成同龄人眼中的"英雄"或是无人敢惹的"学校霸王"。

不会屈服却会"变形"的"叛逆者"

在中国有一档收视率很高的纪实类节目，叫做"变形计"。大致内容是，城市里的"叛逆"少年，从养尊处优的城市环境来到偏远贫穷，生存条件艰苦的农村地区生活，在农村新"爸妈"的引导教育下，经历一段"苦日子"，从而洗心革面，重新做

---

[1] A life role exchange program on Hu'nan Satellite TV, China

中国湖南卫视一档生活类角色互换节目

thoroughly reformed themselves and turn over a new leaf after experiencing a period of "hard days" under the indoctrination of the new rural "parents". Almost every episode will narrate one or several "rebellious" teenagers that "changed into" good kids who are sensible, grateful, and learn to be considerate and caring to parents.

Initially, in educating and managing these kids, their parents and teachers in cities had abandoned them, and they are almost desperate about their education and management of their characters, behaviors, and attitudes towards handling things, and they had no way to make them understand the principles of learning, living and behaving by indoctrinating. Only their parents, due to family affection, still hope to make the future of these problematic teenagers turn for the better in some way. So, this program, the moment being launched, was trusted by these parents a lot. They are quite

人的故事。基本上每期节目，都会有一个或几个"叛逆"少年被"变形"为懂事感恩，知道体谅关爱大人的好孩子。

起初，在教育管理方面，这些孩子们都已经被城市里的家长和老师所放弃，家长和老师对于他们的性格、言行、处世态度的教育管理几乎绝望，已经没有办法，来通过说教使他们明白学习、生活和做人的道理。唯有父母因为亲情，仍然希望能用什么办法，可以让这些问题少年的未来出现转机。于是这档节目出现后，便很受这些家长们的信赖，他们很愿意让自己"叛逆"的孩子们，通过改变生活环境的方式改变自我。"变形"前他们是学校的"霸王"、家里的"皇帝"，到哪儿都是肆无忌惮，为所欲为。没钱了就张口给父母要，不给就发脾气，摔东西，然后赌气出门，泡酒

willing to let their "rebellious" kids change themselves by changing their living environment. Before the "change", they were the "overlords" in school and the "emperors" in family. Wherever they go, they did whatever they wanted unscrupulously. When they had no money, they would ask their parents for it, and, if money was not given, they would lose their temper, throw something, and then went out in anger --- going to bars, Internet cafes or dance halls, drinking alcohol and then fighting. . . Eventually, they had to let their parents take them home from the police station. At school, a very tiny problem would cause them to yell, shout, scold, even punch and kick, totally merciless. Whether the teachers or the classmates, they had to center on them at all times. To them, the rules and systems, respecting teachers and friends are merely bullshit, whoever offended them would be hurt by them, they "never yielded" then.

In these kids' eyes, no reason

吧网吧或是舞厅、喝酒，然后打架…最后不得不让父母从警察局把他们领回家。在学校，稍有不顺轻则大喊大叫，破口大骂，重则拳脚相加，毫不留情。不管是老师还是同学，在他们面前，一律要以他们为中心。什么规章制度，尊师敬友，在他们那里都是浮云，谁惹他们，他们就会伤害谁，那时的他们"永不屈服"。

在这些孩子们看来，没有

could make them surrender their rights --- a freedom to behave at will similar to baby's cry, which all humans can comprehend. At least in terms of human nature, it's inherently legitimate to defend and pursue freedom in human society regardless of what it would cause to others if to claim such freedom.

After being put in the tough rural environment, initially they still persisted their own way, defying all the restraints and management around them and the earnest and kind remonstrations of the new "parents": Disrupting class disciplines, clashing with classmates, contradicting teachers, and even damaging properties, and venting dissatisfactions. Gradually they discovered that, however, they still received tolerance and care far more than those around them under extremely tough living conditions, and they got to feel touched --- they would shed tears in certain times and occasions. They gradually realized that their past behaviors are hateful

任何理由可以让他们交出自己身上的权利——一种类似于婴孩啼哭，所有人类都能体会的，可以按照自己意愿去做的自由。主张这种自由，先不管会给别人带来什么，至少从人性的角度来看，捍卫并追求自由，在人类社会具有先天的正当性。

到了生存艰难的农村环境以后，一开始他们仍然是我行我素，藐视周围所有的约束和管理，还有新"爸妈"的苦口婆心。随意破坏课堂纪律，与同学冲突，顶撞老师，甚至破坏财物，发泄不满。但慢慢的他们发现，在极其艰苦的生存条件下，他们仍然得到了比身边人多的多的宽容和关爱，他们开始有了被触动的感觉——在某些时间和场合，他们的泪水会从眼中流下来。他们逐渐意识到自己以往的言行是可恨的，开始明白自己过往的言行，给别人带来的伤害是那么的沉重。因为任性、鲁莽，要让朴实善良，从不惹事的农村"爸妈"花掉一年的积蓄，去给人家道歉，赔偿损失；他们看到了，为了生活，

and they got to understand how painfully others were hurt by their past behaviors. Due to their willfulness, recklessness, their simple while kind rural "parents" had to spend their one year's savings to apologize to others and compensate for their losses; they got to see that, in order to make a living, their rural "parents" were reluctant to spend money on getting treated when they were ill and they had to endure the pain to work in the fields. . . All these made them start to "change", and the essence of the process of such "change" is that the "rebels" --- "rebellious" teenagers --- who began to surrender their rights (freedom) and stopped doing whatever they want would really change into sensible and thankful kids.

"Rebels" Surrender "Rights"

What makes the "rebellious" teenagers who "never yielded"

农村"爸妈"有病舍不得花钱去医治，要忍着病痛下地干活…这些都让他们开始"变形"，而"变形"的实质过程，就是"叛逆"的少年开始交出权利，不再为所欲为，交出权利（自由）的"叛逆者"，也真的很快就变成了懂事感恩的好孩子。

"叛逆者"交出"权利"

究竟是什么原因让"永不屈服"的"叛逆"少年主动交出

surrender their rights voluntarily and change into obedient and sensible kids on earth? Is there a more powerful force making them feel scared? Obviously not, the energy that these rebellious teenagers have is enough to confront any external forces attempting to make them yield. Such threats and violence as fisting and cudgeling will not make them scared but more ferocious. The human nature of pursuing freedom makes "rebellious" teenagers defend their freedom with more fierce rebellion. Meanwhile, their behaviors demonstrate the inherent and rather powerful inner strength of human life. From the perspective of life, the rebellion of "rebels" is inherently legitimate. Facts have proved that, for freedom, their conduct is usually reckless and unstoppable.

Then, when will these "rebellious" teenagers restrain themselves or even surrender their rights? Now that external coercive powers cannot make them yield,

自己的权利，从而变得听话懂事呢？是有更强大的力量让他们觉得恐惧吗，显然不是，这些叛逆少年身上的能量足以对抗任何试图让他们屈服的外在力量。拳头棍棒和暴力威胁不会让他们恐惧，反倒会让他们变得更加凶猛。因为人类追逐自由的天性，使得"叛逆"少年会用更加猛烈的反抗来捍卫自己的自由，同时他们的行为也彰显了人类生命固有且十分强大的内在力量，从生命的角度来看，"叛逆者"的反抗具有先天的正当性。事实证明，为了自由他们的表现也常常是不计后果，不可阻挡。

那在什么时候，这些"叛逆"少年才会收敛甚至交出权利呢？既然外在的强制性力量无法使他们屈服，那他们是不是就永远不会放弃自己的权利，一味

will they never give up their rights, and blindly pursue freedom and then do whatever they want? This can be concluded through the TV program "X-change" which records real changes. If these "rebellious" teenagers are free enough to hurt the innocent and make others painful and sorrowful, and the people hurt by them are still tolerating and caring about them, their hearts will be touched. They begin to change their own cognitions and concepts. They originally thought that the relationship among people is just strife, and only to satisfy themselves blindly like a baby can they survive. When they see the kindness of the human world, human rationality makes them aware of their own serious defects, and which are common to everyone under certain circumstance. This is why they deal with others by fierce means without being ashamed. But once they find someone who can surmount

的追求自由，继而随心所欲呢？通过那档真实的"变形"节目，可以得出结论。如果这些"叛逆"的少年足够自由，自由到他们可以伤害无辜，让别人痛苦难过，并且被他们伤害的人们却还在宽容、关爱着他们，这时的他们内心就会有触动。他们开始改变自己的认知和观念，他们原本以为人与人之间就是争斗的关系，人活着就要像婴孩一样，一味地满足自己才能存活。当他们看到人类世界的善良时，人类的理性让他们意识到自己的严重缺陷，而这种缺陷是某种情形下人人都有的，这也是他们用凶狠的手段对付他人而不觉可耻的原因。可他们一旦发现能够克服这种缺陷的人，他们会觉得这样的人是可敬的，这些人做到了大多数人（包括叛逆者自己）都做不到的事情——能够克服人性中的不足,彰显人性之善良（忍耐宽容、关爱和不伤害）。应该说，是比他们拥有更大能量的人们，身上所表现出的善良，让"叛逆"少年发生了变化。经历了善良的少年，开始去克服自私任性

such defects, they will think that such a person is respectable, and such kind of people have done what most people (including the rebels themselves) can't do --- able to surmount the defects in human nature and demonstrate the kindness of human nature (tolerance, forgiveness, care and harmlessness). It should be said that it is the kindness shown by people with greater energy than them that has changed the "rebellious" teenagers. Teenagers having experienced the kindness begin to surmount their selfish and willful desires and claims. To reduce the pain caused to them by the humiliation of human rationality, the first step they shall do is usually to surrender their rights (freedom) and stop doing whatever they want. They want to "change" themselves, and use this method to repent in exchange for comfort and satisfaction.

的欲望要求。为了减弱人类理性的耻辱感给自己带来的痛苦，第一步他们要做的通常都是交出自己的权利（自由），不再为所欲为。他们要自己"变形"，并用这种方式来忏悔，以换取慰藉和满足。

"Good Kid"

Whether good kids who have always been sensible and obedient, or "rebels" who have surrendered rights and "changed", they all indicate a common trait in them --- aware of the importance of self-restraint and self-discipline. No longer indulge their own desires and claims, turning the "right expansion" status of doing whatever they want (a state of unrestrained pursuit of freedom) into a state of being cautious, not hurting others easily, and trying the best to self-discipline. They realize that only to use their energy on overcoming their inner human defects can they be recognized, accepted and agreed with by others. Too much homework, can I not do it? No. A good kid is aware that he/she must endure and work hard to complete the homework, and whether a student can complete the homework or not represents whether he/she

"好孩子"

不管是一直懂事听话的好孩子，还是交出权利、"变形"成功的"叛逆者"，在他们身上都显现出一种共同的特质，那就是这些孩子们明白了克己自律的重要性。不再放纵自己的欲望要求，让为所欲为的"权利膨胀"状态（无节制追求自由的状态），变为谨慎、不轻易伤害别人，努力自律的状态。他们意识到只有把自己的能量放在克服内在的人性缺陷方面，才能取得别人的认可和赞同。作业很多，可以不写吗，不行。好孩子知道，必须懂得忍耐和刻苦，才能完成作业，能否完成作业，就代表着这个学生是否称职和优秀。在这个过程中，孩子们必须放弃自己的权利，想要舒适、睡懒觉不去学校的本能和欲望，都要被克服掉。换句话说，这些人人生而有之的权利（自由），在这个时候必须被放弃。因为只有放弃了这些权利，孩子们才能完成父母和老师给他们设定的目标任务，而这些目标任

is competent and excellent. In this process, kids must give up their rights, and the instinct and desire to be comfortable, to sleep and not go to school must be all surmounted. In other words, such rights (freedom) that all people are born with must be given up in such case. As only to give up such rights can the kids complete the goals and tasks set by their parents and teachers, and such goals and tasks will become the basis and conditions for the kids to gain a foothold in society in the future.

Good kids who are obedient and sensible are strong, as they understand very early they can give up freedom in exchange for progress. They start practicing overcoming the defects of human nature very early to clear the obstacles when moving forward. Although they don't dare to indulge themselves easily, in terms of pursuing freedom and showing humanity, they seem to be somewhat "cowardly", and they voluntarily gave up

务将会成为孩子们未来在社会上立足的基础和条件。

听话懂事的好孩子们是坚强的，因为这些孩子们很早就明白了，用放弃自由去换取进步的道理，他们很早就开始练习，通过克服人性的缺陷来清除自己前行时的障碍。尽管他们不敢轻易放纵自己了，从追求自由，张扬人性的角度看，他们近似乎有些"懦弱"，他们主动放弃了原本属于自己的自由和权利。但这样的"懦弱"却是人类社会所必须的，如果大家都不放弃合乎本性却不符合理性的那部分自由（权利），这个世界就

the freedom and rights that they owned. But such "cowardice" is necessary for human society. If no one gave up the freedom (rights) that is in line with nature but not in line with rationality, the world would become what as described in "Leviathan" --- clashes and strifes among people will become unimaginable due to the unlimited expansion of human desires. Considering that the order of human society needs to be maintained, kids who practice giving up rights from an early age are strong and kind. They surmount difficulties to give up freedom (rights) in order not to affect or harm others, and not to disrupt the rules and order around them. Meanwhile, they will master rich knowledge and skills needed for human survival and development by giving up freedom and self-restraint and tolerance so as to gradually become "strong" --- a kind of "strength" that is not from instinct but rational, rule-based, and beneficial for others

会成为《利维坦》中所描述的那样，人与人之间的冲突和争斗会因为人类欲望的无限扩张而变得不可想象。从人类社会秩序需要维护的角度看，从小练习放弃权利的孩子们，是坚强善良的，他们克服困难舍弃自由（权利），为的是不影响伤害别人，不破坏身边的规则秩序。与此同时，他们也会通过舍弃自由和克己忍耐，去掌握丰富的人类生存发展所需要的知识技能，让自己逐渐变得"强大"，一种不是来自本能，但却理性、讲规则、对他人和社会都有益处的"强大"。

and society.

"Rebellious Teenagers"

The kids themselves and the environment they live in are not good or bad, just like the adults and their world, the fittest survive. Kids who follow what their teachers and parents say, are not naughty and work hard usually get a lot from them: Toys and delicacies, as well as recognition and encouragement from teachers and honors from schools. These kids have a deep understanding of how to give up freedom (rights) in their teenage years, and they have long been familiar with how to use a smaller part of freedom in exchange for greater gains.

Most of the kids who were born very stubborn, brave, and fearless will not well obey what their parents and teachers say. They only believe in their own feelings and perceptions, such physical punishments like cudgeling don't work well for

"叛逆少年"

孩子们本身以及他们所处的环境，无所谓好坏，正如成人和他们的世界一样，适者生存。听从老师、父母的教导，不淘气顽皮，努力学习的孩子们，通常从家庭和老师那里会得到很多东西。有玩具和美食、也有来自老师的肯定鼓励和学校的荣誉。这些孩子们，对于如何放弃自由（权利），在少年阶段已有较深的体会，很早就熟悉了如何用较小部分的自由，去换取更大的收获。

如果有些孩子，天生就十分倔强，胆量大，无所畏惧，那么这样的孩子，大多不会很好的听从父母和老师的话。他们只相信自己的感觉和认知，棍棒和体罚对他们不太有效，他们不会屈服于外在的强迫性力量。慢慢的，在家不听话，在学校不

them, as they will not yield to external coercive powers. Gradually, being disobedient at home, not studying and not observing disciplines at school become their features. It's not because they willfully do so, but because of the cognition and concept that always exist in their mind --- "Why do I have to be like that, I think I should be like this." Later on, they begin to change from being disobedient to disruptors of the rules of order --- contradicting their parents and teachers, violently clashing with classmates, and seriously violating school disciplines. . . As they are still holding on to an idea --- "I want to be free anyway, and everything that binds me is wrong." To break through the restraints and confinement in their eyes, they will bravely choose to break the confinement and break free. Such things as parental requirements, school disciplines, civilizedness and etiquette, etc., can all be restraints

学习、不遵守纪律，就成为他们的特征。不是因为他们故意要这样，而是在他们的心里始终会有这样的认知和观念——"我为什么要那样，我觉得我应该这样。"再往后发展，他们开始从不听话变为秩序规则的破坏者，和父母老师顶嘴，与同学暴力冲突，严重违反学校纪律…因为他们的心里仍在坚持一个念头——"我就是要自由，所有一切束缚自己的东西都是不对的"。为了冲破他们眼中的约束和禁锢，他们会勇敢的选择打破禁锢、挣脱束缚。诸如父母要求、学校纪律，文明礼仪等等，都算得上他们眼中的约束和禁锢，他们不惜背上"坏孩子"的名声，也要去实现"捍卫自由"的目标。虽然这样的做法，通常不会被世俗社会认可和肯定，但从人类权利的本质属性（可以按照自己意愿去做的自由）——自由这个角度来讲，这些"勇敢的坏孩子"是最能代表人类本来面目的，他们身上所表现出的言行特征、动机目标，正是所有人内心深处都曾反复思虑、渴慕得到的东西。

and confinement in their eyes. To achieve the goal of "defending freedom", they'd rather get the disrepute of "bad kid". Although it's generally not recognized to do so by the secular society, in terms of the essential attribute of human rights (the freedom to behave at will) --- freedom, such "brave bad kids" can best represent the true colors of humans. The features of behaviors, motivation and goals shown in them are the very things that everyone has repeatedly thought about and yearned for deep in their hearts.

Kids Can All Become the Mainstay of An Undertaking Whether "Good" or "Bad"

The strength and kindness of "good kids" and the bravery and self-confidence of "bad kids" are both necessary for human society. Sensible kids begin to learn how to self-discipline at a very early age, give up their unreasonable

无论"好坏"都能成为栋梁之才

"好孩子"身上的坚强善良，"坏孩子"身上的勇敢自信，都是人类社会所必需的。懂事的孩子们，很小就开始学习如何自律，放弃自己的不合理欲望和要求，努力学习知识技能，用较小的自由（权利）换取更

desires and claims, work hard to learn knowledge and skills, and use smaller freedom (rights) in exchange for greater benefits. Whereas the kids who may not seem sensible but are honest and brave but unwilling to give up freedom have a more real life in spite of continuous bumpiness and blunders along the way as they grow up. They have demonstrated the power of life with disobedience and resistance. The spirit of pursuing freedom and defending rights that they demonstrated is what all humans yearn for, as well as a prerequisite and condition for people to perceive happiness.

The homeland of mankind needs to be designed, planned and constructed with wisdom, and a lot of professional talents are needed to satisfy this. Obviously, in such case, the brave and obstinate and unruly "bad kids" don't have any advantages, as their nature determines that they are unable to get the chance to master such knowledge and skills. Only to

大的利益收获。而虽显得不太懂事，但却诚实勇敢，不愿放弃自由的孩子们，尽管成长过程中一路磕绊和跌撞，但他们的生命却因此更加真实。他们用不服从和反抗，展现出了生命的力量，他们所彰显出的追逐自由和捍卫权利的精神，是所有人类共同向往的，也是人们能够感知幸福的前提和条件。

人类的家园，需要智慧来设计、规划和建设，而这些事情需要很多专业型的人才才能满足。勇敢而难以驯服的"坏孩子"，这时显然不具备任何优势，因为他们的本性决定了他们无法获取机会，去掌握这类知识技能。一个人的学习、理解和记忆是必须要放弃部分自由（权利）才能实现的，需要选择放弃安逸舒适的权利。而

give up some freedom (rights) can one attain the goals of learning, understanding and memorizing. He/she needs to choose the right to give up comfort. While the kids who became obedient and sensible at a very early age have worked hard to accumulate knowledge. They had learned to give up smaller freedom in exchange for something more meaningful since a very early age. They will utilize the knowledge and practices they have learned and accumulated bit by bit over time in exchange for various skills and experiences needed in human society. They will become engineers, doctors, lawyers, entrepreneurs, salespeople . . . etc. to contribute their ingenuity to the homeland of mankind so as to make the planet where mankind lives more harmonious and beautiful. They'll become the mainstay of the undertaking of human society when the knowledge and skills they have exchanged for by giving up freedom satisfy the needs of

从小听话懂事的孩子们，一点一点的努力积累知识，很早就学会了放弃较小的自由，去换取更有意义的东西，他们会用一点一滴，日积月累所学到的知识和实践活动，去换取各种各样人类社会所需要的技能和经验。他们会成为工程师、医生、律师、企业家、推销员…等等，来为人类的家园，贡献自己的聪明才智，让人类居住的这个星球更加和谐美丽。他们通过放弃自由，而换取的知识技能，在满足了人类社会的需求，转化为人们认可的价值时，他们就成为了人类社会的栋梁之才。

human society and convert into values recognized by people.

"Good kids" can become the mainstay of the undertaking for sure. But how about the brave and self-confident "bad kids" who fail to learn knowledge and skills as they never want to give up freedom (rights)? Can they create value for human society by obtain the recognition from their compatriots by virtue of their nature and abilities? Such rebellious kids represent the true side of mankind. What they show us is uncarved, original and simple. But they are short of rationality as they are so real that they have unearthed the true colors of human nature. Their spirit of defending rights and the courage to pursue freedom, however, are indeed necessary for human society. When their compatriots encounter foreign invasions and when the basic order of human society is disrupted, those "rebels" who are willing to surrender their rights for the sake

"好孩子"能成为栋梁之才，那些勇敢自信始终不肯放弃自由（权利），未能学会知识技能的"坏孩子"们该怎么办呢？他们可以凭借自己的本性和能力，得到同胞们的认可，进而为人类社会创造价值吗？这些叛逆的孩子们，代表了人类真实的一面，他们所表现出的面目是未经雕琢的，是原始而简单的，只不过因为太真实，显露出了人性的本来面目，缺少了理性的成分。但他们捍卫权利的精神和追逐自由的勇气，的确是人类社会所必须的，在同胞们遇到外敌入侵时，在人类社会的基本秩序遭到破坏时，那些心甘情愿为了人类社会而交出权利的"叛逆者"们，就会勇敢地担当起保护同胞，捍卫人类社会秩序的重任。这时，他们一样满足了人类社会的迫切需要，他们的价值也因此得以实现，曾经的"坏孩子"就会成为栋梁之才，成为不折不扣的英雄。

of human society will bravely take on the responsibility to protect their compatriots and defend the social order of mankind. In such case, they have also satisfied the urgent needs of human society, and as a result, their value is realized. Those who were once "bad kids" become the mainstay of the undertaking and out-and-out heroes.

Qualities in Kids

Whether the obedient and sensible "good kids" or the egoistic "bad kids" who behave at will, they can all reflect the good qualities of humans.

The innate feature of humans --- only when their desires are satisfied can they be happy --- lead to many legitimate (to satisfy desires so as to pursue happiness) but unreasonable (infringe the freedom of others) situations in the continuation of everyone's life. For example, there is only one water source somewhere but

孩子们身上的品质

不管是听话懂事的"好孩子"，还是我行我素、唯我独尊的"坏孩子"，在他们身上都能折射出人类所具有的优良品质。

由于人类的先天特征——满足欲望才能快乐，导致了每个人在生命的延续过程中，会出现很多具有正当性（满足欲望追逐快乐），但却不合理（侵犯他人自由权利）的情形。比如，在一个地方只有一个水源，但有很多人需要使用。那么因为生存需要，谁可以饮用，谁不可以饮用呢？从生命的角度

many people need it. Then, to survive, who can drink and who cannot? From the perspective of life, anyone who needs to drink can drink. Both parties of each interpersonal conflict arising from water are legitimate as water is not created by mankind. In order to continue life, it is a right of human to find water sources. And everyone has an equal right to get water. The "equal" mentioned here means that everyone shall be allowed to get the water and reasonable reserves needed for individual life (to be determined by the rules formulated by all). If one occupies too much water resources and hence undermines the rules and fairness of water-taking, his/her behavior will be irrational.

Having gradually understood and accepted the above similar principles from a very early age, the kids begin to consciously restrain and adjust their own desires and demands in dealing with all resources and conflicts.

来讲，凡是需要饮用的都可以饮用，每次由于饮水出现的人际冲突，无论哪一方都具有正当性，因为水不是人类所造之物。为了延续生命，寻找水源，是人的权利。并且每个人取水的权利是平等的，这里的平等就是每个人都可以得到个体生命所需之水以及合理的储备（由众人制定的规则来确定）。如果一个人占用了过多的水资源，而破坏了取水的规则和公平性，那么这个人的行为就不合乎理性了。

孩子们从小慢慢明白接受上述类似的道理之后，在对待所有的资源和矛盾冲突时，就开始有意识地自觉约束调整自己的欲望和诉求。他们知道满足欲望可以让自己快乐，但他们也在日常生活的过程中，逐

They are aware that satisfying their desires can make themselves happy but they gradually realize in their daily life that it is unreasonable to indulge their desires --- they may incur fierce resistance and attacks when their behaviors affect or even harm the interests of others (rights/ freedom). So, humans learn to restrain themselves and give up unreasonable rights (freedom) from a very early age. The more obedient and sensible a kid is, the more rights he/she has to give up. Such kind of kids choose to suppress their own desires as they do not want to affect the interests of others. This is a valuable quality. Such kind of kids will basically, relying on the knowledge and skills they have mastered, become powerful constructors of human society when growing up.

Likewise, one more good quality is reflected by another group of kids, who own a firm belief and fearless spirit in

渐意识到放纵自己的欲望是不合理的——当自己的言行影响甚至伤害到他人的利益（自由权利）时，可能招致很激烈的反抗和攻击。因此，人类在很小的时候就学会了收敛，放弃不合理的权利（自由）。越是听话懂事的孩子们，放弃的权利就越多，这些孩子们因为不愿影响伤害别人的利益，而选择压抑自己的欲望要求，是一种很可贵的品质，这样的孩子长大之后基本上都会依托自己掌握的知识技能，而成为人类社会的有力建设者。

同样的，还有一种优良的品质，在另外一群孩子们的身上得到体现，这些孩子对权利（自由）的捍卫追逐，有着坚定的

defending and pursuing rights (freedom). Their behaviors are, however, usually awfully unreasonable as they are unwilling to give up their rights, obey their parents and teachers, and even totally disregard the interest of others in satisfying their own desires. In their parents and teachers' eyes, they cannot be good kids but be disobedient kids or even "bad kids" only. But their instinct to defend rights and pursue freedom is a good quality that humans must own to survive, defend against foreign invaders in critical moments.

Integrate into Society & Grow to Manhood

In a modern civilized (civilization symbolizes a harmonious order among social members) society, most kids have to undergo the process of education and edification by school, which is also a process on how parents, teachers and the

信念和无所畏惧的精神。不过，由于他们不愿放弃自己的权利，不愿顺从父母老师，在满足自己的欲望时更会毫不顾及他人的利益，因此其言行通常很不合理。他们在父母、老师的眼中，算不上好孩子，只能是不听话的孩子，甚至是"坏孩子"。但他们身上那种捍卫权利，追逐自由的天性，却是人类在求生、抵抗外侵等危急时刻所必须的优良品质。

融入社会长大成人

在现代文明（文明象征着社会成员之间和谐的秩序）社会，绝大部分的孩子都要经历学校的教育和训化过程，这个过程也是父母老师以及社会教导孩子们如何理性的放弃权利（自由），与周围的人们和谐相处，学会遵守规则的过程。为了维系人

society teach kids how to give up their rights (freedom) rationally, get along with the people around them and learn to obey the rules. In order to maintain the basic order of human society, this process seems quite necessary. And, in this process, kids can also learn necessary knowledge and skills, which are the prerequisites for them to earn a living and create value in the future. Most kids will, having gone through the process of education, and integrate into society in some way. There will inevitably be, however, some kids, who are cannot accept education at school for various reasons, integrate in society directly at a certain stage of life regardless of the level of economy civilization of human society.

Having integrated into the society, they gradually begin to earn a living on their own. They become an adult in the real sense when they grow to an age recognized by the society. In a modern civilized society,

类社会的基本秩序，这个过程显得十分必要。并且在这个过程中，孩子们还可以学到必要的知识技能，这些知识技能是他们以后谋生，创造价值所必须的前提条件。绝大多数的孩子在接受教育的过程结束之后，都会以某种方式融入社会。不过，无论人类社会的经济水平和文明程度如何，总会难免有一些孩子们，由于这样那样的原因，没有办法接受学校的教育，而在人生的某个阶段，直接融入社会。

融入社会之后，他们开始慢慢地独立谋生，当年龄达到社会认同的时候，他们便是一个真正的成年人了，也会成为真正意义上的社会成员。在现代文明社会，孩子们长大成人后，他们身上的权利（自由）也会

when kids grow up, their rights (freedom) will also have another name --- civil rights, or to say, the rights (freedom) that a member of a society deserves.

Civil rights are neither like people's initial rights e.g. the same rights as baby's cry nor like the rights that humans could have during the periods of social development when human nature was severely confined. Civil rights are gradually formed under circumstances and conditions where human society is relatively civilized and people's awareness of rights (freedom) has generally developed. In ancient Greece, there was once the appellation "citizen"[1]. But the rights that the then "citizens" were entitled to are quite different from the civil rights to talk about below.

The "civil rights" mentioned here is the result of gaming

有另外一个名字——公民权利，或者说是作为一个社会成员所应享有的权利（自由）。

公民权利不同于人们最初的权利，就是类似婴孩啼哭一样的权利，也不同于人性被严重禁锢的社会发展时期人类所能拥有的权利。公民权利是在人类社会相对文明，人们的权利（自由）意识普遍舒张的环境条件下逐渐形成的。古希腊曾有过"公民"的称谓，但那时的"公民"享有的权利，和下面所要讲述的公民权利相差较多。

这里的公民权利，是人类社会成员互相博弈的结果，是人

---

[1] *Politics* by Aristotle [Ancient Greece], translated by Wu Shoupeng, the Commercial Press, 1965 edition, p. 113.

[古希腊] 亚里士多德：《政治学》，吴寿彭译，商务印书馆 1965 年版，第 113 页。

among the members of human society. They are rational rights (appropriate rights) recognized and protected by the social contract entered into jointly by people after compromising and giving up their rights, as well as human rights (freedom) that will, after being sculpted, not disrupt the normal order of society and infringe the legitimate interest of others. Every member who has grown to manhood and integrated into society shall fully enjoy these basic human rights (freedom).

Legitimate and Rational Civil Rights

The biggest difference between a citizen and a person in the common sense lies in that, a citizen is of strong sociality. Such identity symbolizes that, a person is a member of a certain human group. He/she and other members within the same group have entered into a contract concerning how to exercise their original

们妥协和放弃权利之后共同达成的社会契约，所承认和保护的理性权利（适当的自由）；是被"雕琢"之后，不会影响破坏社会正常秩序，不会侵害他人正当利益的人类权利（自由）。每一个长大成人，融入社会的成员，都应当完全充分地享有这些基本的人类权利（自由）。

正当且理性的公民权利

公民和普通意义上的人最大区别在于，公民具有很强烈的社会性，这种身份标志着一个人是某个人类群体的成员，他（她）和同一群体之内的其他成员，就如何行使自己的原始权利（类似婴孩的啼哭——一种可以按照自己的意愿去做，满足自我，追求快乐的自由）达成了一种契约，这个契约约束所有的群

rights (rights similar to baby's cry --- a freedom to behave at will, to satisfy self and to pursue happiness), and which restrains all group members to give up unreasonable rights and claims and only retain those basic rights that are beneficial to both himself/ herself and other members, and which will usually explicitly protect everyone's basic rights by means of coercive power (public power).

Such contract has several types and manifestations. But there is one thing in common --- it aims to clarify the boundaries of people's rights, whichever type or manifestation it is. A monarchic contract clarifies the rights of a monarch; an aristocratic contract protects the rights of the nobilities; and a democratic contract stipulates the rights of the people. But only those defined rights that almost everyone is equally entitled to can be called "civil rights". How many rights one can have shall not be determined per his/her identity.

体成员放弃不合理的权利要求，只留下对自己和其他成员都有益处的基本权利，这个契约也通常都会明确以强制力（公权力）的方式保护大家的基本权利。

这样的契约有多种类型和表现方式，但无论何种类型方式，有一点都是相同的——这种契约都是为了明确人们权利的边界。君主制契约会明确君主的权利，贵族制契约会保护贵族的权利，民主制契约会规定人民的权利，但只有近似乎人人平等的权利界定，才能称得上是公民权利。公民不以身份来决定拥有权利的多少，只要你是这个群体的成员，你就拥有和他人一样的权利，你也应该和他人一样放弃不合理的原始权利。按照这样的公民制契约所组成的人类社会群体，可

As long as you are a member of this group, you shall have the same rights as others, and you shall also give up unreasonable original rights like others do. A human social group formed by such a citizenship contract can be called a civil society ---- this is a human social group in which everyone is equal in terms of rights (freedom).

Which legitimate and rational civil rights do people have after they give up some of their original rights? The first one is the right to subsistence. A member of a civil society must have the freedom to seek what needed to live by various means. Simply a civil society doesn't allow people to make a living by means that violate the contract as it will affect or damage the interest of other social members. Everyone agrees, for the group's common interest, to stipulate to give up such rights by contract and punish those social members violating the contract with coercive power (public power). If some group

以称为公民社会——从权利（自由）的角度来讲，这是一种人人平等的人类社会群体。

在人们放弃了部分的原始权利之后，正当且理性的公民权利会有哪些内容呢？生存权是第一个，一个公民社会的成员，必须拥有自由去通过各种手段谋取生存所需，只是公民社会不允许人们使用违反契约的方法手段来谋生，因为那样会影响侵害其他社会成员的利益，大家为了群体的共同利益，用契约的方式约定放弃这样的权利，并且同意用强制力（公权力）惩罚违反契约的社会成员。如果群体内某些成员，由于一些原因无法获取生存所需的资源而使生存权受到威胁，那么公民社会允许这些人用其他方式直接获取生存所需的资源——接受资助，一种来自他人和群

members cannot obtain the resources needed for survival for some reasons, and which threatens their right to subsistence, a civil society will allow them to obtain resources needed for survival by other means --- to accept financial aid, a gratuitous aid from other people and groups. This also reflects the excellent qualities of human nature and the value pursuit of human society. Besides the right to subsistence, the economic right is another very important right of citizens. "Economy" is the prerequisite and condition for the multiplication of human society. Only when there exists economic phenomenon can human society be maintained. Human needs e.g. food, clothing, housing and travel, etc. all need to be satisfied through economic activities. In terms of the essential process, economic activities include two main steps: value creation and value exchange, e.g. the process of farming, harvesting and exchanging for other products.

体的无偿援助，这也体现了人性当中的优秀品质和人类社会的价值追求。生存权之外，经济权利是公民的又一个非常重要的权利。"经济"是人类社会繁衍生息的前提和条件，只有存在经济现象，人类社会才能维系，人类的衣食住行等需求都要靠经济活动来满足。就本质过程来看，经济活动可以归结为两个主要步骤：价值的创造和价值的交换，比如农夫耕作、收获、换取其他产品的过程。简而言之，公民的经济权利就是社会成员拥有创造、交换价值，满足需求的权利（自由）。因着经济权利的需求，还有相应的受教育权和劳动权的产生，只有掌握必要知识技能且能劳动的人，才能创造出价值。公民的另一个重要权利，是参与社会管理的权利，或者称作"政治权利"，也即人们对于其所处的群体秩序和运行机制有权利发表观点意见，有权利提议变革，甚至是宣布退出契约，收回原始权利。具体可以表现为言论的自由，批评社会管理者的自由，抗议的自由等等，但

In short, the economic right of citizens is the right (freedom) of social members to create and exchange value and satisfied their needs. Due to the generation of the demand for the economic right and the corresponding right to education and labor right, only those who have mastered necessary knowledge and skills and are able to work can create value. Another important right of citizens is the right to participate in social management, or "political right", namely the right of people to express their opinions about the order and operating mechanism of the groups they belong to, to propose reform, or even to declare to quit the contract to recover their original rights. Its specific manifestations include freedom of speech, freedom to criticize social managers, freedom to protest, etc. But the political right of a civil society also has clear boundaries. Also, the exercise of such rights cannot violate the contract or arbitrarily infringe the legitimate

公民社会的政治权利也有明确的边界，行使这样的权利同样不能违反契约，不能肆意侵害其他社会成员的正当利益和社会的正常秩序。

interest of other social members and the normal order of society.

In addition to the above rights, which are more important ones, citizens have other rights. But all civil rights have a common feature, that is, they are all the basic human rights that are determined after citizenship contract adjustment, and they are all derivatives of the original rights of mankind.

What "value" Is?

What is "value" For humans, this is a term not applicable to the world of lower creatures, for which "value" or "valueless" doesn't matter; only humans can discuss value. "Value" is extremely "subjective", that is, it can be understood as that "value" has different meanings for different people. But in general, "value" represents a kind of "usefulness", which can be embodied in a labor product or in a person's behaviors, and can be tangible or intangible.

除此之外，公民还有其他的权利，上述几种权利只是较为重要的部分。不过所有的公民权利，都具有一个共同的特征，那就是它们都是经过公民制契约调整之后，而确定下来的人的基本权利，都属于人类原始权利的衍生物。

"价值"是什么

"价值"是什么？对于人类来讲，这个词汇无法用于低等生物的世界，只有人类才能讨论价值，对于低等生物无所谓有没有"价值"。"价值"带有极强的"主观性"，也就是可以理解为对于不同的人，"价值"的含义也会不同。但总体上来说，"价值"代表着一种"有用性"，这种有用性可以体现在一个劳动产品上面，也可以体现在一个人的言语行为之中，可以是有形的，也可以是无形的。只要他们是"有用的"，就会具有"价

They will have "value" as long as they are "useful". For example, if a person who takes something too hard intends to commit suicide, and an experienced and wise elder persuades him patiently. Because of whom this person gets to understand the principle that life is valuable and precious, and regain the confidence and courage of life. For this person who once intended to commit suicide, such elder's wisdom and words are the most "valuable" then. Likewise, for a hungry and thirsty passerby, tasty food will be the most "valuable".

It is questionable that the longer the working time is, the higher the value will be. Labor is not directly equivalent to value. Labor sometimes cannot be regarded as true value whether it undergoes the necessary value stage or the surplus value stage. Let's exemplify it as well: In the 19th century, heroin was refined out and synthesized and used as a medicine for humans to inhibit and relieve certain

值"。打个比方，一个想不开的人，要寻短见，另一位阅历丰富、充满智慧的长者，对他进行了耐心疏导，这个人便明白了生命可贵的道理，又重新找回了生命的信心和勇气。对于这个曾经要寻短见的人，长者的智慧和话语，便是当时最有"价值"的。同样，一个又饿又渴的路人，美味的饮食，才是最有"价值"的。

劳动时间越长，价值就越高的说法，是值得商榷的。同样一个例子来说明，劳动并不直接等同于价值，无论是否经过了必要的还是剩余的阶段，劳动有时算不上真正的价值。19世纪，海洛因（Heroin）被提炼合成出来，并作为药物用来抑制缓解人类疾病的某些症状。但后来人们发现使用这种"药物"的病人出现了极其严重的依赖成瘾问题，意识到海洛因对人类具有巨大的危害，许多

symptoms of diseases. But later it was discovered that patients who took this "medicine" had an extremely serious problem of dependence and addiction, and it was realized that heroin is a huge harm to humans. So, many countries began to legislate to prohibit the production and sale of it and defined it as a drug. In such case, we can also say that heroin cannot be used to satisfy human needs, regardless of the dosage and duration. On this premise, let's analyze the behavior of continuing to refine, process, synthesize and sell heroin while being fully aware that it has been classified as a drug that seriously harms humans. First, such behavior falls within human labor as it also requires the laborers' time and energy. There should be no objection to the above conclusion, but can such labor create value? Or to ask, the longer the working time for this is, the more value it will create? Supposedly it is only valuable to such workers

国家开始立法禁止制造和销售这种物品，并将其定义为毒品。这时我们也可以说，海洛因不能用来满足人类的需求，无论多少的剂量和期限都不行。在此前提下，我们来分析明知已被定性为严重危害人类的毒品，却仍在提炼加工、合成销售海洛因的行为。首先，这样的行为属于人类的劳动，需要耗费劳动者的时间和精力。上述结论应该不会有人反对，但这样的劳动可以创造出价值吗？或者说，这样的劳动时间越长，其创造出的价值也会越多吗？恐怕只是对这些劳动者及其雇主才有价值，让他们可以用这种方式赚钱发财，满足他们对金钱的欲望。人类社会的绝大多数成员，都不认为这样的劳动可以创造价值。因为，这样的劳动不仅不能满足人类的需求，反而会给人类带来严重的危害。至于他们的行为满足了自己和吸食毒品者的需要，则可以解释成这些人的需求是不合理的，满足这样的需求，不是真正的价值。社会成员的需求究竟是合理的还是不合理的，公民社

and their employers, and enables them to make money in this way to satisfy their desire for money. Most members of human society don't think such labor can create value. Because such labor cannot satisfy the human needs, instead, it causes serious harm to humans. As for the argument that their behavior satisfies the needs of themselves and drug users, it can be so interpreted: their needs are unreasonable, as it is not true value to satisfy such needs. A civil society shall determine by contract whether the needs of social members are reasonable or not on earth, that is, citizens restrain and confine unreasonable desires and needs and only retain the basic rights and reasonable needs not harmful to others and the society by giving up unreasonable rights (freedom).

So, in human society, only when a tangible or intangible carrier shows its "usefulness" in satisfying the needs of human society members that meet the

会会通过契约的方式确定下来，即公民们通过放弃不合理的权利（自由）来约束禁锢不合理的欲望需求，而留下对他人和社会无害的基本权利和合理需求。

因此，在人类社会中，有形的、无形的载体在满足人类社会成员符合契约要求的需要时，显现出的"有用性"，才是真正的"价值"（有用且合理）。

requirements of the contract can it have "value" (useful while reasonable) in the real sense. Whilst those carriers and their features that fail to satisfy the needs of human society or satisfy unreasonable needs don't have true value, as they are not "useful or rational". They are not only useless but also harmful to human social groups. They shall not be advocated and protected. They can only be considered as a useless and meaningless process of human activities, or "useless work". The features of true value make it quite distinct from the value stated in the "Surplus Value Theory".[1] The latter is based on and directed by reasonable needs of human society, and is "usefulness" that can be embodied in various tangible and intangible carriers. This approach of describing value can be called "Demand Value Theory".

那些没有满足人类社会需求或是满足了不合理需求的载体及其特性，不是真正的价值。因为它们不具有"有用性或是合理性"，对于人类社会群体，非但无益反而有害，不应提倡和保护，它们只能算是没有作用意义的人类活动过程，或者称为"无用功"。真正的价值所表现出来的特征，使其非常明显的区别于"剩余价值论"中所描述的价值，它是以满足人类社会合理需求为前提和导向的，是能够体现在各类有形、无形的载体之上的"有用性"，这种描述价值的方法，可以称作"需求价值论"。

---

[1] *Das Kapital* by Marx[Germany], translated by Jiang Jinghua and Zhang Mei, Beijing Publishing House, Beijing Publishing Group Co., Ltd, 2012 edition, p.40-41.

[德] 马克思:《资本论》，姜晶花、张梅译，北京出版集团公司北京出版社 2012 年版，第 40-41 页。

Why Humans Create Value?

The value of the human world means that the reasonable needs of human society can be satisfied. Countless various needs are contained in one's clothing, food, housing and transportation. Only when the needs are properly satisfied by the value created can humans survive and multiply. The thousands of years' long human history is a history of constant value creation by mankind. The accumulation and development of all walks of life have contributed to the sublimation and refinement of the value creation process one time after another. From typography to today's 3D printing, and from tying knots for keeping records to today's automated Internet..., Value have always been being created nonstop by humans themselves around the needs of human society. Do any of them exist in isolation from

人类为什么要创造价值

人类世界的价值，意味着可以满足人类社会的合理需求。一个人的衣、食、住、行当中囊括了数不清的各种各样的需求，只有需求被创造出的价值适当满足时，人类才能生存繁衍下去。浩瀚的几千年人类历史，就是一部人类不断创造价值的历史，各行各业的沉淀和发展无不是对价值创造过程的一次又一次升华与提炼。从活字印刷术到今天的 3D 打印，从结绳记事到今天的互联网自动化…都是在围绕人类社会的需求，而由人类自身不断创造出的价值。他们当中有一样是脱离了人类社会的需求而孤立存在的吗？没有。没有需求，就没有价值，但有时不是没有需求，而是当时的人们没能立即发现需求，那时的需求可能是潜在的，需要挖掘，互联网经济时代尤其如此。但无论如何，价值都不应脱离人类的需求而孤立存在。

the needs of human society? No! Were there no needs, there would be no value. But sometimes it's not because there are no needs but because people fail to tap needs immediately. The needs then may be latent and needs to be discovered. This is true especially in the Internet Economy Era. But in no case shall value exist in isolation from human needs.

It is precisely because the needs of human society are satisfied by the value created by human activities that mankind has never become extinct in the cruel evolution process on this planet for thousands of years. With their own value creation, humans' various needs including needs for food, clothing, housing, transportation etc. can be satisfied, and mankind can multiply and thrive till today. From this perspective, if human society is wanted to advance, value must be created. Humans create value first for their own survival, existence and development so as to discover higher levels of human

正是因为人类活动创造的价值满足了人类社会的需求，所以在这个星球几千年来的残酷演绎进程中，人类始终未曾灭绝。藉着自身的价值创造，人类的衣食住行、各种需求才得以满足，人类才能繁衍生息直至今天。从这个角度来讲，人类社会想要前进，就必须创造价值，人类创造价值首先是为了自身的存续和发展，进而发现更高层次的人类需求和目标，然后更多地创造价值。只有这样我们才能不断地前行，去验证人类世界的美好愿景和终极意义。

needs and goals, and then to create more value. Only in this way can we continue to move forward to verify the good vision and ultimate meaning of the human world.

Besides, the answer to the question of whether human is an evolved creature or a created creature is also quite valuable, as it concerns mankind's most fundamental physical and psychological needs --- the desire and pursuit of happiness. The answer to this question, if it can be recognized by people, will become the most valuable thing in the world. Such value will make people understand how to be happy, which needs to be created with human wisdom and is very meaningful, as it satisfies humans' fundamental needs of pursuing happiness.

Connotation of Economic Right

People's right to subsistence is intuitive and relatively easy to

另外，人是进化之物，还是受造之物，这个问题的答案也极具价值，因为这个关乎人类最根本的生理和心理需求——对幸福的渴慕追求。这个问题的答案，如果能够得到人们的认同，便会成为人世间最有价值之物。这种价值会让人们明白如何才能幸福，这种价值需要人类的智慧创造，并且很有意义，因为它满足了人类追求幸福的根本需求。

经济权利的内涵

人们的生存权利较为直观，也相对容易去解释和理解。但

interpret and understand. But one's economic right is not so easy to thoroughly understand. What is economy? Different perspectives will lead to different answers. Some explain it as efficiency, while some explain it as the process of production, exchange, distribution and consumption.

But in terms of its essence and core meaning, the economy in human society shall mainly refer to activities of value creation and exchange to satisfy mankind's the reasonable needs. When the reasonable needs of human society are discovered in certain way, corresponding value that can satisfy these needs will be soon created. Initially, these needs may not be well satisfied, but with constant growth of humans' technological experience in value creation and increasing value created by people, the extent to which human needs are satisfied will become deeper and broader. For example, in human history, a demand for word printing

一个人的经济权利, 却不是那么简单就可以理解的透彻。什么是经济, 不同的视角会有不同的答案, 有解释成效率的, 也有解释为生产、交换、分配和消费过程的。

但就其实质和核心意义来讲, 人类社会的经济应该主要是指满足人类合理需求的价值创造和交换活动。当人类社会合理的需求以某种方式被发现, 可以满足这些需求的相应价值就会很快被创造出来。起初, 可能这些需求不能被很好的满足, 但随着人类创造价值的技术经验不断增长, 人们创造的价值会越来越多, 人类需求被满足的程度范围也更加深入广阔。比如, 人类历史上由于传播信息的需要, 产生了对文字印刷技术的需求, 对这种需求的满足就经历了从古代的活字印刷到今天电脑排版打印的漫长过程, 人类需求被满足的进程, 也是价值不断被创造出来的过程。虽然满足的是同一种需求, 但满足的程度却在不断加深。在这个过程中, 不同层级的价值会出现在不同的人类历史阶段,

technology emerged due to the need to spread information. The satisfaction of such need has undergone a very long process from ancient typography to today's computer typesetting and printing. The process of satisfaction of human needs is also a process in which value has constantly been being created. Though what to satisfy is the same need, the extent of satisfaction has constantly been being deepened. In this process, different levels of value arise in different stages of human history. But the value is "useful" to the local people then whichever level it belongs to. One kind of need can be satisfied once a kind of value is created. But the problem is how all needs in human society can be satisfied as the needs are countless. The value creation of one person or a group of people is impossible to satisfy everyone's needs. So, it becomes a necessary mode for the development of human society that as many people as possible participate in

但无论处于那一层级的价值，对于当时当地的人们都是"有用"的。一种价值被创造出来，一种需求会被满足，但问题是，人类社会的需求多不胜数，如何满足所有的需求，一个人或是一群人的价值创造不可能满足所有人的需求，于是尽可能多的人参与价值的创造，并且实现价值与价值的交换，就成为了人类社会发展的必须模式，而所有这些活动就构成了人类社会的经济。一位精通活字印刷的宫廷官员，只靠印刷术是无法耕种庄稼，收获粮食的。虽然，他会从宫廷得到生活所需，但不能改变的事实是，粮食是由农民耕种得来，印刷品和粮食所承载的两种价值，对于官员和农民，在具体的社会经济模式下，会以某种方式进行交换，并最终使他们的需求都得到满足。因此，只有通过价值的创造和交换，人类社会的需求才可能得到满足，人类才会繁衍生息，社会才能进步。其中人们创造价值和交换价值的自由，就构成了人类的经济权利。

value creation and realize value-to-value exchange, and all these activities constitute the economy of human society. A palace official proficient in typography is unable to cultivate crops and harvest food only by printing. Though he will obtain what he needs from the palace, an unchangeable fact is that grain is cultivated by peasants and farmers. And the two kinds of value carried by printed matter and grain would exchange between the two in some way and ultimately satisfy the needs of both under the specific socio-economic mode. So, only through value creation and exchange can the needs of human society be satisfied, can humans multiply and thrive, and can society progress. Of which, the freedom of people to create and exchange value constitutes human economic right.

In other words, human economic right is one's freedom to satisfy the reasonable needs of himself/herself and others by creating and exchanging value.

换句话说，人类的经济权利就是，一个人可以通过创造价值和交换价值，来满足自己以及他人合理需求的自由。

How People Realize the Economic Right?

For human society, people's economic right is very important. If no one is engaged in economic activities (value creation and exchange), this world will be on the verge of collapse or extinction, as various human needs cannot be satisfied. The essence of economic activities is value creation and exchange. For the multiplication of humans, humans must constantly be engaged in economic activities with value creation and exchange as the content so as to satisfy various needs that emerge in human society. So, the freedom to be engaged in economic activities must also become a human right. This is a basic prerequisite for maintaining the needs of humans, as well as a necessary condition for the progress of material production of the society.

How to exercise such an important right? First, obstacles

人们如何实现经济权利

对于人类社会来说，人们的经济权利是非常重要的，如果没有人从事经济活动（价值的创造和交换），那么这个世界就会濒临崩溃或是灭绝，因为人类的种种需求，将不能被满足。经济活动的实质内容就是价值的创造和交换，为了人类的繁衍生息，人类必须要不断的从事以创造和交换价值为内容的经济活动，才能满足人类社会出现的各样需求。因此，从事经济活动的自由，也必须成为人类的权利，这既是维系人类自身需求的基本前提，也是社会物质生产进步的必备条件。

该如何行使这样重要的权利呢？首先，应该给人类挖掘

shall be cleared away for humans to tap their own reasonable needs, the legitimate needs of humans shall not be hindered or confined. In old times when the productivity was very low, it was an urgent need for most people to have a filled-up granary. As the productivity and the grain output improve, people no longer take the problem of food and clothing as the primary goal to solve. Because such human need at a lower level has been well satisfied. Except for some areas that have not been well satisfied for various reasons, most inhabitants of this planet are no longer afraid that hunger will come again someday. However, as the granary fills up, the spiritual world of mankind gradually becomes empty. People begin to pursue spiritual enjoyment, and a growing need for literary and artistic creation emerges. In such case, the value carried by the fruits of labor of litterateurs and artists will exceed that represented by the grains cultivated by peasants

自身合理需求扫清障碍，不能阻碍禁锢人性的正当合理需求。在生产力低下的旧时代，能有充盈的粮仓，是大多数人的迫切需求，随着生产水平和粮食产量的提高，人们会不再把温饱问题作为首要目标来解决。因为人类的这个较低层次的需求已经被很好的满足了，除了部分地区由于种种原因还未能实现以外，这个星球的大多数居民都不再害怕，有一天饥饿会重新来临。不过伴随着粮仓的充盈，人类的精神世界却慢慢开始空虚，人们开始追求精神享受，对文学艺术创造产生了越来越强烈的需要。这个时候，文艺工作者的劳动成果所承载的价值，会超过农民种植粮食所代表的价值。同样都是劳动，在相对均等甚至是更短的时间内，为什么创造出的价值，给人们的感觉却不同量呢？这个问题从根本上来讲，是因为它们满足人类需求的程度不同，一个是迫切且难以满足的精神艺术需要，另一个却是普通且容易满足的基本生理需求，因此在多数人不再在意温饱需

and farmers. Both are labor, but why do people feel that the value created by them differs in a relatively equal or even shorter time? Fundamentally, this is because the extent to which they satisfy human needs differs. One is an urgent and insatiable spiritual and artistic need; the other is an ordinary and easy-to-satisfy basic physiological need. So, the latter appears to be relatively less important and valuable when most people no longer care about food and clothing needs. It's the first step of human economic activities to excavate reasonable human needs. Only by knowing what mankind really needs can there be goals for value creation and can economic activities be launched.

After clarifying people's needs, what to do next is to create human fruits of labor that can satisfy these needs and carry value using human wisdom and labor, which can be either tangible or intangible, e.g. wise men's words and opinions, which show

求的时候，后者就显得相对不那么重要、有价值了。挖掘人类的合理需求，是人类经济活动的第一步，只有知道了人类真正需要什么，价值的创造才有目标，经济活动才会启动。

在明确人们的需求之后，接下来要做的就是用人类的智慧和劳动，去创造出能够满足这些需求，承载价值的人类劳动成果，这种劳动成果可以有形的形式出现，也可以无形。比如，智者那给人指点迷津的话语和观点，关键时刻可以拯救人的

someone how to get onto the right path, can save one's life at critical moments. This is de facto value, and it can also be deemed as a variant of human economic activities. A wise person discovers the needs of the person he or she is to save, and then satisfies him (her) utilizing his or her wisdom to rekindle his/her confidence and courage to live. This is a value creation that can save lives. In this process, the wise person saves a person's life utilizing his or her wisdom. The wise person will reap corresponding rewards and win respect from his/her compatriots and draw attention from others. Such a process is value creation and exchange, and the value of each member of human society must be reflected through creative activities that can satisfy the needs of others or the society.

This abstract example suggests that the key to people's exercise of the economic right is to be able to create tangible or intangible fruits of labor

性命。这是当然的价值，也可以看作是人类经济活动的变体，智者发现了所救之人的需求，而后用自己的智慧去满足他（她），使其重新燃起生活的信心和勇气，这是一种可以拯救生命的价值创造。智者在这个过程中，用他（她）的智慧拯救了人的性命，智者会收获相应的回报，赢得同胞的尊重和他人的关注。这样的过程就是价值的创造和交换，人类社会每个成员的价值都要通过能够满足他人或社会需求的创造活动而体现出来。

从这个抽象的例子当中，还可以看出，人们行使经济权利的关键在于要能够创造出满足人类合理需求、承载价值的有形或无形的劳动成果，然后以

that satisfy reasonable human needs and carry value, and then exchange them in an appropriate way so as to get different needs of human society satisfied.

适当的方式进行交换，从而使不同的人类社会需求都能得到满足。

Where Surplus Value Is?

剩余价值在哪里

Value is the usefulness carried by objects that can satisfy human needs. So, how does such usefulness meeting human needs come about? Can value be created only in a tangible and visible form? Will intangible and invisible things have value? To answer these questions, we need to look at a process of value creation.

"To the people, food is heaven." If humans want to multiply and thrive, what needs to satisfy first is the demand for food. For such need, peasants and farmers act as the main value creators. They sow, cultivate, and harvest grain, and then satisfy all consumers by exchange. The cost they paid seems to be unequal in

价值是能够满足人类需求的客体所承载的有用性，那么这种满足人类需求的有用性，是如何产生的呢？价值是不是只能以有形的、看得见的方式被创造出来，无形的、看不到的东西会有价值吗？回答这些问题，需要我们看一个有关价值创造的过程。

"民以食为天"，人类若想繁衍生息，首先要满足的需求，就是对饮食的需求。对于这种需求，农民充当了主要的价值创造者。他们播种、耕耘、收获粮食，而后通过交换满足所有的消费者。他们付出的成本和交换粮食所得的财物相比，从形式上看好像不相等，成本较低，收获较多。有一种经济理论，解释这种现

form, with lower cost and more harvest compared to the properties or goods obtained from the exchange of grain. An economic theory interprets this phenomenon as the formation process of surplus value. It believes that it is visible and tangible labor that create all value. It artificially and forcibly divides laborers' labor time into two parts: one part creates cost value; the other creates surplus value. This theory intends to tell us that those who possess surplus value are immoral and unrighteous people exploiting the value of others. The theory ever set off a shocking wave of hatred for wealth value in human history, which caused countless people to get bankrupt and lose life, and caused costly disasters to human society. Such conclusions are not alarmist talk, nor are they rootless trees or sourceless water, and can be proved simply by in-depth analysis of the process of value creation and exchange.

Let's take the above example

象为剩余价值的形成过程，认为是看得见的有形劳动创造了所有价值，把劳动者的劳动时间人为地强制地划分为两部分，一部分创造出成本价值，一部分创造出剩余价值。这种理论试图说明，占有剩余价值的人，是不道德的，是剥削他人价值的不义之人。这种理论在人类历史上曾经掀起仇恨财富价值的惊天骇浪，这种仇恨让不计其数的人倾家荡产，丢掉性命，给人类社会带来了沉重的灾难。这些话不是危言耸听，更不是无根之木，无源之水，这样的结论只需要深入分析价值的创造和交换过程就可以证明。

还以上面的事例来分析，农

for analysis: to cultivate crops, peasants and farmers need, in addition to seeds, to sow, weed and manage. In this process, some labor is tangible while some intangible, that is, some is visible while some invisible. Visible labor e.g. obtaining seeds, sowing seeds, watering and irrigation, weeding, etc.; whilst invisible labor includes thinking about how to obtain seeds, when to sow, how to manage, etc., and which plays a more direct and important role in forming of the value contained in the fruits of labor. For example, a peasant/farmer's grain output is much higher than that of others due to timely sowing and proper management; or his/her grain harvested is tastier as he/she has chosen better varieties based on his past cultivating or farming experience. In the system of viewpoints of the above theory, the labor that can be seen by people is interpreted as the cost of value; while the invisible labor that cannot be seen by people and has

民耕种农作物，不仅需要种子，还需要播种、除草和管理，在这个过程中有些劳动是有形的，有些是无形的，也就是说有些能看得见，有些看不见。能看到的有形劳动如获取种子、播种、浇水灌溉、除草等过程，看不到的无形劳动包括了思考如何获取种子、何时播种、怎样管理等，并且这些无形劳动对于劳动成果所蕴含的价值形成会起到更为直接重要的影响作用。比如一位农民的粮食产量由于播种及时，管理得当，而远远高于其他的耕作者，或是凭借他以往的耕作经验，选择了更为优良的品种，从而使其收获的粮食更加美味。在上述理论的观点体系中，人们看得见的劳动，被解释为价值的成本，而人们看不见的且对价值形成作用更大的无形劳动却被忽略，无形劳动形成的价值，被认为是有形劳动的增值部分。这种理论也认为由劳动者创造出来的劳动产品，增值部分都被特定人群无偿占有了，这个过程叫做剥削。可是如果没有无形的劳动，人们该如何选择哪些

a greater effect on value formation is ignored. The value formed by intangible labor is considered to be the added value of tangible labor. This theory also believes that the added value of the products created by the laborers is all possessed by a certain group of people for free --- this process is called "exploitation". Was there no intangible labor, however, how should people choose: which labor has value and can satisfy reasonable human needs; and which labor couldn't satisfy human needs and instead would harm? All these questions have to be answered in reliance upon human invisible labor. If there were no capitalists and rulers, which kind of product to produce, how about the output, how about the quality standards and how to sell smoothly will all become challenges. Workers will not be able to continue the process of value creation normally. If failed to produce and create, the value that satisfies human needs

劳动是有价值的，可以满足人类合理需求，哪些劳动非但不能满足人类需求反而是有害的呢？这些问题都要依靠，人类的无形劳动来解决。如果没有资本家和管理者，工人生产何种产品，产量多少，质量标准怎样，如何顺利销售，都将成为难题，工人们将无法正常继续价值的创造过程。不能生产创造，满足人类需求的价值就会无从产生，人们为了生产创造的投资和成本也会无法收回，因为不能满足需求，没有价值的产品，没有人愿意交换。因此，只有资本家和工人通力协作，价值才能被创造出来，满足人类的需求。也就是说，无形劳动和有形劳动的完美结合，才是价值形成的根本原因，离开了无形劳动，单靠有形劳动创造价值是非常困难的。反之亦然，资本家和管理者的空想也无法生产出可以满足人类需求的产品。资本家和工人之间，可以互相通过有形和无形的劳动，满足对方的需求，对于彼此这也是一种价值。他们的结合，会生产出合适的产品，来

wouldn't generate, nor would people's investment and cost for production and creation be recovered, as no one wants to exchange for valueless products that cannot satisfy their needs. So, only through cooperation between the capitalists and the workers can value be created to satisfy human needs. That is, the perfect combination of tangible labor and intangible labor is the very root cause for value formation. It's tough, apart from intangible labor, to create value by tangible labor alone, vice versa, capitalists and managers cannot produce products that can satisfy human needs simply by thinking. Capitalists and workers can satisfy each other's needs through tangible and intangible labor --- this is a value for each other too. Their combination will produce suitable products to satisfy the needs at higher levels and of more people. In this process, what we see is just that the combination of tangible labor and intangible labor jointly

满足更高层次，更多人群的需求。在这个过程中，我们看到的只是无形劳动和有形劳动的结合，共同创造出了满足人类需求的价值，所谓的"剩余价值"始终没有出现。

create value that satisfies human needs; and the "surplus value" has never appeared.

What Political Right Is?

Among human rights, the political right is a very special one. And what makes it special is that it is not an original right, and appears in certain circumstance. The "certain circumstance" mentioned here refers to the circumstance when humans choose to live together in groups and form a certain social contract. Whether a monarch-subject contract in a monarchic society or a civil contract in a law-based democratic society, political right will emerge when the contract comes into play.

Such right is essentially a freedom for human group members to participate in social management. Who to rule and lead human society, how do leaders generate, how to maintain the internal order of human groups, and how to formulate

政治权利是什么

在人的权利当中，政治权利是很特别的，特别之处在于它不是一种原始权利，它只在特定的情形下才会出现。这里的特定情形是指，当人类选择群体聚集生活，且形成一定的社会契约之时。无论是君主社会的君臣契约，还是法治民主社会的公民契约，当契约发挥作用的时候，政治权利便出现了。

这种权利实质上是一种人类群体成员参与社会管理的自由。由谁来统治领导人类社会，领导者如何产生，人类群体内部秩序如何维系，社会规则怎样制定等都是政治权利的内容。人类群体必须通过这样的方式才能在与大自然的搏斗之中生

social rules, ... are all content of political right. Only in this way can the human groups survive the struggle with nature, and can the basic social order necessary for human production and life be maintained. Political right includes a lot of content concerning social management, but in terms of its external form, it is mainly manifested in the freedom of speech and participation in decision-making of social members, namely the freedom to make comments, criticism and suggestions in respect of agendas and matters on social management and to vote on related agendas. Political rights do not need to be exercised by social members all the time. Such right is only used when needed. When leaders change, social rules are made, or managers solicit social opinions, all social members are required to exercise the political right to satisfy the needs of handling social and public affairs. Specifically, it is manifested in all possible ways

生不息，才能维持人类生产生活所必须的基本社会秩序。作为政治权利，虽然包括了很多与社会管理相关的内容，但就其外部形式来看，主要表现为社会成员的言论自由和参与决策的自由，也就是对社会管理相关议题和事项，提出意见、批评和建议，以及对相关议题事项进行表决的自由。政治权利并不需要社会成员无时无刻的行使，这种权利只在需要之时才使用，领导人更迭之时，社会规则制定之时，管理者征求社会意见的时候，都需要社会成员通过行使政治权利去满足处理社会公共事务的需求，具体表现为言论、建议、批评、表决等有助于解决社会公共事务的所有可能的方式。

that help solve social and public affairs, e.g. speech, suggestion, criticism and voting.

But such right will vary greatly as the social contract differs. For example, the political right of social members in an autocratic monarchic society are much more restricted and narrowed than those of members in a law-based democratic society. Because the autocratic monarchy featuring with absolute obedience does not allow subjects to have too much freedom and choices. In other words, under such social system, the humans' right --- the freedom to behave at will --- is substantially constricted, and the political right is very few. Instead, in a law-based democratic society where the awareness of rights is generally awakened and human rights and claims are highly expanded, the political right of social members is in an uptrend of continuous expansion. People have to vote to determine the leaders they deem competent, as well as

但这种权利会随着社会契约的不同，而出现很大的差异。比如君主专制社会之中，社会成员的政治权利相比较民主法治社会之中社会成员的政治权利，是要被限制和缩小很多的。因为以绝对服从为特征的君主专制，不容许臣民有过多的自由和选择。换句话说，这种社会体系之下，人类的权利——可以按照自己意愿去做的自由，受到了极大的约束，政治权利更是少之又少。相反，在权利意识普遍觉醒，人的权利要求高度膨胀的民主法治社会，社会成员的政治权利则呈现出不断扩张的趋势。人们要投票决定自己认为能够胜任的领导人，要通过投票确定他们认为合理的社会管理规则和基本原则，人们会对不负责任的领导人和官员提出质疑和弹劾，要求官员对与其有关的社会危害后果承担责任。

the social management rules and basic principles they deem fit. People will question and impeach irresponsible leaders and officials, and require officials to bear the responsibilities and liabilities for the harmful social consequences incurred by them.

So, in general, political right can be deemed as the right (freedom) of every social member to participate in social management when there is a human group that produces and lives together and a social contract is formed within the group. The important content of civil political right is mainly manifested in the freedom of social members to make comments and suggestions on social and public affairs and participate in decision-making.

Other Civil Rights

Obviously, the right to subsistence, the economic right and the political right are very important rights among civil

因此，总体上政治权利可以被视为，当出现共同生产生活的人类群体，且形成群体内部的社会契约之时，每一个社会成员参与社会管理的权利（自由）。公民政治权利的重要内容，主要表现在社会成员对社会公共事务有提出意见建议以及参与决策的自由。

其他的公民权利

很显然，生存权利、经济权利和政治权利是公民权利当中非常重要的权利，因为它们直接关系到人们的生存和安全。

rights, as they are directly relate to people's survival and safety. They don't represent, however, all of civil rights in spite of their great importance. There are also lots of rights derived from them, e.g. the right to obtain relief, and the right to education required to master knowledge and skills, etc. as mentioned above. So, it's impossible for us to list all the civil rights using words in detail. In a word, all the freedoms of members of civil society to satisfy their reasonable needs all fall within the scope of civil rights.

The original right of mankind is a freedom to behave at will. The original rights adjusted by the contract of a law-based democratic society (a kind of contract that all social members are entitled to participate to formulate and embody the equality of all) are called "civil rights". The source of civil rights is still the original rights of mankind. It discarded the unreasonable and harmful elements in the original rights by

不过，虽然它们很重要，但也代表不了公民权利的全部内容。还有很多衍生出的权利，比如上面提到的获得救济权、还有掌握知识技能所需的受教育权等，因此我们无法用文字将所有的公民权利都详尽地一一列举。总的来说，公民社会的成员所有满足自己合理需求的自由，都应属于公民权利的范畴。

人类的原始权利，是一种按照自己意愿去做的自由。经过民主法治社会契约（一种全体社会成员都有权利参与制定的，体现人人平等的契约）调整的原始权利，被称为公民权利。公民权利的根源仍是来自人类的原始权利，它以特定社会契约的方式摒弃了原始权利当中不合理、有害的成份，比如人性的贪婪、过度的情欲、嫉妒和仇恨等等。这里的社会契约可以表现为宗教信仰、道德习俗、

specific social contract, e.g. greed in human nature, excessive lust, jealousy, hatred, etc. The "social contract" mentioned here can be manifested in various forms e.g. religious belief, morality, custom, laws, legislations, etc. All thoughts, viewpoints, values and rule systems generally recognized and accepted by members of a specific social group can become substantive content of social contract. Since civil rights essentially aim to satisfy the reasonable human needs, any civil right shall be the rights of social members as citizens as long as they are not prohibited by the social contract of a law-based democratic society. So, the denotation and scope of civil rights are very extensive. Including some unacceptable freedoms, they still fall within civil rights.

A case in point is the freedom of "extramarital affair". Human emotional need is much higher than that of other creatures, and it is a necessary condition for human

法律等多种形式，凡是被特定社会群体成员普遍认可接受的思想观点、价值理念和规则体系，都可以成为社会契约的实质性内容。由于公民权利在本质上是为了满足人类的合理需求，只要没有被民主法治社会契约禁止的，都应是社会成员作为公民的权利，因此公民权利的外延和范围是十分广阔的。包括一些让人难以接受的自由，仍然属于公民权利。

很典型的一个例子，就是"婚外情"的自由。人类对于情感的需求远远高于其他生物，获得感情是人类幸福快乐的必要条件。所以，多数现代文明

happiness to obtain affection. So, most modern civilized societies (law-based democratic societies) do not absolutely prohibit the right (freedom) of their members to engage in such behavior. In other words, "extramarital affair" still falls within civil rights. The reason why it is not absolutely prohibited is that such behavior satisfies human emotional and physiological need, and is, like original rights, inherently legitimate. From another perspective, however, such behavior has a great harmful effect, especially for the spouses and kids of both sides in an "extramarital affair", the harm of the "extramarital affair" to them is far above the effect of physical trauma. The value of such behavior is only to satisfy the emotional and physical need of both sides in an extramarital affair, those who they hurt are the relatives around them, what they damage is the marriage and emotional order of the society. So, such behavior is not advocated

社会（民主法治社会）没有绝对禁止其成员从事这种行为的权利自由，换句话说，"婚外情"仍是公民权利的一种。之所以没有绝对禁止，是因为这种行为满足了人类的情感生理需求，具有类似原始权利的先天正当性。但从另一角度看，这种行为却具有很大的危害作用，特别是"婚外情"双方的配偶和孩子，"婚外情"对于他们的伤害已经远远超出了肉体创伤带来的影响。这种行为的价值，仅在于满足婚外情双方的情感和生理需求，伤害的是各自身边的亲人，破坏的是社会的婚姻情感秩序。所以，这种行为不被人类社会所提倡，但鉴于其先天的正当性，也没有将其绝对禁止，只在一定层面的社会契约，诸如道德习俗之中予以谴责。

by human society, but considering it is inherently legitimate, it is not absolutely prohibited. It is only condemned within social contract e.g. morality, custom, etc. at a certain level.

Ubiquitous Social Contract

Human society own many features, including collectivity, sociality, cooperativeness, etc., a most prominent feature should be the contractual nature of human society. What is contract? A contract in the common sense refers to the agreement of multiple parties --- an agreement formed by people in a certain way in order to achieve specific goals on certain issues and matters. Such agreement can be tangible or intangible, and can be entered into in an explicit manner or by tacit understanding. For example, laws made by the representatives of the people are tangible contracts; morality and custom formed by the

无处不在的社会契约

人类社会的特征很多，有群体性、社会性、协作性等等，其中最突出的一个特征应该是人类社会的契约性。什么是契约，通常意义上的契约，是指多方当事人的合意——就某些问题和事项，人们为了实现特定目标，以某种方式所形成的约定。这种约定可以是有形的，也可以是无形的，可以用明示的方式达成，也可以用默契达成。有形的契约如民众代表制定出的法律，无形的如信仰潜移默化而成的道德习俗，明示的如公布的规则，默契的如社会成员自律而成。

imperceptible belief are intangible contracts; announced rules are explicit contracts; and contracts formed by social members' self-discipline are tacit understanding.

Due to lack of water in an area, people living there can only get water from the only nearby water source. Initially, due to inadequacy of water, people who got there to get water often had to scramble violently to obtain priority access to water. In the end, someone lost life in fighting for water, which everyone believes should have not happened. Everyone in this world has the right to get the water needed for life. If someone wants to deprive others of the right to get water, he (she) will be opposed and rejected by everyone, as such behavior is illegitimate in the human world. It hinders people from realizing their most original right to subsistence, it is unjust. Later, someone sets a sign near the water source, hoping that everyone could line up to get water in order based on their

一个地区，因为缺水，居住在这里的人们只能到附近唯一的一处水源取水。起初，由于水源水量不充沛，到那里取水的人们常常要通过暴力争抢的方式，获得优先取水的机会，最后就出现为了争水有人丢掉性命的事情，大家都觉得这样的事情不应该发生。这个世界上的每一个人都有取用生命所需之水的权利，如果有人想要剥夺其他人取水的权利，他（她）就会被大家反对和排斥，因为这种行为在人类世界是不正当的，它会阻碍人们实现最原始的生存权利，具有非正义性。后来，有人在水源附近立下标记，希望大家能够按照到达水源的先后顺序排队取水，大家看到这样的提议，便都自觉排队取水，绝大多数人都会自觉避免因为取水而武力争斗。再到后来，大家又想了一个办法，按照附近居民各自居住的区域，分时

arrival. Seeing such a proposal, everyone begin to line up consciously to get water, and most of them would consciously avoid fighting for water. Later on, they work out one more way: to get water at different times according to the areas in which nearby residents live to avoid crowding due to too many people at the same time, and the maximum water amount per person per time is stipulated too.

In the above assumed example, the social contract recurs in many forms. Initially, it is a contract of violent combat and winners first, which appears intangibly. It is a naturally-formed order as no one proposes, nor they discuss such an issue. Lining up to get water by setting sign, and jointly discussing getting water at different times fall within the scope of the contract entered into explicitly and tangibly.

So, social contract is a mode of behavior that is spontaneously selected, acquiesced or recognized

段前去取水，避免同一时段取水的因人多而拥挤，并且规定了每人每次最大的取水容量。

在上面这个假定的例子当中，社会契约就以多种形式反复出现。起先是暴力争夺，强者先取的契约，这种契约是以无形的方式出现的，因为没有人提议或是大家商议这样的问题，属于自然形成的秩序。再后来的立下标记排队取水和共同商议分时段取水，则属于以明示、有形的方式达成契约。

因此，社会契约就是在人类社会群体内，由全体成员自发选择、默许或是共同认可的行

by all members within a human social group. Such contracts are ubiquitous in human society, from beliefs, morals and laws to waiting in queue, observing the order, etc. in daily life, all fall within the scope of social contract.

Sum-up to "About Right"

Human right is the freedom of a person to behave at will. Human right is initially manifested as unrestrained original rights --- all rights and freedom like baby's cry. People's original rights are inherently legitimate as such freedom satisfies one's own needs and can bring satisfaction and happiness. Many original rights of a person are, however, irrational and will usually affect the legitimate rights and interest of others and the basic order of the human community due to absence of even slight restrictions and restraints.

So, when people choose to

为模式。这样的契约，在人类社会无处不在，大到信仰、道德和法律，小到日常生活中的排队等候、遵守秩序等等，都属于社会契约的范畴。

权利篇之结语

人的权利就是一个人能够按照自己意愿去做的自由。人的权利最初表现为不受约束的原始权利——所有的类似婴孩啼哭的权利自由。人的原始权利具有先天的正当性，说其具有正当性，是因为这种自由满足了一个人的自身需求，能够给其带来满足和快乐。但一个人的原始权利，由于未加丝毫限制和约束，有很多是不合乎理性的，会常常影响破坏他人的正当权益和人类群体的基本秩序。

所以，当人们选择群居和

live in groups and live together, human group members must choose to restrict their respective original rights in some way in exchange for a stable order within the group and stable basic interest of each group member. Such way of restricting rights usually appear in the form of contract, which can be tangible or intangible, and can be entered into explicitly or by tacit understanding. All behavior patterns or rules that are commonly recognized and accepted by the human group members fall within the scope of human group contract. The human rights adjusted by group contract can no longer be called original rights. Because people have to give up unreasonable desires and claims under the restraints of contract, and they can only claim those legitimate original rights.

As the human group contract was developed and improved to a certain extent, monarch-subject social contract in the age of the monarch developed into equal

共同生活，人类群体成员必须选择以某种方式限制约束各自的原始权利，以此来换取群体内秩序的稳定和每一个群体成员的基本利益处于安定的状态。这种限制权利的方式，通常以契约的形式出现，它可以使有形的，也可以是无形的，可以公示，也可以通过默契达成。凡是人类群体成员共同认可接受的行为模式或是规则，都属于人类群体契约的范畴。经过群体契约调整过的人类权利，就不能再称作是原始权利了，因为在契约的约束之下，人们要放弃不合理的欲望和要求，只能主张正当且合理的那部分原始权利。

当人类群体契约发展完善到一定程度，由君主时代的君臣社会契约发展到民主法治社会的平等社会契约时，这些被契约调整过的人类原始权利，

social contract in a law-based democratic society, these human original rights adjusted by contract began to have a resounding name --- civil rights --- by virtue of the fairness within the social group and the society and the personality and identity attribute of general equality of social group members.

Civil rights grew out of the original human rights, and are the original rights adjusted by the group social contract. In essence, citizen rights still fall within original human rights; simply people dispose some of their own rights that violate the social contract, are irrational, and might endanger the legitimate rights and interest of others or disrupt the social order, voluntarily obeying the restraints of the social contract to which they are subject and giving up the above unreasonable rights. In view of the greatest feature of rights ---- freedom, all freedoms that can satisfy human needs are human original rights. So, in terms of denotation and

便因着社会群体内部的公平性，以及社会群体成员普遍平等的人格身份属性，而有了一个响亮的名字——公民权利。

公民权利脱胎于人的原始权利，是被群体社会契约调整过的原始权利，从本质上来讲，公民权利仍然属于人的原始权利。只是人们把自己身上一些违背社会契约，不合乎理性，有可能危害他人正当权益或者破坏社会秩序的权利进行了处分，自愿服从所属社会契约的约束，放弃上述不合理的权利。鉴于权利的最大特征——自由，所有可以满足人类需求的自由都是人的原始权利。因此，在外延和范围上，人的原始权利是非常广阔的，即便是依据民主法治社会契约，放弃部分权利以后的公民权利也仍然包括很多——生存权利、经济权利、政治权利、受教育权、获得救济权等远不能涵盖其全部内容。

scope, human original rights are very extensive. Even civil rights after giving up some rights according to the contract of a law-based democratic society still include a lot of rights --- the right to subsistence, economic right, political right, right to education, right to relief, inter alia.

It can be believed that the human original rights adjusted by the contract of a law-based democratic society but not restricted or prohibited constitute all of the civil rights.

可以这样认为，被民主法治社会契约调整过，但没有被限制或禁止的人类原始权利，组成了公民权利的全部。

权力篇
About Power

Defects in Human Nature

In human society, youths without belief will easily get together to drink, boast, talk about everything scornfully if they have no chance and environment to create value or fail to learn and master the knowledge and skills needed for value creation for various reasons. They will resent people who create value. There is an inborn hatred in mankind. Such hatred will provoke the impulse of destruction and violence when they see that others are happier and more satisfactory than themselves. Destroying is a main way for such group of people to keep them mentally balanced. At a dark night, in a street for which street lights have just been installed, those who have a painful and dark heart will kick the innocent street light poles with their feet at night again and again, and no one dare to stop them, and finally a street light fails

人性的不足

在人类社会当中，没有信仰的青年人，如果没有机会和环境去创造价值，或者由于种种原因没能学习掌握创造价值所需的知识技能，便容易聚到一起，喝酒、说大话、谈天说地且满口不屑。他们会对创造价值的人群产生愤恨，人类在骨子里有一种与生俱来的仇恨，当他们看到别人过的比自己幸福美满时，这种仇恨便会挑起破坏和暴力的冲动。破坏是这类人群保持心理平衡的主要方式，一个夜里漆黑的街道上，刚被装上了路灯，但心理痛苦阴暗者，在夜里会用脚一下一下地狠踹那根无辜的路灯杆，且无人敢拦，终于有一天那盏路灯不亮了。一群好事且游手好闲的人聚在一起喝酒，酒后多半都会无事生非，或是殴打他人、破坏财物发泄无名火，或是饮酒过程中彼此发生暴力冲突，最后血腥收场。这样的事情，在人类社会当中，特别是

to shine one day. When a group of dawdlers gather together to drink alcohol, most of them will make trouble out of nothing, or beat others, destroy properties and vent their anger without justified reasons, or violently conflict with each other in drinking, and finally ends up with a bloody scene. Such things often happen in human society, especially among those who have no spiritual beliefs and don't understand self-discipline, the reason for which is the defects in human nature, or to be called "human inferiority". The defects or inferiority in human nature refer to the inherent sin of some of human original rights. To satisfy such unreasonable even evil human needs, human words and deeds become "evildoings".

In terms of human nature, humans would easily feel painful without value for comfort. Because the desires and claims of human original rights will start to expand and break out if their needs cannot be satisfied for long, and

没有精神信仰，不懂自律的人群当中经常发生，究其原因是由于人性的不足，或叫做人的劣根性。人性的不足或劣根性，是指人类身上部分原始权利所固有的罪恶性。为了满足此类不合理甚至是邪恶的人类需求，人类的言语和行为就会变成"恶行"。

从人性角度来看，如果没有价值的慰藉，人类是很容易感到痛苦的，因为需求不能被满足，时间久了，人类原始权利的欲望和要求就开始扩张和爆发，而这些原始权利常常会给人带来无法抑制的邪恶感。人

such original rights will usually result in an insuppressible sense of evil to people. The more human needs are satisfied, the better the unreasonable original rights will be suppressed, and the defects and inferiority in human nature will be less likely to be exposed. But there are always times when, and occasions where people cannot suppress their own unreasonable desires and needs. These can indirectly prove that defects in human nature are the root cause of many problems in the human world.

"Unspoken Rules" Derived from "Inferiority"

At a well-known hospital somewhere had a constant flow of patient coming for it to see the doctor and consequently suffered traffic jams and lack of parking space. To solve this issue, the hospital figured out a very good solution for vehicle parking:

类的需求被满足得越多，不合理的原始权利就会被抑制得越好。人性的不足或劣根性就越不容易显露出来，但总有时间和场合会有人无法抑制自己不合理的欲望需求，这些可以间接印证人性的不足是人类世界很多问题的根源。

"劣根性"衍生出 "潜规则"

某地一家很有名气的医院，由于前来看病的人络绎不绝，就常常出现车辆拥堵，无处停放的情况。为此，医院采用了一个很好的车辆停放办法来解决上述问题。就是在院内设计了环形道路，车辆从进口处驶入，然后沿着环形路寻找车位，如

To design a ring road in the hospital. Vehicles drive in from the entrance and then look for a parking space along the ring road; if they can't find one, continue to drive along the ring road until find one after a car leaves. Such a rule well alleviated the chaotic traffic in the hospital due to too many cars which resulted in lack of parking place. This is an effective management rule recognized and accepted by people.

Since specialized managers were employed for it, however, the effect of this rule had changed. Several cars were looking for parking spaces on the ring road, but a manager at road side was talking with someone on his phone, he said loud: "Come here, here is a parking space... "There was a parking space beside him, but was occupied by a warning pile, which was very light and could be removed or put back anytime. Drivers of other vehicles couldn't use this parking space without the consent of the manager. Most of

果找不到，就继续环行直至有车离开出现空的车位。这样的规则，较好的缓解了车多无处停放，导致医院内交通秩序混乱的局面，是一种有效并得到人们认可的车辆停放管理规则。

但自从引入专门的管理人员之后，这种规则的效果就出现了变化。好几辆车在环形道路上寻找车位，而路边的一位管理人员正在用手机和别人通话，只听到他大声的说：你过来吧，这里还有一个车位…在他的旁边有一个车位，但被警示桩占起来了，不过这个警示桩很轻便，可以随时拿掉，也可以随时放上。其他车辆的驾驶人员如果未经这名管理人员同意，是用不上这个车位的，绝大多数人都认为管理人员是代表医院维护车辆停放秩序和规则的，理应自觉服从。但实际情况是，

them believed that these managers were maintaining the order and rule for vehicle parking on behalf of the hospital and they ought to obey them consciously. But the truth is that the managers were making use of the rule recognized and accepted by the hospital and everyone to attain their own goals to gain personal benefits.

In such case, the methods the managers adopted to gain personal benefits are distorted rules --- unspoken rules. Only by attaching to the effect of the original rules can unspoken rules play a role to enable certain people to enjoy benefits differing from others'. Unspoken rules reflect unfairness, and only those who know them can benefit from them. Unspoken rules will not be accepted by most people as the purpose of human social members to formulate and observe rules is to restrict people's unreasonable rights (freedom) and maintain the order of human society. Whereas unspoken rules only benefit a few

管理人员在利用医院和大家都认同的规则去实现自己的目的，获取私利。

这个时候管理人员为了获取私利所采取的方式方法，便是变了味道的规则——潜规则，这种潜规则必须依附于原先制定的规则效力才能发挥作用，使特定的人享受到和他人不一样的好处。潜规则体现出不公平性，知道且会利用它的人才能从中得到好处。潜规则不会被多数人所接受，因为人类社会成员制定遵守规则的目的就是为了限制人们不合理的权利自由，维持人类社会秩序。而潜规则却只会让少数人受益，这种强烈的不公平属性，决定了人们必定会反对它。少数人利用潜规则的最终结果，也只能是破坏人类社会秩序。因此，潜规则的出现是和人类社会追

people. Such strong attribute of unfairness determines that people will definitely oppose them. The final result of utilization of unspoken rules by a few people will be disrupted order of human society only. So, the emergence of unspoken rules is obviously contrary to the original intention of human society to pursue order and fairness.

Then, where do unspoken rules come about? The behavior of making use of and performing unspoken rules is a breach to the promises made in the original rules. Manipulators of unspoken rules are familiar with the features and essentials of the rules. He/she will make use of these advantages to enable certain people to benefit from the rules without complying with the rules. Investigating the root causes, breaching the promises made when formulating the rules to unscrupulously gain personal benefits suggests that unspoken rules of human society are derived from human fraud and

求秩序公平的初衷明显相悖的。

那么，潜规则究竟从哪里来？利用实施潜规则的行为，是对当初设定规则所作承诺的背弃，潜规则的操控者熟知规则的特征和要领，他（她）利用这些优势，让特定的人不需符合规则要求，也能享受规则带来的好处。究其根源，背弃制定规则时的承诺，不择手段地获取私利，说明人类社会的潜规则正是来自人类的欺诈和贪欲，来自人类身上顽劣且难以克服的不合理欲望和需求——人性的缺陷（劣根性）。

greed, and from the unreasonable human desires and needs that are stubborn and insurmountable --- the defects in human nature (inferiority).

Rules of Human Society

Due to inferiority in human nature, people will usually choose to restrain people's unreasonable desires and needs with certain contract or rule applicable to certain social groups so as to provide a stable and order environment for people who work and live together.

In the monarchic human society, loyalty and obedience to the monarch were the basic consensus of social members. All people believed that the noblest emperor or king, honored the son of heaven, could absolutely not be treated the same as common people. Common people were willing to be fully reverent and respectful to the noble king, and in turn the king also believed

人类社会的规则

因为人类的劣根性，为了能让在一起共同生产生活的人们有一个安定的秩序环境，人们通常会选择在一定的社会群体内部适用某种契约或规则，来约束人们不合理的欲望和需求。

在君主制的人类社会当中，忠君和服从是社会成员的基本共识，大家都觉得贵为天子的皇上或是国王，与庶民百姓是绝对不能等同待遇的。普通人愿意对尊贵的国王毕恭毕敬，而国王也觉得像对待孩子们那样去对待自己的百姓是他的应尽职责。只要这样的规则得到大家共同认可，这样的人类社会便会出现人们想要的秩序——百姓在创造价值，提供满足人

that it was his duty to treat his civilians like his own children. As long as such rules would be recognized by everyone, such kind of human society would have the order that people wanted ---- the civilians were creating value to provide various labor products that could satisfy people's needs; and the king would do his best to govern the country and defend the territory. The rules recognized and accepted by social members in such case are also called the king-civilian contract.

The content of the contract in democratic human society is quite different from that of the contract in monarchic society. But there is also something in common, that is, the content of the social contract must be accepted by social members. The "accept" here may be due to threat or fear (for example, people were forced to accept the contract in monarchic countries due to fear of torture). But in terms of the form, a social contract has to be

们需求的各式各样的劳动产品，而国王也会尽心尽力的管理国家，捍卫疆土。这里被社会成员认可接受的规则也叫做国王与百姓之间的契约。

在民主制的人类社会当中，契约的内容和君主制社会存在很大的差别。但也有共同之处，那就是社会契约的内容都要被社会成员接受。这里的接受可能存在受威胁或是恐惧的原因（比如君主制国家由于恐惧酷刑而被迫接受），但从形式上来讲，社会契约必须让全体社会成员接受，才能成为维系社会秩序的有效规则。民主制社会契约，就是为了防止社会成员因为恐惧而接受不平等契约，因此它会明确要求规则应体现每一位

accepted by all social members so that it can become an effective rule for maintaining social order. Democratic social contract is to prevent social members from accepting unequal contracts due to fear. So, it will expressly require that the rules should reflect the rights and options of every social member and that the rules should be formulated jointly by all social members and maintain social order according to such rules.

The importance of social rules or contracts is to restrain and regulate the unreasonable desires and needs of human social members so as to attain the goal of maintaining the basic order of human society. Otherwise, if to organize and operate human society per human nature, chaotic situation, as well as misdeeds e.g. theft, violent sabotage, etc. would be everywhere due to the natural defects of human.

社会成员的权利和选择，由全体社会成员来共同制定规则，并以此维系社会秩序。

社会规则或契约的重要性就在于，约束和规制人类社会成员不合理的欲望和需求，以达到维系人类社会基本秩序的目的。否则，如果按照人类的本性来组建运行人类社会，由于人类的天然缺陷，就会导致出现混乱不堪的局面，偷盗、暴力破坏等行径便会无处不在。

Rules That Need to Be "Guarded"

As long as people choose to produce together and live a socialized life in groups, everyone needs to enter into a contract among them, which is also called "social rules" in order to maintain such basic order of human society. Social contract varies depending on the type of society. In spite of different content, the main feature is similar --- such contract rules must be generally recognized and accepted by social members, whether accepted actively or accepted forcibly because of fear. But unfair contracts that scare most people cannot maintain social order for long, and will eventually be substituted by new social rules.

In general, there have been two types of contract rules in human society since the recorded era of human history --- monarchic contract and democratic contract.

需要"值守"的规则

只要人们选择在一起共同生产，过群居的社会型生活，那么为了维系这种人类社会的基本秩序，大家就需要达成一种他们之间的契约，这种契约又称作社会规则。不同的社会类型，会出现不同的社会契约，虽然内容不同，但主要特征都是相似的——那就是这样的契约规则要得到社会成员的普遍认可和接受，无论他们是主动接受还是迫于恐惧而被迫接受。不过，不公平、让多数人恐惧的契约，是不能长久维系社会秩序的，终将被新的社会规则所替代。

从有记载的人类历史时代开始，总的来说人类社会出现过两大类型的契约规则——君主制契约和民主制契约，这是依据社会成员的身份是否平等

The classification is based on whether social members have an equal status or not. Regardless of whether the contract types are the same, however, some basic rules are applicable to the contract rules of all human societies, like prohibiting extremely unreasonable human desires e.g. fraud, theft, harm, adultery, etc. No society will openly allow such behaviors to occur in human groups.

Although prohibited by social rules, such behaviors still occur from time to time due to the natural defects of human desires and needs. It is not because people don't know that such behaviors are prohibited by social rules, but because a considerable number of people cannot restrain and confine their own unreasonable even evil desires and needs by self-discipline in many times and occasions. So, generally accepted rules, without force to protect, would be easily violated and trampled. People who follow the

而做出的区分。但无论契约类型是否相同，有些基本的规则，是适用于所有人类社会契约规则的，比如禁止欺诈、偷盗、伤害、奸淫等人类极不合理的欲望需求，没有哪个社会会公然许可这样的行为发生在人类群体之中。

尽管被社会规则所禁止，但由于人类自身欲望需求所存在的天然缺陷，这些行为仍会时有发生。其缘由不是因为人们不知道这些行为已被社会规则所禁止，而是在很多时间和场合，有相当数量的人无法通过自律来约束禁锢自己不合理，甚至是邪恶的欲望需求。所以，人们普遍接受的规则，如果没有力量保护，就会被轻易违反践踏，会让遵守规则的人们受到伤害，社会秩序遭到破坏。如果一部分人不合理的欲望需求得不到有效禁锢，紧跟着就会有越来越多的社会成员收回

rules would be harmed, and the social order will be disrupted. If some people's unreasonable desires and needs cannot be effectively confined, more and more social members will take back their original rights (freedom) that they originally surrendered for forming the society. It is for self-defense and satisfaction of self-needs for people to do so. In such case, the social contract rules will lose their effect.

To avoid the barbaric status of human society where everyone fight against others, people prevent the situation of destroyed rules and social disorder in a way: To form a public right belonging to all social members and the entire social group through transfer of rights among people, which, as is authorized by everyone, has a great coercive power --- a unilateral dominating force: can directly force the targeted objects to obey the requirements of public rights without negotiation. For example, social members will,

他们原本为了组建社会而交出的原始权利（自由），人们这样做是为了自卫和满足自我需求，这时社会契约规则就会失去作用。

为了避免人类社会出现人人争斗的野蛮状态，人们通过一种方法来防止规则遭受破坏，社会失去秩序的局面出现。那就是通过人们的权利让渡，形成一种属于所有社会成员和整个社会群体的公共权利，这种公共权利因为获得了大家的授权，所以具有很大的强制力——一种单向的支配力，不需要协商，可以直接迫使作用对象服从公共权利的要求。比如抓到了偷窃的人，社会成员不再用自己的原始权利去私自惩罚小偷，而是要把他交给社会群体中的某些部门，比如警察局和法院，

having caught a thief, no longer punish him personally with their original rights, but hand him over to certain departments in the social group e.g. the police station and the court, and then the police and judges will represent public rights to investigate, collect evidence against him, convict and punish him. Such way is to manage the social order via social rules instead of the original rights of social members lest the natural defects of original rights drag mankind into endless fights.

Hence, such police, judges, government officials, and other members of human groups who can maintain the rules and defend social order of human society become the "guards" of social contract rules.

"Public Rights" Controlled by "guards"

To maintain the order of operation of human society, most social members are willing to

然后由警察和法官代表公共权利，对其进行调查取证，定罪处罚。这样的方式就是通过社会规则来管理社会秩序，而不是用社会成员的原始权利来进行，以此避免原始权利的天然缺陷会将人类拖入无休止的争斗当中。

这些维护规则，捍卫人类社会秩序的警察、法官、政府官员，还有其他能够起到这种作用的人类群体成员，就成为了社会契约规则的"值守者"。

"值守者"掌控的"公共权利"

为了维护人类社会的运行秩序，绝大多数社会成员都愿意以让渡部分原始权利的方式，

authorize an organization or a certain type of persons by transfer of original rights to exercise some of the original rights belonging to themselves on their behalf, e.g. punishing violators of social rules, and implementing violence against social members who violate the rules. Because such original rights are highly dangerous and destructive to humans themselves, most people choose to voluntarily surrender their rights to avoid chaos in society due to different extent and standards in exercise of such rights by individuals.

Such original rights transferred by such social members, by gathering and making public in some way, will become a public right --- a freedom belonging to all social members, and a freedom to behave as per the common will of social members. Because such freedom reflects the common will that all social members require to take certain actions, e.g. implementing violence to and punishing those who violate social

授权给某个机构或是某类人员，让他们来代替自己行使原本属于自己的一部分原始权利，比如对违反社会规则者进行惩罚，对违反规则的社会成员实施暴力等。这些原始权利由于对于人类自身具有较高的危险性和破坏性，因此绝大多数人都选择主动交出权利，以避免由于个人行使这样的权利，尺度标准不一而给社会带来混乱。

这些社会成员让渡出来的原始权利，经过一定方式的汇聚和公示，会成为一种公共权利——一种属于全体社会成员的自由，一种按照社会成员共同意愿去做的自由。由于这种自由，体现了全体社会成员要求做出某些行为的共同意愿，比如对违反社会规则的人实施暴力、进行惩罚等。因此，这种公共权利具有明显的单方强制性——这种权利由于得到社会成员的普遍认可和授权，它的

rules and so on. Such public right is obvious unilaterally coercive --- exercise of such right does not require the consent of the targeted objects as it is generally recognized and granted by social members. To exercise such right cautiously, however, social contract rules will usually set strict procedures and requirements for its implementation to avoid mistakes and counter-acting force that disrupts social order in the exercise of public rights.

In view of the above features of public right, when the guards of the social contract rules --- police, judges, soldiers and government officials --- control public rights in the name of managing and maintaining social order with the authorization by social members, such force that represent the common will of social members, derived by transfer of human original rights and has unilateral coercion will get another name --- political power --- due to its important effect to the entire

行使无须征得作用对象的同意。不过为了慎用这种权利，社会契约规则通常会对其实施设置严格的程序和要求，以避免公共权利的行使出现错误和破坏社会秩序的反作用力。

鉴于公共权利的上述特征，当社会契约规则的值守者——警察、法官、军人和政府官员们，经过社会成员的授权，以管理维护社会秩序的名义掌控公共权利时，这种代表社会成员共同意愿，由人类原始权利让渡衍生而来，且具有单方强制性的力量，便由于其对整个社会的重要作用，而有了另外一个名字——政治权力。

society.

Human Society Needs "Political Power"

Political power has unilateral coercion, and the legitimacy of such public right comes from the authorization of every social member. Social members transfer by way of authorization some of their original rights, which belong to themselves but will cause instability and destruction to the human groups if they are allowed to be exercised by individuals at will, to social public organizations, and which will hand them over to qualified "guards" of social contract rules who meet the requirements to exercise.

Why exercise of one's own rights by himself/herself will cause destructive effects to the group to which he/she belongs? This is due to the natural defects of human --- "inferiority", e.g. the human desires and needs for hatred and destruction. Many people, having caught a thief,

人类社会需要 "政治权力"

政治权力具有单方面的强制性，这种公共权利的正当性，来源于每一位社会成员的授权。社会成员以授权的方式将原本属于自己，但如果任由个人随意行使，却会给人类群体带来不稳定和破坏作用的部分原始权利，让渡给社会公共机构，由这些机构交给符合资格和条件的社会契约规则"值守者"来统一行使。

为什么属于自己的权利，由自己行使却会给所在群体带来破坏作用呢？这是由于人类的天然缺陷——"劣根性"导致的，比如人类仇恨和破坏的欲望需求。人们抓到了小偷，有不少人会想把小偷打死，因为愤怒——这人偷我的财物，他竟敢偷我

want to kill him due to anger --- "This guy stole my belongings, he even dared to steal my things"; and some people will become increasingly angry when thinking about it, and eventually lose mind and control. If they were to exercise their right to retaliate against the thief, the thief would be likely to lose his life because of the theft. In the process, the cruel side of human would be fully revealed. The thief might need money to serve his elderly and children, or he couldn't restrain or surmount the evil desire to steal. . . Whatever the reason, there is rarely something that needs him to pay the cost with his life. So, in order to embody the pursuit of good value, satisfy the reasonable needs of all compatriots, and enable more people to feel happy, most social members will agree to hand over such persons and matters to public organizations for treatment. To human society, it is also another kind of value creation to get such people punished appropriately via

的东西，一些人会越想越气愤，以致最后失去理智和控制力。如果由他们自己行使报复小偷的权利，这个小偷很有可能因为偷窃而丢掉性命，在这个过程中人类残暴的一面将展现无遗。这个小偷或许需要财物去侍奉自己的老人和孩子，或是他自己无法抑制克服偷窃的邪恶欲望…但种种原因，里面罕有需要他付出生命作为对价的。因此，人类社会为了体现美好的价值追求，满足所有同胞的合理需求，让更多的人获得幸福快乐的感觉。绝大多数社会成员都会同意，将这样的人和事，交给社会公共机构去处理。通过一种相对公允的力量，来让这样的人受到适当的惩罚，帮助他们悔过自新，这样的过程对于人类社会也是另一种价值创造。因为，这个过程给了窃贼新的人生机会，满足了他们重新做人的合理需求，同时这样做也会让其他社会成员感到用了特别的方式创造出价值。

a relatively fair force to help them turn over a new leaf. Because this process gives the thieves a new opportunity in their life and satisfies their reasonable needs to renew themselves. Meanwhile, doing so will also make other social members feel that they have created value in a special way.

Human society needs a relatively fair force to deal with various situations and issues that social members cannot or are not suitable to directly solve in order to maintain its own order and stability. To attain such a goal, members of human society form, by way of transfer of their original rights to social public organizations, the power to manage and maintain the order of human society --- political power.

Different Social Public Organizations

Since the recorded era of human history, many types of contracts have emerged successively in

人类社会为了维护自身的秩序稳定，需要一种相对公允的力量，来处理各种各样社会成员不能或不适宜直接解决的情形和问题。为了实现这样的目标，人类社会成员便使用让渡原始权利交给社会公共机构的方式，结成这种管理维护人类社会秩序的力量——政治权力。

不同的社会公共机构

自有人类历史记载以来，人类社会先后出现了很多种契约类型，但总体上可以社会公

human society. But in general they can be divided into two types by the attribution of social public rights (political power): the monarchic contract (including aristocratic contract) --- the political power is controlled by a few people e.g. the king; and democratic contract --- the political power is exercised jointly by all social members in some way. Corresponding to different social contracts, the public organizations that control political power in human society also have many manifestations.

Under the contract of the monarchic society, the king or tribal chiefs and their various organizations and officials are the public organizations managing the society. According to the cognition of social members, the king, chiefs and their subordinates can control public rights for some reason (or authorization from the unknown world, or their worship to them). Only when everyone believes that the political right to manage

共权利（政治权力）的归属而分为两大类：一类是君主制（包括贵族制）——政治权力属于国王等少数人掌控，一类是民主制——政治权力由全体社会成员以某种方式共同行使。相对应不同的社会契约，人类社会掌控政治权力的公共机构，也有多种表现形式。

在君主制社会契约下，国王或是部落首领以及他们下属的各类机构和官员，是管理社会的公共机构。在社会成员的认知当中，国王、首领及其下属由于某种原因（或是来自未知世界的授权，或是自身对他们的膜拜）是可以掌控公共权利的，大家都认为管控社会的政治权力由这些人来掌握和实施，才具有正当性和有效性。为此社会成员不反对在人格层面，国王、首领以及官员的地位高过

and control the society shall be mastered and implemented by such people can it be legitimate and effective. To this end, social members didn't object to the status of the king, chiefs and officials higher than themselves at the level of personality. Members of a monarchic society were willing to accept personality inequality and social hierarchy. They believed that the foregoing persons had talent or abilities beyond common people. They agreed such public organizations to play a role so as to maintain the order of society.

In an aristocratic contract-regulated society, there was also a system of public organizations similar to that of a monarchic society. Also, there would also be the king and officials. Simple the control of the king and chiefs over public power was dispersed by the aristocratic members in the control of the political power of the society due to the formation of the aristocratic class and the expansion of aristocratic forces.

自己，君主制社会的成员会愿意接受人格不平等和社会等级，他们认为上述人员具备天赋或是超出常人的能力，他们支持这些公共机构发挥作用，以维系社会的运行秩序。

在贵族制契约调整的社会当中，同样有一套类似于君主制社会的公共机构体系。也会有国王和官员，只不过由于贵族阶层的形成，以及贵族势力的扩张，贵族成员在掌控社会政治权力方面，分散了国王和首领对公共权力的控制力度。但总体上，社会民众对于公共机构以及国王、首领和贵族的认知，基本无异于君主制社会。社会成员仍然处在——他们比我们更优秀，更适合掌控政治

But in general, the cognition of the public of the society to public organizations and the kings, chiefs and nobles was basically no different from that of monarchic society. The social members were still in a hierarchical society of unequal personality --- "they are more suitable for controlling the political power as they are better than us". But in such case public organizations still played an important role in stabilizing the social order.

When it comes to the era of democratic contract, the situation has changed a lot. Due to the development of news and information dissemination, the knowledge and skills of social members have been improved comprehensively, and their self-confidence and personal abilities have greatly enhanced. In such case, people generally begin to have the claim for the right of equality and freedom. Social members think that there are no special classes who are inherently

权力——这样一种人格不平等的等级社会之中，不过公共机构此时依旧发挥着稳定社会秩序的重要作用。

到了民主制契约时代，情况就有了很大的变化。由于咨讯和信息传播的发达，社会成员的知识技能全面提高，自信心和个人能力极大地增强，这时人们普遍有了平等自由的权利主张和要求。社会成员觉得在人格层面，没有天生就比自己更强，更适合掌控政治权力的特别阶层。人人平等是这个时代的显著特征，社会成员需求日益多元化，权利（自由）意识迅速提升，人们开始通过代议制民主，实现由全体社会成员共同行使公共权利（政治权力）的目的，

better than them and more suitable for controlling political power at the level of personality. Equality of all is the distinctive feature of this era. The needs of social members are increasingly diversified, and the awareness of rights (freedom) has increased rapidly. People begin to attain the goal of exercising public rights (political power) by all social members through representative democracy. To organize social public organizations, e.g. president, parliament, government, judge, prosecutor, etc. by election or authorization to appoint. Having entered this era, social public organizations have become more diverse and effective. As under such contract rule, almost all social members have the opportunity to participate in the political life of the society. Group wisdom plays an important role in the operation of social public organizations. Also, the application of political power becomes practical and efficient. An unprecedented new

选举组成或是授权任命组成社会的公共机构，比如总统、议会、政府、法官、检察官等等。进入这个时代，社会的公共机构就显得更加多样化，也更加有效了。因为在这种契约规则之下，几乎所有社会成员都有机会参与社会的政治生活，群体智慧在社会公共机构的运行过程中，起到了重要作用，政治权力的运用也显得务实高效，社会秩序出现了前所未有的新局面。

pattern comes into being to the social order.

Necessary while "Savage" Political Power

In essence, political power is still a right --- a freedom to behave as per the will of the subject of right. In terms of the form and operating mode, however, political power is different from rights in the common sense. It is condensed after all social members transfer some of their original rights to public organizations. The freedom reflected by political power is at a stronger level. Every social member allows social public organizations to exercise such right without the consent of the subject. Because such right, after the transfer of right and authorization by social members, is not only legitimate, but also reasonable. Even if it sometimes causes pain or harm to the subject, it is necessary for the human

必要却"狰狞"的政治权力

政治权力从其本质上来讲，仍是一种权利——一种按照权利主体的意愿去做的自由。但从其形式和运行模式来看，政治权力又不同于普通意义上的权利，它是全体社会成员将原本属于自己的某些原始权利让渡给社会公共机构之后凝结而成，政治权力所体现出的自由度更加强烈。每一个社会成员都允许社会公共机构在行使这种权利时，无需经过当事主体的同意。因为，在经过社会成员的让渡授权之后，这种权利不仅具有正当性，而且具有合理性，即便有时会给当事主体带来痛苦或是伤害，但这是人类群体为了维系内部秩序所必需的，群体成员接纳、认可这样的自由。因此，这样一种人类社会的权利——公共权利，又称政治权力、权力，除了自由

groups to maintain internal order. Group members recognize and accept such freedom. So, such a right of human society --- public right --- is also called "political power" or "power", in addition to the essential feature of freedom, it also has one more feature --- coercive domination.

Because power is condensed from the authorization of social members (the transfer of original rights), power is legitimate to human society. Accordingly, power exhibits an obvious feature of coercive dominance. Such coercive domination can affect and deprive the subject's various interests ranging from freedom of speech and deeds, property interests, to personal rights, and even the right to life. So, it can also be said that the power condensed from human original rights is "savage". Under the monarchic contract, a person who disobeyed the king's order might be decapitated. In this way, the king would let his subjects know

这一权利的本质特征之外，又多了强制支配性的特征。

因为，权力是由社会成员的授权（原始权利让渡）凝结而成，所以权力对于人类社会既有正当性，又有合理性，权力因此表现出一种很明显的强制支配性特征。这种强制支配性可以影响、剥夺当事主体的各种利益，小到言行自由、财产利益，大到人身权益，甚至是生命权利。因此，也可以说由人类原始权利凝结而成的权力是"狰狞"的。在君主制契约下，一个违抗国王命令的人，是可能被砍掉头颅的，国王会以这种方式，让自己的臣民知道，违反社会契约是要付出代价的，尽管他可能没有意识到他（她）和臣民之间存在这样的契约。但国王手中的权力，客观上的确是这种契约的产物，社会成员为了

that they would pay if violate the social contract, though he might not be aware that there was such contract between him/her and the subjects. But objectively the power of the king is a product of such contract. For the sake of safety and stability, social members were all willing to let the king and his officials exercise some of their original rights that belonged to them. Also, they might not realize that those rights belonged to them. But objectively the king's power did come from their obedience and acceptance. Likewise, under the democratic contract, if a social member severely violates the social rules formulated by the public through representative government system --- the law--- he may also be imposed death penalty by corresponding public organizations, a case in point is when killing an innocent child with a gun. Under the above circumstances, it is because the king and the judicial officials under the democratic contract

安全和稳定，都愿意由国王及其官员来行使原本属于自己的部分原始权利，他们也可能并没有意识到那些权利原本属于自己，但国王的权力客观上的确来自他们的服从和接纳。同样在民主制契约下，一个社会成员如果严重违反了民众通过代议制制定的社会规则——法律，他也有可能被相应的社会公共机构施以极刑，比如他用枪杀害了无辜的儿童。 在上述情形下，无论是国王，还是民主契约下的司法者，都是因为掌控了权力，才可以剥夺社会成员的生命而不被谴责，从人性的角度来看，这时的权力都显得十分"狰狞"。

both controlled the power that can deprive social members of their lives without being condemned. In terms of human nature, the power in such case appears to be very "savage".

Power to Protect Rights

The source of power is the transfer of the original rights of the members of the human group. The members of the human group transfer some of their original rights --- e.g. the right to punish those who violate the rules of the social contract, and the right to retaliate against those who endanger their legitimate rights and interests, the right that needs to be constrained when obeying the rules, etc. --- to public organizations that represent the common will of the human group, which will exercise such rights closely related to the internal order of the human group on their behalf.

As power comes from the

保障权利的权力

权力的来源是人类群体成员的原始权利让渡，人类群体成员将自己的部分原始权利，比如处罚违反社会契约规则者的权利，报复危害自身正当权益者的权利，在遵守规则时需受约束的权利等，让渡给代表人类群体共同意志的公共机构，由他们代为行使这些和人类群体内部秩序密切相关的权利。

因为权力来自人类的原始

human original rights, it is condensed from the original rights that members of human groups voluntarily transferred (or were forced to surrender). So, such power is legitimate in human society, and it is also a necessity of human society. A common while convincing example is the maintenance and control of traffic order in human society. All social members have the freedom to travel and transportation, and no one wants their such right to be interfered and restrained. As the population and transportation vehicles increase, however, problems arising from transportation are increasingly serious in human society, and eventually resulted in traffic congestions. People realize that everyone should not exercise such right at will. There should be a rule to restrain people's such right, and the purpose for it is eventually to ensure everyone's freedom of passage. So, traffic rules have emerged. All vehicles

权利，是人类群体成员自愿让渡（或是被迫交出）的原始权利凝结而成，所以在人类社会，这样的权力具有正当性和合理性，也是人类社会的必需之物。一个常见且有说服力的例子，就是人类社会关于交通秩序的维护和管控，所有的社会成员都有出行和交通的自由，没有人愿意自己的这种权利受到干涉和约束。但随着人口和交通工具的数量增多，人类社会因为交通出现的问题越来越严重，以致于最后拥挤不堪，无法通行。人们意识到大家不应该随心所欲的行使这项权利，应该有个规则来约束人们的这项权利，约束大家的目的，最终还是为了保证每一个人的通行自由。于是，交通规则出现了，凡是朝着一个方向通行的车辆或是人员要靠近路的一侧行驶，以避免和对面方向驶来的车辆和人员相撞。遇到十字路口，要根据指挥人员或是信号灯光的指示前行，不能随意通行。通过这样的规则，人们很好地解决了交通拥堵无秩序的问题，这样的规则，也很好地保护了每一位社会成

or people moving in one direction shall drive or walk close to one side of the road to avoid collisions with vehicles or people coming from the opposite direction. When coming to a crossroad, shall proceed as per the instructions of the traffic commander or the signal lights, and shall not pass through at will. Through such rules, people have well solved the issue of traffic congestion and disorder, and, such rules have well protected the freedom of passage of every social member. However, if such rules rely solely on the self-consciousness and self-discipline of social members, it will exist in name only. Due to the natural defects of human and the unreasonable desires and needs that are insurmountable, there will be many people who break the rules in order to satisfy their selfish desires. This will cause fewer and fewer people to obey the rules (restraining their own rights/freedom), and finally cause the rules to be fully invalidated,

员的通行自由。但这样的规则，如果仅靠社会成员的自觉和自律，就如同虚设，因为人类自身的天然缺陷，以及难以克服的不合理欲望和需求，会出现很多为了满足私欲而去破坏规则的人，这样会使遵守规则（约束自己的权利自由）的人越来越少，以至最后规则完全失效，人们的通行自由失去保障。因此，人们在设定交通规则之后，通常都要将自己为了维护交通秩序而让渡出的部分权利交给社会公共机构，由他们管理处罚违反交通规则的社会成员，以维护交通秩序，保障社会成员的原始权利——交通自由。

and people's freedom of passage will become unsecured. So, after setting traffic rules, people will usually deliver some of their rights that have been transferred to maintain traffic order to social public organizations, which will manage and punish social members who violate traffic rules so as to maintain traffic order and protect the original rights of social members --- the freedom of transportation.

In terms of the fundamental purpose, power is condensed from some original rights that social members voluntarily transfer (or are forced to surrender) in order to guarantee their more important rights (freedom). So, it can also be said that power is established by social members to secure their rights.

Power Controllers

Some of social members' rights, after being transferred and surrendered, will appear in the

从根本目的上来讲，权力是社会成员为了保障自己更重要的权利自由，而自愿让渡（或被迫交出）的部分原始权利凝结形成。因此，也可以这样说，权力是社会成员为了保障权利，才被人们设立存在的。

权力的掌控者

社会成员将部分权利让渡交出之后，会以权力的形态出现在社会公共机构——诸如政府、

form of power in social public organizations e.g. the government, police station, court, etc., where there are some specified persons who control power on behalf of such public organizations --- They are generally called "officials".

For example, officials in charge of traffic (also known as traffic police) exercise the power condensed from the transfer of some of social members' power on behalf of the public organization that manages the traffic order of the society. They can seize and punish social members' vehicles according to certain procedure without being condemned. There is no room for social members to resist them, because the legitimacy and reasonableness of such power determines that it is legitimate (recognized and affirmed by most social members) as such power is a unilaterally coercive public right of human society because it is condensed form social members' rights. But such kind of justice will disappear in some cases due

警察局、法庭等地方，而在这些机构内，会有一些代表公共机构具体掌控权力的人，通常这些人被称作——官员。

比如负责交通的官员（也被称作交通警察），他们便代表管理社会交通秩序的公共机构，行使社会成员让渡凝结而成的权力，他们可以按照某种程序查扣处罚社会成员的交通工具，而不被谴责，且不容反抗。因为这是社会成员的权利凝结而成，是人类社会的公共权利，带有单方强制性，其本身具有的正当性和合理性，决定了这种权力的正义性（被绝大多数社会成员认可和肯定），所以不容反抗。不过这种正义性，却会因为权力掌控者的原因，在某些情况下消失。

to the power controllers.

One case is that the power controllers are not eligible or qualified, e.g. officials not appointed or authorized by the king in a monarchic society, officials not recommended or elected by the people in a democratic society, etc. In such cases, exercise of power by the above officials would be unjust and social members would resist such power. Because power is in essence formed by transfer of rights, now that social members can surrender their original rights, they can absolutely take back the rights surrendered by them as necessary as well. The reason for people to take back their rights in such case is that such power controllers are not qualified to exercise their original rights.

One more case is that the exercise of power is not based on established procedures and rules. Power is most likely to infringe the original rights of social members in exercising though

一种情况是，权力的掌控者不具备资格。例如在君主制社会，官员没有被国王任命和授权。在民主制社会，官员没有经过民众的推荐选举。这样的情形，都会使上述官员在行使权力时，不具有正义性，社会成员会反抗这样的权力，因为从本质上来讲，权力由权利让渡形成，社会成员可以交出自己的原始权利，也完全可以在必要的时候收回自己交出的权利。这时人们收回权利的理由，就是这样的权力掌控者不具备资格行使人们的原始权利。

还有一种情况是，权力的行使没有依据既定的程序规则。由于权力具有很强的单方强制性，虽然它以保障权利而被设立存在，但在行使过程中，权力却最容易侵犯社会成员的原

it is set to secure rights due to the strong unilateral coercion of power. To surmount such defects, the operation of power in almost all types of human societies shall follow preset procedures and rules. Three-time memorial to the throne and five-time memorial to the throne before executing a death-penalty prisoner in a monarchic society [①], as well as notice/notification, hearing, and statement of defense prior to administrative punishment in a democratic society are all manifestations of such requirement. If the operation of power does not follow the rules and procedures, such power will accordingly lose its justice since it is extremely likely to infringe social members' rights --- social members will take back the original rights that belonged to them because of this.

始权利。为了克服这样的缺陷，几乎所有类型的人类社会，权力的运行都要遵循事先设定的规则程序。君主制社会中，死刑犯行刑前的三复奏、五复奏，民主制社会中，行政处罚前的告知听证和陈述申辩，都是这一要求的体现。如果权力的运行，没有遵循规则程序，由于这样的权力极其容易侵犯社会成员的权利，因此也会失去正义性——社会成员会藉此收回属于自己的原始权利。

---

① *The Political Essentials of the Zhenguan Era* by Wu Jing (The Tang Dynasty, China) (Volume 8), translated by Pian Yusai and Pianhua, Zhonghua Book Company 2009 Edition, （"The Criminal Law: Article 31"）p. 212.

（唐）吴兢：《贞观政要》（第 8 卷），骈宇赛、骈骅译，中华书局 2009 年版，（刑法第三十一）第 212 页。

Another case will also cause the exercise of power to lose justice, that is, power controllers abuse the power under their control for personal gain, and which is also called "corruption". An example is a traffic policeman's illegal behavior of not punishing the owner of a vehicle upon unauthorized private receipt of money or property from such owner after seizing it. Such power has lost the justice due to the loss of fairness and violation to the purpose of securing rights and maintaining justice.

Respectable Power Controllers

Due to the insurmountable natural defects and "inferiority" of mankind, in order to maintain the basic order of the society, members of human society will usually choose to transfer or surrender some of their original rights to condense the unilaterally coercive power to maintain the

还有一种情况也会让权力的行使失去正义性，那就是权力的掌控者，将自己控制的权力，滥用于谋取私利，这样的情形，也被称作"腐败"。比如，查扣交通工具的交通警察，私自收取当事人的财物，而不处罚他们的违规行为。这样的权力由于失去公平，背离了权力保障权利和维护正义的宗旨目标，而不具有正义性。

令人尊敬的权力掌控者

由于人类自身难以克服的天然缺陷和"劣根性"，人类社会成员为了维系社会的基本秩序，通常会选择让渡交出部分原始权利来凝结成，具有单方强制性的权力，来维系人类社会的正常秩序。人们允许权力来分配重要资源，制约社会成员的不合理欲望需求，以实现

normal order of human society. People allow power to allocate important resources and restrict the unreasonable desires and needs of social members so as to attain the goal of stable social order.

At a T-junction in the evening, everyone and every vehicle on the street rush through this junction. The junction gets congested with vehicles very soon as no one is willing to yield to others actively and don't know when to yield. In such case, everyone's rights are in an expanded status. Their arbitrary personal will have caused everyone to lose the basic traffic order, and then cause their right --- freedom to transportation --- to be constricted and fail to realize smoothly.

In such case, a device representing power or a person controlling power is most needed by people to appear. Such a device can be a signal light, which is conferred with the power to force pedestrians and vehicles to pass as per its instructions. If someone

社会秩序安定的目标。

在夜幕就要降临的丁字路口，街上的每一个人、每一辆车都争先恐后的通过这个路口。因为大家都不肯主动避让，也不知何时该避让，路口很快就被通行车辆堵得水泄不通。这个时候，每个人的权利都处于扩张状态，这些随心所欲的个人意志，导致大家失去了基本的交通秩序，进而每个人的权利——交通自由，都受到了约束，无法顺利实现。

在这种情况下，人们最需要一个代表权力的设备或是掌控权力的人出现，这样的设备可以是信号灯，它被人们赋予了强制行人车辆按照其指示通行的权力，如果有人违反信号灯的指示通行，人们又授权更高层级的权力掌控者（或是设备）

passes through in violation to such instructions of the signal light, then people will authorize power controllers (or devices) at higher levels to record and punish such behavior. For example, to record the behavior in violation to the instructions of a signal light with camera, and then impose penalties on them e.g. points deduction, fine, etc. The signal light here can also be replaced by traffic police. Pedestrians and vehicles passing through the junction shall obey the instructions of the traffic police. Under the instructions of the traffic police, wait to yield to other pedestrians or vehicles and then pass through the junction. Such kind of command will enable all vehicles and people to pass through a T-junction in a time as short as possible.

And everyone will be in awe of the police carefully directing traffic in the middle of the road when they pass through such a junction smoothly. Their work is of great significance as they

来记录和处罚这样的行为。比如，用摄像头记录下违反信号灯指示的行为，然后给予扣分、罚款等处罚。这里的信号灯也可以用交通警察来替代，在路口通行的行人和车辆需要服从交通警察的指挥，在交通警察的指示下，等待避让其他车辆，然后通过路口，这样的指挥会让所有的车辆和人员，用尽可能短的时间，来通过这个丁字路口。

当人们顺利通过这样的路口时，看着马路中间认真指挥交通的警察，每个人的心中都会肃然起敬。尽管他（她）们只是在做好自己的本职工作，但由于他们创造出了真正的价

create value in the real sense that satisfies the reasonable needs of most people and embody the common will of social members though they are just doing their own jobs they ought to do. Their images will also appear great and prestige in people's hearts. Such power controllers will certainly be respected by most social members. This can be proved by the fact that people in a country spontaneously sent burials to policemen who were shot dead due to retaliation.[①]

值, 满足了多数人的合理需求, 他们的工作体现出社会成员的共同意志, 因此意义非凡。他们的形象在人们的心中也会显得高大威严, 这样的权力掌控者也一定会受到绝大多数社会成员的尊敬, 某个国家人们自发为由于报复而被枪杀的警察送葬就充分证明了这一点。

"Mutated" Power

"变异" 的权力

Normal power is necessary for all sorts of human unions. Power is necessary whether for the kings and nobles in a monarchic society or for the elected officials in a democratic society so as to maintain the basic running order of

正常的权力, 是所有类型的人类联合体所必需的。无论是君主制社会当中的国王和贵族, 还是民主制社会的民选官员, 为了维护人类联合体的基本运行秩序, 克服人类自身的天然缺陷和 "劣根性", 权力都

---

① *Xi´an Daily* (Xi'an, China): "Around 20,000 police and citizens gathered in New York to see off a Chinese police", published in *Netease News*, http://news.163.com/15/0106/04/AF8HVH4D00014AED.html, access time: 15:46 Mar 7, 2017.

西安日报 (西安):《两万名警民齐聚纽约送别华裔警察》, 载网易新闻, http://news.163.com/15/0106/04/AF8HVH4D00014AED.html, 访问时间: 2017 年 3 月 7 日 15: 46。

a human union and surmount the natural defects and "inferiority" of mankind. Power exists for realizing effective restriction to the original rights of members of human groups. To be precise, power is established in some way to restrain the unreasonable needs of social members (from either the unknown world or the transfer of people's rights). It is the very existence of power that gets unreasonable human needs effectively restricted lest the chaos depicted in "Leviathan" occur in human society.

On the other hand, however, there is no room for people to resist power as power is a unilaterally coercive public right that represents the public will of the society. So, without a direct and effective power control system, power is extremely likely to infringe the legitimate and reasonable rights of social members. In such case, power will mutate and become a destructive force that harms the social order

是必要的，权力的存在是为了实现人类群体成员原始权利的有效制约。准确的说，权力是为了遏制社会成员的不合理需求，而以某种方式被设立存在（或来自未知世界，或来自民众的权利让渡）。正是由于权力的存在，人类的不合理需求才被有效约束，人类社会才不至于陷入《利维坦》所描绘的混乱场景之中。

但另一方面，由于权力代表了社会的公共意志，是一种带有单方强制性的公共权利，不容社会成员反抗。因此如果没有直接有效的控权体系，权力也极其容易侵犯社会成员正当合理的权利，这个时候权力便会发生变异，成为祸害人类社会秩序的破坏性力量。变异的权力对于社会的危害，并不亚于自然灾难。我们可以先看一个例子，在一个国家级贫困地区的农村，几位妇人坐在路边

of mankind. The harm caused by mutated power to the society is no less than that caused by natural disasters. Let's first take an example. In a country-level poverty-stricken rural area, several women sit on a stone by the side of the road, doing needlework while chatting. One woman says, "One child shall be enough as long as he/she will be excellent, needless to have too many children", another woman says, "It makes sense! As long as one child becomes an official, your whole family will benefit from him/her. Whatever celebration takes place in your family, all kinds of people around you will come for you to celebrate whether they are in a close relationship with you or not. "The other woman immediately replies, "You are right! Look at our village secretary or village head, a lot of people come for them when there are celebrations in their families. If he/she becomes an official of the provincial or even the central government, far more

的石头上, 边做针线活, 边聊天。一位说, "孩子们不要多, 只要有一个有本事就行"。另一位说, "就是, 只要有一个做了官, 全家人都跟着享福, 家里过个什么事, 大车小车、什么人都来了。" 对方马上回应说, "就是, 你看现在做个村支书、村长, 家里过什么事, 人都很多。要是在国家、省里做个官, 那还不更厉害。"

people will come for you."

The power of an official described by these village women is the very mutated power. In such case, the power doesn't exist to secure the legitimate rights of most people of the society and maintain social order any more. The power controlled by such officials is to seek benefits for themselves and a few people. Because according to the essential attribute of power, social members don't need to please them. Their power ought to be used to protect the legitimate rights of social members and maintain social order. When the situation described by the above village women becomes common in human groups, it means that power has mutated. In such case, the power controllers serve those who flatter and please them. Such power has lost its targeted functions of maintaining social order and protecting legitimate rights of the public and consequently becomes a tool for the power controllers to seek

村妇们口中描述的官员手中的权力，便是变异的权力。这种权力不再是为了保障社会多数人的正当合理权利，和维护社会秩序而存在。这样的官员所掌控的权力，是在为自己和少数人谋取利益，因为按照权力的本质属性，社会成员无需讨好他们，他们手中的权力是应该为保护社会成员的正当权利，维护社会秩序而发挥作用的。当上述村姑描述的情形，在人类群体当中普遍出现的时候，就说明权力发生了变异，权力的掌控者只在为讨好、取悦他们的人群服务，这样的权力已经失去了维护社会秩序和保护公众正当权利的目标作用，而成了掌控者谋取私利的工具手段。一部分社会成员为了取得权力的保护，或是不被权力侵害剥夺属于自己的正当权利，而不得不去讨好官员，让他们得到额外的好处和利益。在这种社会环境下，懂得如何取悦官员的人们，会获取不正当的利益，而弱势群体和不愿意讨好官员的人们，则很有可能因

personal gains. In order to be protected by power, or not to be infringed or even deprived of their own legitimate rights by power, some social members have to please officials and enable them to obtain extra benefits and interests. In such social environment, those who know how to please officials will gain illegitimate benefits; while those who are among vulnerable groups and unwilling to please officials are likely to lose their benefits they could have enjoyed due to arbitrary intervention by power. Human society will gradually lose fairness and order due to such mutated power.

"Mutated" Power Requires "Soil"

Normal power can be operated under the "sun". Every corner of power can be seen very clearly by social members. People are able to know in detail when it starts to take effect, according to which

为权力的肆意干预，而失去原本他们可以享有的利益。人类社会由于这种变异的权力，会逐渐失去公平和秩序。

"变异" 的权力需要 "土壤"

正常的权力，可以在"阳光"下运行。权力的每一个棱角，社会成员都可以看得很清楚，它什么时候开始发挥作用，依照什么程序发生作用，作用力有多少，人们都能知道的很

procedures it takes effect, and how much acting force there will be. People have a sense of awe for power, but they are never afraid that power will hurt themselves wantonly. Because such power is generally recognized and accepted by social members. Even if such power punishes some social members and causes them pain, other members will believe that such result is justified and reasonable. Reasons are required for normal power to be activated, and must be operated according to the established procedures. Whether one can enjoy the shelter of power or be punished by power depends entirely on what he/she has done. Regular power will not interfere with the rights and freedom of social members.

But "mutated" differs from normal power. Social members will be afraid of such power. Because people don't know when such power will take effect, according to which procedures it will take effect, and how much

详细。人们对于权力会有敬畏感，但绝不害怕权力会肆意伤害自己。因为这样的权力得到了社会成员的普遍认可与接受，即便这种权力处罚了某些社会成员，给他们带来了痛苦，其他成员也都会认为这种结果是正当合理的。启动正常的权力是需要理由的，且必须按照既定程序来运行，人们能否享有权力的庇护，或是受到权力的惩罚，完全取决于自己做了什么，正常的权力不会无缘无故去触碰社会成员的权利自由。

但"变异"的权力，就和上面的情形大不一样了。社会成员会对这样的权力感到恐惧，因为人们不知道什么时候，这样的权力会发生作用，会按照什么样的程序发生作用，作用力有多大，这些都让人们对于"变

acting force there will be. All these doubts make people fear "mutated" power, worrying that it will deprive them of their own legitimate interests anytime. Let's take traffic police as an example again to illustrate how mutated power scares people. The power controlled by the traffic police is established to secure the freedom of passage of social members and maintain traffic order. When such power is operated for this purpose, people will not have any worries and anxieties. But once such power is not operated solely for the freedom and order of the social members, the situation will become awful. If the salaries of those who control such power cannot be secured, and they have to consider increasing their financial income when exercising their power, various unreasonable fines and fees will arise. Fines are imposed forcibly against traffic violations for which persuasion could have been adopted, or issues against which fines can be imposed

异"的权力感到恐惧，担心它随时会夺去属于自己的正当利益。还用交通警察的例子来说明，变异的权力是如何让人们感到恐惧的。交通警察手中掌控的权力，是为了保障社会成员的通行自由，维护交通秩序而被设立存在的，当这种权力为了这个目标运行时，人们不会有担心和顾虑。可一旦这项权力不完全是为了社会成员的通行自由和秩序而运行时，情况就会变得非常糟糕。如果掌控这项权力的人们，工作薪水待遇得不到应有的保障，迫使他们不得不在行使权力时，考虑增加经济收入的问题，各式各样不合理的罚款收费项目就出现了。原本可以说服教育的交通违规行为，就必须处以罚款，或是找出可以罚款的问题，让人们有苦说不出。这样的情形多了，人们就开始害怕交通警察，每当看到他们，就会主动选择绕道而行。对于这种变异的权力，人类社会不会允许它长久存在下去，这样的权力不是为了大多数社会成员的正当合理权利而运行，不具有正义性。

are carped, causing unspeakable troubles to social members. As more and more such situations occur, people start to be afraid of the traffic police. And they will actively take a detour whenever they see them. Human society will not allow such mutated power to exist for long as such power is not operated for the legitimate rights of most social members and thus is unjust. So, if most social members get aware of the truth, they will take back their original rights in some way and no longer voluntarily yield to the domination and control of such power. It can be inferred from this conclusion that "soil" is required by mutated power and its operation, that is, the purpose and trace of such power must be hidden and cannot be known by most social members. Otherwise, people will take back some of their original rights that formed such power, and consequently such power will lose the prerequisite for it to take effect --- justice (the establishment

因此，如果大多数社会成员都知道了事实真相，他们就要以某种方式收回自己的原始权利，不再自愿服从这项权力的支配和管制。从这个结论可以得出，变异的权力及其运行是需要"土壤"的——那就是这种权力的目的和运行轨迹，必须被隐藏起来，不能被大多数社会成员知道。否则，人们就会收回形成这项权力的那部分原始权利，这项权力会失去发挥作用的前提条件——正义性（设立这项权力被绝大多数社会成员认可和肯定，进而自愿交出部分原始权利来凝结成这样的权力。）

of such power is recognized and affirmed by most social members, and then voluntarily surrender some of their original rights to condense into such power).

The Power of Truth

It can be inferred from the above analysis that "mutated" power does not exist for the purpose of maintaining normal social order and the legitimate rights of social members. Such power requires certain "soil" to hide the truth of its purpose and operating process, and to benefit a few people concealingly in a mode that is not clearly understood by most social members. Such means and ways differ from the social contract rules accepted and recognized by everyone, they are concealed and unjust and are usually called "unspoken rules".

"Mutated" power and unspoken rules are awfully harmful to the internal order of human society. They will cause human society

事实真相的威力

由上面的分析可以得出，"变异"的权力不是为了维护正常社会秩序和社会成员的正当合理权利而存在的，这种权力需要特定的"土壤"，来掩藏其目的和运行过程的真相，通过不被大多数社会成员清楚了解的模式隐蔽的使少数人获益。这样的方法手段与大家接受认可的社会契约规则不同，具有隐蔽性和非正义性，通常又叫做"潜规则"。

"变异"的权力和潜规则对人类社会内部秩序的危害特别大，它们会让人类社会失去公平，会让绝大多数社会成员的

to lose fairness and damage the legitimate interests of most social members. So, they are not accepted by most social members. Any power established by human society or formed in some way (there also exists the situation that the reason why people surrender their original rights is from the unknown world of mankind) is to safeguard the legitimate rights and interests of most people and maintain a balanced social order in the name of justice (recognized by most people). Once people find that power is infringing the interests of most people, it will lose its justice. Also, such power will no longer be recognized by social members. People will take back their original rights that have condensed such power by various means. As a result, control and operation of power will, lie sourceless water, eventually cease to be.

It can be said that the power to safeguard the interests of a few people by concealed non-disclosed

正当利益受损。因此，它们不被绝大多数社会成员所接受，人类社会所设立的权力或是以某种方式形成的权力（人们让渡交出自己原始权利的理由，也存在来自人类未知世界的情形），都是以正义之名（绝大多数人的认可），维护绝大多数人的正当合理权益，维持社会秩序的平衡。一旦人们发现权力在侵害多数人的利益，权力便会失去正义性，这样的权力也会不再被社会成员认可，人们就会用各种方式收回凝结这项权力的原始权利，权力的掌控运行，就会成为无源之水，并将最终不复存在。

可以这样说，通过隐蔽不公开的方法手段——潜规则，去维护少数人利益的权力，是"变

means ---unspoken rules --- is "mutated" power. Normal power is operated openly, and the operation ought to follow the rules and procedures preset by people. The operation of some normal powers, though is not disclosed, is also a kind of reasonable concealment authorized and recognized by social members. "Mutated" power will cause terrible harm to human society. Then, how to overcome power's mutation to avoid its harm?

It's quite simple --- to disclose the truth. Because power is condensed from the original rights of social members. If most social members have seen the harm that mutated power has caused to the society and take back their original rights, the mutated power will lose its authority and effect when people see the truth. Let's take an example for analysis, most social members will agree to pay taxes to the state after earning income for the purpose of ensuring the social order and the fund needed

异"的权力。正常的权力是公开运行的，是应遵循人们预先设定的规则程序的，尽管有些权力的运行没有公开，那也是经过社会成员授权和认可的合理性隐蔽。"变异"的权力，会给人类社会造成很大危害，那么该如何克服权力的变异，避免它的危害呢？

方法其实比较简单——公布事实真相。因为，权力是由社会成员的原始权利凝结而成，如果绝大多数社会成员都看到了变异的权力给社会造成的危害，而收回自己的原始权利，变异的权力便会在人们明白真相之时失去权威和效力。这里可以分析一个例子，绝大多数社会成员都会同意在获得收入时，给国家缴纳税款，目的是为了保障社会秩序和正常运转所需的经费，给官员、警察、法官、军人等人员提供薪水待遇，这样人们才能在遇到问题和危险

for normal operation of the society to provide salaries to officials, police, judges, soldiers, etc. Only by doing so can people get help and protection when encountering problems and dangers. Generally, people will actively cooperate with tax officials on behalf of the state to pay the payable taxes. Because, social members accept to do so and will surrender some of their original rights to condense into tax officials' taxation power; and in turn people provide what is needed to maintain human social order. Once people find that the taxes collected by tax officials have not been used for legitimate items, but have been squandered or wasted by a few people, they will take back those rights when they get aware of the truth. As a result, the power of tax officials will lose its justice very soon, and will eventually dissipate and collapse. As for when and how to take back their original rights, it depends on when and how many people get aware of the truth.

时，得到帮助和保护。通常情况下，人们都会主动配合代表国家的税务官员，缴纳该缴的税款，因为社会成员接受这样的行为，大家会让渡交出一部分原始权利，来凝结成税务官员的征税权，人们用这种方式提供维持人类社会秩序之所需。可是一旦人们发现，税务官员收取的税款，并没有用于正当合理的项目，而是被少数人挥霍浪费掉了，人们便会在知道真相之时，收回那些权利，税务官员的权力会很快失去正义性，并最终消散瓦解。至于人们何时收回，以何种方式收回他们的那部分原始权利，则取决于人们在什么时候知道真相，有多少人知道真相。

As the truth allows social members to see whether their original rights are being used correctly, and then decide whether to take them back. So, the greatest power of truth is that it can make "mutated" power lose the recognition of most people --- justice, and then disintegrate such unacceptable power.

Another Key Role of Truth

Regarding people's almost limitless original rights, it's tough to define which are legitimate and which are not. Way too many people make their life go on while blindly getting their desires and needs satisfied. One will feel painful and will not find happiness if his/her desires and needs cannot be satisfied. But it's seldom possible to draw a correct conclusion as to which of people's desires and needs shall be satisfied and which shall not be satisfied on earth just

由于事实真相可以让社会成员看清楚自己的原始权利是否被正确使用，进而决定是否收回它们。因此，事实真相最大的威力就在于，它可以非常迅速地使"变异"的权力失去多数人的认可——正义性，进而瓦解这种不被人们接受的权力。

事实真相的另一个 重要作用

对于人们几乎浩瀚无边的原始权利来讲，哪些是正当合理的，哪些是无理和不正当的，是一个很难去准确界定的问题。有太多的人都在盲目地满足欲望需求中，继续着自己的生活。如果一个人的欲望需求得不到满足，那么他（她）就会觉得痛苦，会找不到幸福快乐的感觉。可是人的欲望需求，究竟哪些应当被满足，哪些应被抑制或摒弃，在很多时候单凭个体的认知和判断，是无法得出正确结论的。比如"婚外情"的自由，属不属于一个人的正当权

relying on individual cognition and judgment. For example, it's quite controversial whether the freedom of "extramarital affairs" falls within the scope of legitimate human rights or not.

The reason why humans choose to live in groups is to unite more human wisdom, and gather more production and life experiences so as to lay the foundation and choose a direction for human multiplication, development and progress. Appropriate and rational answers can probably found for conclusions that one cannot draw if it is placed among a social group to be judged by more social members. Regarding whether some of human desires and needs can be satisfied or not, shall also make more social members know and understand what the crux for this problem is, and then let them express their opinions, herewith mainstream opinions can be formed among people in most cases. Like in the above example, if let all social members to vote

利，就会出现很大的争议。

人类之所以选择群居生活，就是为了联合更多的人类智慧，汇集更多的生产生活经验，为人类的繁衍生息和发展进步奠定基础，选择方向。一个人不能得出的结论，如果放在社会群体当中，让更多的社会成员去评判，多半都能找到适当理性的答案。对于人类的部分欲望需求是否可以满足的问题，也应该让更多的社会成员知道，明白症结所在，然后由大家发表看法，绝大多数情况下都能形成人们的主流意见。比如上面的例子，如果让全体社会成员来表决，一个人该不该满足"婚外的（不包括某些社会契约允许的一夫多妻）"情感和生理需求，基本上意见会比较统一——不应当满足一个人对婚外情的需求。除了婚外情的当事人可能会有很多理由去证明婚外情的正当性，多数人对这一问题

as to whether a person should satisfy his/her emotional and physical needs of "extramarital (excluding polygamy permitted by certain social contracts)", the opinions will basically be uniform --- shouldn't. Except those who involved in an extramarital affair may have many reasons to prove the legitimacy of an affair, most people's view or opinion on this issue will reflect rationality and justice, and is more conducive to maintaining the order of marriage and emotion in human society. So, none of human social contracts will explicitly protect the original right of "extramarital affairs" in the form of rules. Moreover, not only such right cannot be protected, but also they will be condemned by the lower-level social contract—moral consensus because of extramarital affairs. There is a very important step in this process of development from subjective cognitive judgment of an individual to the final rational decision of a group of people, that

的看法和观点，都会体现出理性和公道，也更有利于维护人类社会的婚姻情感秩序。因此人类社会契约，都不会用规则的形式来明确保护"婚外情"的原始权利，并且不仅得不到保护，当事者还会因婚外情受到较低层级的社会契约——道德舆论的谴责。在这个过程中，从个体主观的认知判断，发展到群体最后的理性抉择，中间有一个很重要的环节，就是问题的发生经过和危害后果，必须详实地呈现在多数社会成员面前。比如，应让人们知道"婚外情"是如何产生的，它给家庭和爱人子女造成了什么样的伤害…这些事实真相，是让社会成员做出正确抉择的前提和条件。离开了事实真相，人们便会盲目而不知所措，人们会分不清哪些情感才是真实可靠的，不会伤害他人，破坏家庭。

is, the whole story of the problem and its harmful consequences must be presented to most social members in detail. For example, people shall be made aware of how an "extramarital affair" occurred, and which kind of harm it has caused to the family, the children and the spouse. . . These facts are the prerequisites and conditions for social members to make correct choices. Without the facts, people will be blinded and overwhelmed. They cannot identify which emotions are true and reliable, and will not harm others or destroy the family.

So, another important function of facts is to help people identify and choose legitimate original rights, and abandon unreasonable desires and needs, so as to better maintain human social order.

因此，事实真相的另一个重要作用，就是帮助人们甄别选择正当合理的原始权利，摒弃不合理的欲望需求，从而更好地维护人类社会秩序。

If No Truth Available

The spread of the truth enables social members to exercise the most

如果没有了事实真相

事实真相的传播，使社会成员对于权力的掌控者，能够

direct and effective supervision over power controllers, and to learn whether their rights are being used correctly by them, so as to decide whether to take back their original rights or continue to surrender or transfer them to form power and support the authority of such power controllers (the influence that enables social members to voluntarily surrender their original rights). Meanwhile, the spread of the truth can also allow social members to see more clearly satisfying which original rights will be harmful to mankind and the order of human groups, and hence restrain these unreasonable desires and needs.

But once the truth has no chance of free spread, most social members cannot see the truth, then in such case human society will easily become crisis-ridden and disorderly. The first is the wanton use of power, it cannot be proved whether the public rights coming from the public are seeking benefits for most social

实施最直接有效的监督，及时了解自己的权利是否被权力掌控者正确使用，从而决定是收回自己的原始权利，还是继续让渡交出自己的权利形成权力，并拥护权力掌控者的权威（能让社会成员自愿交出原始权利的影响力）。同时，事实真相的传播，也能让社会成员更加清楚的看到，对哪些原始权利的满足，是有害于人类自身和人类群体秩序的，进而对这些不合理的欲望需求进行约束。

可是一旦事实真相没有了自由传播的机会，多数社会成员看不到事实真相，那么这时的人类社会就很容易变得危机四伏，秩序混乱。首先是权力的肆意妄为，因为没有人知道它究竟是如何运行的，源自公众的公共权利，是不是在为多数社会成员谋取利益，就不能被证实。并且最可怕的是没有

members as no one knows how it is operated. Most terribly, without the truth, even if the power controllers commit things that infringe on the legitimate rights and interests of social members by making use of unspoken rules, they will continue to exercise their power in name of most people as they are unaware of the truth, and such power will still be with effect. The justice of such power in such case is false, however, and it will not always be recognized by social members. It continues to piece together its own authority by deceiving and concealing the truth.

Without the truth, human society will be like a vehicle driving at high speed on a dark highway and a ship with no lighthouse at a dark night, unable to find the direction and be crisis-ridden. After the human history enters the 21st century, more and more useful and important information and news need to be shared by people. Only by learning

了事实真相，权力的掌控者即便利用潜规则做出了侵害社会成员正当权益的事情，但由于多数社会成员并不知情，这些权力掌控者就会仍然籍着多数人的名义，继续行使手中的权力，且这样的权力仍会具有效力。不过，这样的权力此时所具有的正义性是虚假的，它不会一直得到社会成员的认可，它通过欺骗和隐瞒真相，来继续拼凑自身的权威。

如果没有了事实真相，人类社会就好像漆黑公路上高速行驶的汽车和黑夜里看不见灯塔的轮船一样，找不到方向且危机四伏。人类的历史车轮驶入二十一世纪以后，越来越多有用且重要的信息咨询，需要人们共同分享，人们必须了解更多的事实真相，才能让自己不致迷失在诱惑与疯狂之中。比如人类与生俱来的天然缺陷和

more facts will people not be lost in temptation and craziness. For example, the fact that people are born with natural defects and inferiority is not understood and accepted by people, human society will be heavily damaged because of people's evil deeds. A car thief stole a car and found that there was a baby waiting to be fed in it only after driving a long way out. If he understood the natural defects in human nature, he would manage to curb the evil ideas in his mind instead of indulging his cruel idea and deed --- to choke the baby to death, and then bury it and escape. [1] At the time of cruel infanticide, this man had completely lost his mind, and the evil in human nature was revealed. Without the restraint and guidance of religious belief, he committed a crime that even

劣根性，这一事实如果不被人们明白接受，人类社会就会因为人的恶行而千疮百孔。一个盗车贼偷了一辆汽车，开出去很远以后，才发现车上还有一个嗷嗷待哺的婴孩。如果他明白人性的天然缺陷，他就会设法收敛心中的恶念，而不会去放纵残忍的想法和作为——将婴孩掐死，然后掩埋，逃之夭夭。那时那刻，残忍杀婴之时，这个人已经完全失去理智，人的恶性显露无遗，由于没有宗教信仰的抑制和引导，他犯下了连他自己都无法原谅的罪过，只因他不明白这个世界上最重要的事实真相——由于人性存在严重缺陷，人们时时刻刻都需要信仰来帮助自己约束人性之恶。同样的事例发生在有宗教信仰的地方，也就是人们知道这一事实真相的地方——这里的人们明白人性的缺陷客观存在，绝大多数人都选择用信仰

---

[1] *The Criminal of the Case of Car Theft and Infanticide Was Executed on Nov 22nd, 2013,* published in "the Rule of Law" column, Xinhuanet, http://news.xinhuanet.com/legal/2013-11/22/c_118259457.htm, access time: 16:03 Mar 07, 2017.

新华网：《长春盗车杀婴案罪犯 22 日被执行死刑》，载新华网法治，http://news.xinhuanet.com/legal/2013-11/22/c_118259457.htm，访问时间：2017 年 3 月 7 日 16：03。

he himself could not forgive. This is simply because he didn't understand the most important truth in this world --- people need belief all the time to help them restrain the evil in human nature due to serious defects in human nature. Similar cases happen where there is religious belief, namely where people are aware of this truth --- people there understand that defects in human nature exist objectively, and most people choose to self-discipline with belief to overcome evil in human nature. Almost in the same scene, another thief chose to get out of the car immediately, and called the police telling them the exact location of the baby and the stolen car, and then left quickly.[1] In spite of his identity of a thief, he is a person who understands the truth. He has belief deep in his heart, which kept him away from evil

和自律来克服人性之恶。几乎是在同样的场景之下，另一个窃贼选择马上下车拨打报警电话，并告诉警察婴孩和被盗汽车的准确位置，然后迅速离开。尽管他是一个窃贼，但他却是明白事实真相的人，他有内心深处的信仰，这些让他远离了邪恶的念头和行径。他和上面的那个窃贼，最大的不同之处，就是他的内心之中有禁锢，事实真相让他明白有些事情不能做，否则就会陷入无穷无尽的邪恶痛苦之中，这样的痛苦也是人性本能所排斥的。尽管人性存在着诸多缺陷，但从根本上来讲，人类最终追求的是幸福和快乐，而不是痛苦。一个人用恶行（不正当的原始权利）来满足一时的欲望，便意味着这个人给自己召来了挥之不去的内心痛苦和邪恶感。另一个窃贼，只因不知道这个最简单，却也是最重要的事实真相，而犯下了滔天罪过，不仅杀害了

---

[1] Jessica Simeone, Accused carjacker caught on video after stealing jeep with baby still inside, New York Post, http://nypost.com/?s=Accused+carjacker+caught+on+video+after+stealing+jeep+with+baby+still+inside, March 8, 2017 14:23pm.

ideas and conducts. The biggest difference between him and the thief above is that he was aware that something shall be confined in his mind. The truth made him understand that some things couldn't be committed; otherwise he would suffer endless evil pain, which is also what human will repel instinctively. Fundamentally, what human ultimately pursue is happiness instead of pain in spite of defects in human nature. If one uses evil deeds (illegitimate original rights) to satisfy his/her temporary desires, it implies that this person has brought to himself/herself a lingering feeling of inner pain and evil. The thief first mentioned committed a heinous crime simply because he didn't know this simplest while most important truth. Not only did he kill a life, but he also brought himself a tragic ending that his mental pain would not be relieved until he dies.

So, a human society with no truth available would be terrifying

生命，也给自己带来了除去死亡无法解除心灵痛苦的悲惨结局。

因此，没有事实真相的人类社会，是恐怖而不可预测的。

and unpredictable. For a stable human social order, people need truth.

Why Cover up the Truth?

Now that truth is so important to human society, people have the right to know all the facts other than those are prohibited by social contract e.g. personal privacy, state secrets, etc. The reason why people want to know the truth is to better create value, satisfy the legitimate needs of human society, and promote the development and progress of human society. Such right (freedom) can also be called the "right to know" --- a freedom for people to know the truth.

When a mining disaster or other serious safety accident has occurred somewhere, and which has caused a lot of casualties, such news shall be disclosed to the public while rescuing and aiding promptly. Such disclosure can have at least the following effects: 1) to

为了人类社会的秩序安定，人们需要事实真相。

为什么要掩盖事实真相

既然事实真相对于人类社会是如此的重要，那么除了个人隐私、国家机密等社会契约禁止公开的情形之外，人们有权利知道所有的事实真相。人们知道事实真相是为了更好的创造价值，满足人类社会的正当合理需求，推动人类社会发展进步。这样的权利自由也可以被称作知情权——一种人们了解事实真相的自由。

一个地方发生了矿难或是其他严重的安全事故，出现了很大的人员伤亡，那么在迅速进行抢险救助的同时，也应将这样的消息向社会进行公布。这样的公布至少可以起到以下几方面的作用：一是告知大家发生事故的位置区域，防止无关

inform people of the location and area where the accident occurred, preventing irrelevant persons from entering the danger zone; 2) to help collect useful information, obtaining more external support to rescue the endangered people; 3) to speed up figuring out the cause of the accident and sum up the lessons, avoiding recurrence of similar tragedies; 4) to let more social members understand that the endangered workers have paid a high cost in creating value, and thus better cherish their fruits of labor, enabling such people or their relatives to receive legitimate compensation and rewards.

Though doing so cannot save the lives of the deceased and the economic losses caused, it is far better to make up for it timely than turning a blind eye. If not to learn from the truth, similar accidents will recur, and natural disasters will turn into man-made disasters as well. In such a tragic case, the fact and reason are clear. It's the most basic requirement of

人员进入危险地带；二是有利于收集有用信息，获取更多的外部支援去救助落难人员；三是加快寻找事故的原因，总结教训，避免类似的惨剧再次发生；四是让更多的社会成员明白，落难的劳动者在创造价值的过程中，付出了高昂的成本代价，从而更加珍惜他们的劳动成果，使这些人或是他们的亲人家属得到公正合理的补偿和回报。

这样做虽然不能挽回逝者的生命和造成的经济损失，但亡羊补牢远胜于视而不见，不从事实真相中吸取教训，类似事故就还要发生，天灾也会变人祸。在这样的惨痛事例中，事实和情理明晰可见，公布事实真相是多数社会成员的最基本要求，道德、法律等形式的社会契约都会保护人们对这类事件真相的知情权。可是，在这

most social members to disclose the truth. Social contracts in the form of morals and laws will protect people's right to know the truth of such incidents. After such incidents have happened, some people will try their best to conceal the truth. The main reason why they do so is that they are afraid of being punished or losing power and vested interests because of accidents or disasters. If an accident is directly caused by human factors, it is still in line with human nature and reason for the person who has caused the accident to conceal the truth due to fear of being punished. But there is another reason, that is, the accident is indirectly caused by the power controllers' negligence of management and prevention. In such case, the officials shall bear the corresponding responsibilities and liabilities. At least the officials may lose the power originally controlled by him/her, or assume heavier obligations and responsibilities

样的事件发生之后，有一些人却会想尽办法去掩盖事实真相，他们之所以这样做，其中主要原因就是害怕因为事故灾难而受到惩罚或是失去权力和既得利益。如果事故是人为因素直接导致发生的，那么引发事故的人因害怕受惩罚而隐瞒事实真相，尚且符合人性与情理。但还有一种原因，就是事故是由于掌控权力的人疏于管理防范而间接导致发生的，此时官员应承担相应的责任，至少官员很可能因此失去原本由他（她）掌控的权力，或者为此承担更重的义务责任。所以，害怕承担不利后果的官员们大都会利用手中的权力来掩盖事实真相，比如阻止媒体曝光，贿赂记者和上级检查官员，封锁事故区域等等。直接导致事故发生的肇事者，尽管想要隐瞒事实真相，但是他们没有官员的权力，另外他们想要隐瞒的往往只是个人的罪行，而官员们需要隐藏的却是全部的事实真相。官员们隐瞒真相的理由其实也简单——害怕失去权力，受到惩罚。

as a result thereof. So, most officials who are afraid of taking adverse consequences will cover up the truth using their power, e.g. preventing media exposure, bribing reporters and higher-level inspection officials, blocking the accident area, etc. The perpetrators who directly caused the accident want to conceal the truth. But they don't have the power of officials, besides, what they want to conceal is usually only their personal crimes, whilst what officials need to conceal is the entire truth. The reason why officials conceal the truth is actually quite simple --- fear of losing power and being punished.

Because, if people see the truth and understand that such tragic accidents are caused by officials' negligence of prevention and supervision, people will take back the original rights that belonged to themselves from the officials, and what such officials fear most is subsequent large-scale exposure of the truth and

因为，如果人们看到了事实真相，明白这些惨痛的事故是由于官员们疏于防范监管而发生，那么大家就要用各自的方式收回这些官员手中属于自己的那部分原始权利，而这些是官员们最恐惧的事情，没有了权力，紧随其后的就是事实真相的大范围曝光和官员应承担的责罚。

the liabilities and punishment that they are to bear.

Spread of Truth

The truth has extremely important influence and effect on both the power controllers and every social member. With the truth, power controllers cannot exercise their power at will. Because the truth will tell people in time whether the power controllers are using the original rights granted to them by social members, and then decide whether to take back such rights. A power controller who is proved by fact to be obviously unjust, namely a power controller that has not been recognized by most social members, cannot be convincing and authoritative. Social members will not voluntarily transfer their original rights to him (her) to exercise. The root cause is that the power that does not represent the interests of most social members (social members have

事实真相的传播

事实真相无论是对于权力的掌控者，还是每一位社会成员，都具有极其重要的影响和作用。有了事实真相，权力的掌控者就不能随心所欲的行使手中的权力，因为事实真相会及时告诉人们，权力的掌控者是否在正确使用社会成员赋予他们的原始权利，进而决定是否收回这些权利。一个事实证明显然不具有正义性的权力掌控者，也即没有得到大多数社会成员认可的权力掌控者，是不能服众和具有权威性的，社会成员不会自愿将原本属于自己的原始权利让渡给他（她）去行使。其中的根本原因就在于不代表多数社会成员利益（社会成员没有让渡交出自己的权利）的权力，会造成社会不公，破坏人类社会的秩序。

not transferred or given out their rights) will cause social injustice and disrupt human social order.

On the other hand, every social member needs the truth to alert themselves which words and deeds are appropriate and beneficial and shall be recognized and protected by other people and social rules and which words and deeds are illegitimate and shall be constricted and restricted. Such questions will become clear and traceable as most social members see the truth. Only by seeing the truth can people correctly and effectively restrain their own unreasonable desires and needs and avoid harm to others and the society caused by improper words and deeds, and consciously maintain the basic social order. Because if people don't know the truth, they usually cannot make rational and correct choices and then indulge their own evil deeds as humans' instinctive desires are often difficult to overcome.

It is so important, then, how

另一方面，每一位社会成员也都需要事实真相来警醒自己，哪些言行是适当有益的，是应该受到同类和社会规则认可保护的，而哪些言行是无理和不适当的，应当加以限制约束，这样的问题都会因为多数社会成员看到事实真相而变得清晰可鉴，有迹可循。只有看到了事实真相，人们才能正确有效地约束自身的不合理欲望需求，避免不当言行给他人和社会带来的伤害，自觉维护社会基本秩序。因为如果不清楚事实真相，由于人类自身的本能欲望很多时候难以克服，人们常常无法做出理性正确的选择，进而放任自己的恶行。

既然如此重要，那么该怎样

can we let more people know the truth? The most effective way is to let the truth spread freely among social member. The truth itself exists objectively. The means for truth spreading by people who are aware of it has developed from sensory record and word of mouth to spreading through information media and storage devices, and then even the media industry specializing in information spread. The media records and replicates the truth through modern media equipment, and then disclose it using the information or news platform controlled by them. Doing so allows social members to obtain the truth in the fastest time and make rational and correct decisions in the decision-making on the control of individual rights and freedom, so as to facilitate maintaining human social order.

Spreading Medium of Truth

Only when the truth is

才能让更多的人们知道事实真相呢？最有效的方法，就是让真相在社会成员之间自由地传播。事实真相原本就是客观存在的，看到的人，最早是通过感官记录、口舌相传，到后来慢慢发展为通过信息媒介和存储设备，并且出现了专门从事信息传播的媒体业。媒体通过现代化的媒介设备记录复制真相，然后再用其掌握的信息资讯平台面向公众发布。这样可以使社会成员以最快的时间获取事实真相，并在个体权利自由的支配决策中，做出理性正确地抉择，从而有益于维护人类社会秩序。

事实真相的传播媒介

事实真相要让更多的社会

understood by more social members can it give full play to its big role. The truth will make social members sensible, and rationality enables people to satisfy their own desires and needs without affecting the legitimate rights and interests of others. The truth will drive social members to exercise their original rights cautiously, abandon unreasonable rights and claims, and consciously restrain words and deeds that infringe the rights and interests of others, providing preconditions for the formation of a good human social order. Meanwhile, the truth can make power controllers to directly feel that they are being supervised and restrained. Only when their power is exercised to maintain the social rules or the interests of the most people will it not be taken back by social members and then lose the justice (recognized by most social members). Social members who can always learn the truth will end the mutated power.

An indispensable step is

成员明白，才能充分发挥它的巨大作用。事实真相会让社会成员变得理智，理性使人们在满足自己的欲望需求时，不会影响到他人的正当权益。事实真相会驱使社会成员谨慎地行使自己的原始权利，摒弃不合理的权利要求，自觉约束侵害他人权益的言语行为，为形成良好的人类社会秩序提供前提条件。同时事实真相还能让权力的掌控者，直接感受到被监督和约束，当他们手中的权力，是为了维护社会规则或是多数人利益而行使，才不会被社会成员收回，进而失去正义性（大多数社会成员的认可），时刻能够了解事实真相的社会成员，会终结变异的权力。

事实真相要被更多的人知

needed for the truth to be known to more people --- media. Just as its name implies, media is a platform or medium dedicated to spreading the truth. In view of the importance of truth to human society, how to spread the truth is an issue that each kind of social contract needs to solve. Under the monarchic social contract, the emperor and the officials would, in the form of edict and notice, publicize the truth that need to be known to the people, or to attain the goal of punishing evil deeds, warning and education, or directing people to give up their rights (freedom) and obey the law. So, under the monarchic social contract, in addition to word of mouth, people get truth through edicts and notices issued by the emperor and the officials, and such edicts and notices are more authoritative compared to word of mouth. Under the democratic social contract, there are more channels for spreading the truth, and specialized media

道，需要一个必不可少的环节——那就是媒体。顾名思义，媒体就是专门用来传播事实真相的平台或媒介。鉴于事实真相对于人类社会的重要性，如何传播事实真相是每一种社会契约都需要解决的问题。在君主制社会契约下，皇帝官员通过颁布诏令通告的方式，广而告之需要民众知悉的事实真相，或是达到惩戒恶行、警示教育的目的，或是引导民众放弃权利自由、遵守律法。因此，在君主制社会契约下，人们除了依靠口舌相传获取事实真相之外，就是通过皇帝官员的诏令通告了，并且相比较而言，这些诏令通告会更具有权威性。在民主制社会契约下，可以传播事实真相的渠道多了，也出现了专门的媒体机构，电视广播、报纸杂志、网络通讯都是事实真相的媒介。

organizations have emerged. Televisions and broadcasts, newspapers and magazines and online communications are all media for spreading the truth.

Certain methods are needed to spread the truth under whichever kind of social contract. Usually, the most popular way of spreading is the mainstream media in the society. For example, in a monarchic society, people usually could only learn the truth through official edicts and notices when they needed to do so. Whereas in a democratic society, people can satisfy such need through various channels, e.g. government announcements, official newspapers, and non-governmental publications and online media. In addition, after the human society entered the era of information, every social member has chance to spread the truth quickly and conveniently using the mobile Internet technology and their mobile Internet devices due to the popularization and application

不管在何种社会契约之下，事实真相的传播都需要一定的方法途径。通常人们使用最多的传播方法途径，就是这个社会的主流媒体。比如在君主制社会，遇到需要了解真相的时候，民众往往只能通过官方的通告诏令来实现。而在民主制社会，人们可以通过多种途径来满足这样的需求，可以是政府公告，也可以是官方报纸，还可以是民间出版物和网络媒体。另外，人类社会进入信息时代以后，由于移动互联网技术的普及应用，使得每一位社会成员都有机会通过这种技术和手中的移动互联设备，来便捷快速的传递事实真相。这样的媒介方式，以其快速、直观的优势，而成为了人们咨讯传播的主流媒介。

of the technology. Such medium form has, with its advantages of fastness and visualization, become the mainstream medium for the spread of information for people.

We can call such medium form of information spread relying on Internet technology and personal mobile devices "self-media". The emergence of self-media has made human society change at an unprecedented speed and in an unprecedented way. In particular, people's opting of rights and monitor over power are becoming increasingly direct, simple and effective.

An Era in Which Truth Can't Be Hidden

Human society has entered a fully new era, in which all kinds of information and news are, with the help of modern technologies, spreading at an unprecedented speed and in an unprecedented way. It is possible for an event to spread all over the world in a

我们可以把这种依靠互联网技术和个人移动设备，进行信息传播的媒介方式，称作自媒体。自媒体的出现，让人类社会以前所未有的速度和方式发生着改变，特别是人们对于权利的抉择和权力的监控，正在变得越发直接简单和有效。

无法掩盖真相的时代

人类社会已进入一个全新的时代，在这个时代各种信息资讯借助现代科技，正在以前所未有的方式和速度高速传播。只要是发生在这个星球上的事情，就有可能在很短的时间内传遍全世界。在"互联网"出现之前这些是无法想象的，但

short period of time as long as it happens on this planet. These were unimaginable before the emergence of the "Internet". But humans invented computer and established a data Internet system worldwide using their own ingenuity to satisfy the reasonable needs of human society for sharing information resources and create huge value that humans will be proud of.

Soon after more convenient and faster mobile Internet technologies emerged with the development of computer technology and Internet systems. Just as its name implies, such technologies are to allow people to access the global Internet system anytime and anywhere with the help of terminal devices and spread and share the information around them in the first time. Pictures, texts, audio and video data can all be quickly uploaded to the Internet via personal mobile terminals, which may be shared and used by Internet users all over

人类用自己的聪明才智发明了电脑，并在全球范围内建立起了数据互联网体系，用来满足人类社会信息资源共享的合理需求，创造出让人类引以自豪的巨大价值。

随着电脑技术和互联网系统的发展，紧接着又出现了更方便快捷的移动互联技术。顾名思义，这样的技术就是让人们能够借助终端设备，随时随地接入全球互联网系统，第一时间传递分享自己身边的信息资讯。图片文字、音视频资料都可以迅速地通过个人移动终端上传至互联网，进而有可能让全世界的互联网用户共享使用。自从出现了电脑、互联网和移动通讯等信息技术设备，人类社会的资讯传播，变得仿佛比其他任何事情都要简单容易一些，可以影响主导社会成员权利让渡与权力监督的事实真相，

the world. Since the advent of information technology equipment e.g. computer, the Internet, and mobile communication, the spread of information in human society has become simpler and easier than anything else and can influence the truth that dominates transfer of rights and supervision over power by social members. A trend that the truth can't be hidden begins to appear. Because everyone who knows the truth can quickly spread all the information about the truth in a very convenient way, which will then be spread by friends who receive them, and then by friends of friends. . . In such case, the spread of the truth will only become so fast that we cannot imagine.

Several workers clashed with a gatekeeper, and the police went to the scene to deal with the situation and took several people to the police station. But later a woman among them died at the place where the police handled the case. What on earth has caused

开始呈现出无法隐藏的趋势。因为每一个了解事实真相的人，都可以用十分便捷的方式迅速扩散有关事实真相的全部信息，然后是收到讯息的好友扩散，再接下来是好友的好友再次扩散…这种情况下，事实真相的传播速度，只会快到令人无法想象。

几位工人与门卫发生冲突，警察出警到现场进行处理，并将数人带至警察局，但后来其中有一妇人死在办案场所。究竟是什么原因导致悲剧发生，仅凭相关人员的描述无法完全还原事实真相，但有在场人员用移动设备拍下了现场照片并传

the tragedy to happen? The truth cannot be restored completely just relying on the descriptions of relevant personnel. But someone at the scene has taken photos of the scene with mobile devices and uploaded them to the Internet. The photo shows the police stepping on the woman's hair with his feet, and the woman who fell onto the ground seemed to have no strength to resist. Such photo spread on the Internet at an amazing speed. What people do is simply clicking to forward it, but such thing got known to most citizens in just a few days. If this woman committed a crime, she shall be subject to legal sanctions. The police have no power to punish her before confirming her guilt by legal procedures, but the police have the right to control her illegal resistance using force during law enforcement. But obviously the picture can make people feel that the policeman is strong while the woman was lying on the ground. Most people would believe that

至互联网。照片上显示警察用脚踩着那位妇人的头发，而倒地的妇人看似已毫无反抗之力。这样的照片在互联网上以惊人的速度传播着，人们做的只是点击转发，却在短短几天内让多数国民都知道了这样的事情。如果这个妇人有违法犯罪行为，她应该接受法律的制裁。警察在未经法定程序确认其有罪之前，没有权力去惩罚她，但警察在执法过程中有权采用武力控制她的违法反抗。不过照片给人的感觉很明显，一个强壮的警察，一个躺在地上的妇人，多数人会认为这种控制超出了必要限度，再加上妇人死亡的结果，在多数社会成员看到那张照片之后，警察行为的合法性被严重质疑，人们都在思考这位警察的执法行为是否适当。或者说，人们会考虑他能不能代表公众执法，自己还要不要把处置违法者的权利交其行使，在没有获悉全部事实真相之前，仅凭这张照片上的信息，答案多半会是否定的，照片上这位警察的举动最终没有得到多数人的认可。尽管一张照片并不

such kind of control has gone beyond the necessary limit. And, due to the result of the woman's death, most social members would seriously question the legality of the policeman's conducts after seeing the photo. People were all thinking about whether the policeman's law enforcement action is appropriate or not. Or to say, people would consider whether he can enforce the law on behalf of the public and whether they will continue to give him the right to deal with offenders. Before all the facts are known, the answer to these questions will probably be "No" just relying on the information indicated in this photo. And the policeman's action in the photo was eventually not recognized by most people. Although a photo cannot represent the entire truth, people have already begun to question the policeman's behavior. Soon after the photo was exposed, measures were also taken to this policeman to file a case for investigation.

能代表事实真相的全部，但人们已经开始质疑警察的行为，照片曝光不久，这名警察也被采取措施立案调查。

So, after human society entered the era of mobile Internet, it gets very difficult or even impossible to cover up the truth. In this era, the transfer of rights and power supervision of social members become more rational, open and transparent. People will quickly draw a conclusion from enough information as to which original rights of social member are legitimate. The question as to which powers do not represent the interests of the public and are unjust and require social members to condemn or protest against, or to take back their original rights will become easier and simpler than ever.

Unhidable "Unspoken Rules"

Fundamentally, the "unspoken rule" is derived from the defects of human. It means that power controllers benefit a few people who are in a certain relationship with them by hidden unknown

因此，当人类社会进入移动互联时代，掩盖事实真相就变成了一件非常困难，甚至是不大可能的事情，在这个时代社会成员的权利让渡与权力监督，都会变得更加理性和透明公开。社会成员的哪些原始权利是正当合理的，人们会从足够多的讯息之中很快得出结论。哪些权力没有代表公众的利益，不具有正义性，需要社会成员谴责、抗议，或是收回自己的原始权利，都变得比以往更加容易和简单。

难以藏身的"潜规则"

"潜规则"从根本上来讲，是源自人类自身的缺陷和不足，它是权力的掌控者利用隐蔽的、不为人知的方式方法，使少数和自己具有某种关系的人获取利益。这样的利益，如果不通

means. And such benefits would not have been obtained if they were not obtained by "hidden" or "private" means but according to the requirements of the rules agreed upon by social members. More precisely, the emergence of unspoken rules stems from people's dishonesty and their breach to promise. Only if officials promise to maintain social fairness and justice and seek welfare and benefits for social members will people give them the public rights that embody the common will of people --- power. It will be a breach to their original promises if they violate the rules in order to protect the interests of themselves and a few people. Also, those social members who need to seek benefits through unspoken rules have violated their original intention of the transfer of their original rights hoping for social fairness and justice as well. Their behavior of making use of unspoken rules has undermines the social rules generally accepted

过"隐蔽的"或"私下的"方式方法，而是按照社会成员共同认可的规则要求，原本是无法得到的。更准确地说，潜规则的出现是源自人类的不诚信，源自人们对承诺的背弃。官员承诺要维护社会公平正义，要为社会成员谋取福祉利益，人们才会将体现民众共同意志的公共权利——权力，交给他掌握。掌握权力之后，为了维护自己及少数人的利益去违背规则，就是对自己当初承诺的背弃。而那些需要通过潜规则来谋取利益的社会成员，也违背了自己希望社会公平正义而让渡原始权利的初衷，他们利用潜规则的行为，破坏了大家公认的社会规则。

by people.

A condition is required for unspoken rules to play their roles, that is, they must be operated in a "black box" as such "hidden private means" is not generally recognized by social members. Once people who formulated the rules --- all social members find that power controllers are benefiting a few people by making use of unspoken rules, they will condemn and protest against them, and even take back their original rights. In such case, the justice of power will quickly disintegrate as the truth is exposed. So, only if unspoken rules that are not recognized and accepted by social members are used in a hidden way can the justice of power controllers --- the recognition by social members that they need to exercise power --- continue to be maintained.

However, after the human society entered the mobile Internet era, any information or news, no matter when and where, as long as

潜规则要发挥作用需要具备一个条件，那就是它必须要在"暗箱"之中隐蔽地操作，因为这种"隐蔽的、私下的方式方法"并没有得到社会成员的普遍认可，一旦规则的制定者——全体社会成员，发现了权力的掌控者在利用潜规则使少数人获益，他们就要谴责抗议，甚至收回自己的原始权利。这时，权力的正义性会随着事实真相的曝光而迅速瓦解。因此，不被社会成员认可接受的潜规则只有隐藏起来使用，才能继续维持权力掌控者的正义性——他们行使权力时所需要的社会成员的认可。

但是，到了人类社会的移动互联时代，任何信息资讯，不论何时何地，只要出现在人们手中的移动互联设备上，而大家

it appears on the people's mobile Internet devices and everyone is willing to share and spread it, then it will only be a matter of time to get it known by everyone. Advanced Internet technologies and personal mobile devices allow a hot spot event to spread across a country or even the whole world in an astonishingly short time. The same goes for unspoken rules. Once the victims of unspoken rules --- those whose legitimate interests are infringed detect the backdoor deal between the power controllers and the beneficiaries of unspoken rules, they will try everything possible to expose them and disclose the truth to the entire society. Disintegrate the justice of such mutated power with the truth, and expose the illegitimate interests of a few people so as to defend their legitimate rights and interests. It would be very tough to do so in an era without Internet and personal mobile devices. But since human society entered the era of mobile Internet, everything

又愿意分享传播的话，那么被所有人知道，就只剩下时间问题了。先进的互联网技术和个人移动设备，可以让一个热点事件，在令人吃惊的时间里传遍一个国家，甚至是整个世界。潜规则也是一样，当潜规则的受害者——正当利益被侵害的人，一旦发现权力掌控者和潜规则受益者私下的内幕，便会想尽一切办法将其曝光，将事实真相向全社会公布。让事实真相瓦解这种变异的权力的正义性，曝光少数人的不正当利益，从而捍卫自己的正当合理权益。在没有互联网，没有个人移动设备的时代，这是很困难的，但自从人类社会进入移动互联时代之后，一切都变了，特别是对人类社会秩序具有破坏作用的潜规则，也开始"无处藏身"了。

has changed. Especially unspoken rules that have a destructive effect on the order of human society start to "have nowhere to hide".

"Power" That Will Eventually Return to Normal

Mutated power --- namely the power that is operated relying on "hidden private rules (unspoken rules)" and only seeks illegitimate benefits for a few people. Such "hidden private rules" can play their roles only when it is not known to the public. Once it is disclose to the public, the mutated power's selfish feature of benefiting a few people will be revealed, and its justice will disintegrate quickly. People will take back their original rights that belonged to themselves successively, and will no longer voluntarily yield to such mutated power, unless it will be operated as per the established rules and procedures of social members

终将回归常态的"权力"

变异的权力——也就是依托"隐蔽的私下的规则（潜规则）"运行，只为少数人谋取不正当利益的权力。这种"隐蔽的私下的规则"只能在不被公众知悉的时候才能发挥作用，一旦它被公布于众，变异的权力为少数人牟利的自私面目就会原原本本地呈现出来，它的正义性将迅速瓦解。人们会纷纷收回原本属于自己的那部分原始权利，不再自愿服从这种变异的权力，除非它按照社会成员既定的规则程序来运行，回归权力的正常状态——按照规则程序保护大多数社会成员的正当合理利益。否则，变异的权力就会因为曝光而失去效力，并最终消亡。

and returns to the normal state of power --- to protect the legitimate interests of most members as per the rules and procedures. Otherwise, the mutated power will lose its effect due to exposure and eventually vanish.

After human society entered the era of mobile Internet, there are hardly information resources that people want to know but can't find even a bit clue. People can always get relevant information in some way as long as they want to know. The development of modern science and technology has led to incredible breadth and speed of the spread of information of human society. In such an environment, the power that is closely related to social members can become the focus of the public anywhere anytime due to the high speed and convenience of spread of information. It can make unspoken rules that can cause power mutation become increasingly difficult to hide.

What both parties to a

当人类社会进入移动互联时代，几乎不存在人们想知道但却找不到一丁点线索的信息资源，只要人们想知道，总能通过某种方式得到相关的资讯。现代科学技术的发展，已经让人类社会咨讯传播的广度和速度变得不可思议。在这样的环境当中，和人类社会成员息息相关的权力，也因为信息传播的高速便捷性，而时时处处都会成为公众的视野焦点。可以让权力变异的潜规则，这时也变得越来越难以藏身。

一件官司的双方当事人，

lawsuit need most is that the judge handling the case can make a fair and just ruling based on the law and the factual evidence. But in case of an unspoken rule with the judge --- bribe is wanted, the judge will make a ruling that are beneficial to the party from whom he/she can benefit more, The parties have to consider whether to act as per the unspoken rules so as to have a favorable or just ruling. If such doings of the judge cannot be known by the most people of the society, the parties must act as per his unspoken rules in order to finally attain their goals, having a favorable or just a fair ruling. As before people have taken back the original right to condense into this power, the judicial power of the judge is unilaterally coercive power that still has the justice recognized by most people. In other words, the judge is still ruling the case representing most social members. His/her doings are still to maintain social fairness and justice. Although this is false,

最需要的就是，处理案件的法官能依据法律和事实证据，公平公正地做出裁决。但如果法官那里存在潜规则——需要行贿，看谁能让法官得到更大的好处，法官就会做出对谁有利的裁决。那么当事人就要考虑是否按照潜规则行事，以便让自己得到有利的或是公正的裁决结果。假如，法官的这些所作所为，不可能被社会的多数人知晓，那么当事人就必须按照他的潜规则行事，才能最终达到自己的目的，得到对自己有利的，或者仅仅是一个公正的裁决。因为，在人们没有收回凝结这项权力的原始权利之前，法官手中的裁判权，是一种具有单方强制力的权力，仍然具有大多数人认可的正义性，换句话说，法官仍然是在代表多数社会成员来裁判案件，他（她）的作为仍然是为了维护社会的公平正义，尽管是虚假的，但在真相曝光之前，因着人类社会契约之名——人们让渡权利给法官，由法官裁决处罚违反社会规则之人。法官手中的权力，在正常情况下，大多数

people have transferred rights to the judge by virtue of human social contract and such judge is to rule and punish those who have violated the social rules before the truth is exposed. Normally, most social members believe that the power of the judge is irresistible, otherwise, the social contract may allow the initiation of more severe sanctions to punish those who resist the judge for the sake of stable social order and the prestige of the judge.

But the situation will be quite different if the judge and the cases tried by him/her can be supervised by the public. Once the truth of bribery is exposed, the power of the judge will lose the justice. Social members will require such judge to bear the responsibility and liability for violating the social contract. The judge shall control power for the purpose of maintaining social fairness and justice instead of abusing such power to seek personal gain for himself/herself. After entering the

社会成员都认为是不可违抗的，否则为了社会的秩序稳定和法官的威严，社会契约就有可能允许启动更为严厉的制裁措施，来惩罚违抗法官的人。

但假设法官和他（她）审理的案件，能够得到社会公众的监督，情况就会大大不同。行贿的事实，一旦被曝光，法官的权力就会失去正义性，社会成员会要求这样的法官承担违背社会契约的责任，法官应该为了维护社会公平正义而掌控权力，而不能把这种权力滥用于为自己谋取私利。进入移动互联时代以后，将事实真相曝光，成为了一件非常简单的事情，人们只需要拿起手中的智能设备，拍照、录像、录音…法官所做的一切不当之事，便会

era of mobile Internet, exposing the truth has become very simple. People only need to take pictures, videos, and record with their smart devices. . . All the improper things a judge has done will be spread to places as many and far as possible the moment a party clicks with his/finger. The judge will not only lose power herewith, but will also be subject to punishment and be condemned by the public for violating the social contract.

So, there will be less and less chances and conditions for power to mutate in an era of mobile Internet as unspoken rules can find nowhere to hide. The constant exposure of the truth will make the operation of power eventually return to normal and become the "guardian" of the legitimate rights and interests of most social members.

Sum-up to "About Power"

When people choose to live

在当事人手指的点击瞬间，传到足够多、足够远的地方，法官不仅会因此失去权力，还会因为违反社会契约受到惩罚和公众的谴责。

所以，在移动互联时代，随着潜规则的无处藏身，权力发生变异的机会和条件也会越来越少。事实真相的不断曝光，使得权力的运行终将回归常态，成为绝大多数社会成员正当权益的"守护者"。

权力篇之结语

当人们选择群居生活，组

in groups and form a structural human society, to avoid the destructive effect caused by the natural defects of humans themselves on the social order, people all agree to establish a unilateral, coercive dominating force that social members cannot be resist to manage and control the running order of human society. Such public right that represents the common will of social members (a freedom to manage as per the common will of social members). Social freedom is called "power".

Normally, the power that represents the common will of social members is a unilateral coercive dominating force that social members cannot resist. Strict procedures and rules are set for the operation of power of human society lest such force damage and harm the innocent so as to minimize its negative effects. Whether under a monarchic or a democratic social contract, important powers must be subject

成具有结构性的人类社会时，为了避免人类自身的天然缺陷，给社会秩序带来的破坏作用。人们都同意应该设立一种单向的，不容社会成员反抗的强制支配力，来管理和控制人类社会的运转秩序，这种代表社会成员共同意志的公共权利（一种按照社会成员共同意志去管理社会的自由），就叫做权力。

代表社会成员共同意志的权力，正常情况下是一种不容社会成员反抗的单向强制支配力，为了避免这种力量破坏伤害无辜，最大限度地降低它的负面作用，人类社会的权力运行通常都会被设定严格的程序规则。不管是在君主制还是民主制社会契约之中，重要的权力都要接受程序规则的约束监督，比如君主制社会的死刑复奏制度，民主制社会的诉讼程序法等都证明了这一点。

to the restraint and supervision of procedures and rules. This has been proved by, for example, the multiple-memorial system for death penalty in a monarchic society [1] and the procedural law in a democratic society, etc.

Although there are clear rules to follow, it is still likely to happen that power representing the common will of social member will not be operated as per the established rules but be operated as per hidden private "unspoken rules" which seek benefits for a few people inclusive of power controllers in human society due to the human inferiority. Such unspoken rules that do not secure the rights and interests of most social members will cause power to lose its original purposes and goals, and consequently become a means for a few people to obtain illegitimate benefits. For example, a power controller who is entitled

尽管有明确的规则可循，但由于人类的劣根性，在人类社会仍有很大的可能性，出现代表社会成员共同意志的权力不能按照既定规则运行，而是按照为了给权力掌控者等少数人谋取利益的，隐蔽的私下的"潜规则"去运行。这种不保障大多数社会成员权益的潜规则，会让权力失去原本的宗旨目标，而成为少数人获取不正当利益的手段工具。比如，可以任命官员的权力掌控者，不以多数社会成员共同认可的标准去任命管理社会的官员，而是按照谁更能让自己得到好处，谁更听话、与自己更亲密的标准去任命官员，这样的权力此时就不再代表多数社会成员的共同

① *The History of Chinese Legal System*, by Zeng Daiwei, the Law Press, 2001 Edition, p.150.

曾代伟:《中国法制史》，法律出版社 2001 年版，第 150 页。

to appoint an official does not appoints an official for social management as per the standards recognized by most social members but appoints someone who can benefit him/her more and is more obedient and is in a closer relationship with him/her. Such power no longer represents the common interests of most social members, and instead becomes a hidden danger that undermines social order, fairness and justice.

When unspoken rules that allow power to mutate arises in human society, power that is operated following the unspoken rules will be seemingly just and lose the substance of upholding justice. Since hidden private rules exist depending on social contract rules, the power mutated due to its effects and influence will, in the name of the rules make it difficult for the public to detect. The trace of the operation of such power will be hidden, and thus it still own false justice --- most social members will still recognize its

利益，而是成为了破坏社会秩序与公平正义的隐患。

当人类社会出现可以让权力变异的潜规则时，遵循潜规则运行的权力，就徒有正义的外表，却没有维护公义的实质了。由于隐蔽的私下的潜规则是依附于社会契约规则而存在，所以受其作用影响而变异的权力，会假借规则之名让社会公众不易发觉。这种权力的运行轨迹会被隐藏起来，使它仍具有虚假的正义性——多数社会成员仍会认可它的效力。尽管他们可能已经觉察出异常，但出于对社会契约的尊重和认同，社会成员大多仍然选择服从已经变异的权力。在这个时候，

effect. They may have perceived that something has gone wrong, but most social members still choose to obey the mutated power due to respect to, and recognition of the social contract. In such case, the truth has become a powerful weapon to end the mutation of power. The reason why the power that is operated following unspoken rules can still be with effect is that most social members still recognize and accept it and still obey the allocation of social resources and benefits by such power. Once people discover the truth and know that such power does not seek benefits for most people, however, they are no longer willing to obey such power. They will, by virtue of everyone's inborn original rights, take back the rights that belonged to themselves by various means to quickly disintegrate such mutated power that was originally condensed from rights.

So, to what extent and how fast the truth spreads will ultimately

事实真相就成了终结权力变异的有力武器。遵循潜规则运行的权力，之所以还能发生效力，是因为多数社会成员还在认可接受它，还在服从这种权力对社会资源利益的调配。可一旦人们发现了事实真相，知道了这样的权力并没有为多数人谋取利益时，他们便不再愿意服从这种权力了。因着每个人与生俱来的原始权利，他们会以各种方式收回属于自己的权利，迅速瓦解这些已经变异，原本是由权利凝结而成的权力。

因此，事实真相在多大范围内，以多快的速度传播，最

determine when and where the mutated power will end. Especially after human society entered an era of mobile Internet with the rapid flow of information and news, it starts to be difficult to cover up the truth, and there will be less room for unspoken rules to hide. With such changes, the power that represents the common will of social members will eventually restore to its true colors. It will no longer seek benefits for the group of a few people, but will remain to maintain the common interests and basic order of human society.

终决定着变异的权力在何时何地会终结。特别是在人类社会进入信息咨讯高速流动的移动互联时代，事实真相开始难以掩盖，潜规则也越发无处藏身。伴随着这些变化，代表着人类社会成员共同意志的权力，也终将回归它的本来面目，不再为少数群体牟利，而是为了维护人类社会的共同利益和基本秩序而继续存在下去。

权威篇
About Authority

(I)Authority in Human Society

Belief

In the late 1980s, a Nobelist physicist wrote in a book he co-authored with another person named The God Particle: If the Universe Is the Answer, What Is the Question? Such a passage: "A fuzzy swirling light appears in the sky, and a beam of radiance illuminates our man-on-the-beach." In the solemn and climactic chord dub of Bach's Mass in B minor, or perhaps in Igor Stravinsky's piccolo solo "The Rite of Spring", the light in the sky slowly turned into the face of God, smiling, but with an extremely sweet while sad expression. [1]

This passage depicts a

（一）人类社会的权威

信　仰

20 世纪 80 年代末，一位获得诺贝尔奖的世界顶级物理学家在他与别人合著的一本书《上帝粒子：假如宇宙是答案，究竟什么是问题》中，写下了这样一段话：天空中出现了一道炫目的光芒，一束光照亮了我们这位沙滩主人。在巴赫 B 小调弥撒曲庄严、高潮的和弦配乐下，也可能是在斯特拉.温斯基的短笛独奏《春之祭》中，天空中的光慢慢地变成了上帝的脸，微笑着，但带着极度甜蜜的悲伤表情。

这段话，描绘出一位研究事

[1] The God Particle: If the Universe Is the Answer, What Is the Question? by Leon Lederman [America] , Dick Teresi, Translated by Mi Xujun, Gu Hongwei, Zhao Jianhui, and Chen Hongwei, Shanghai Science, Technology and Education Press, 2003 edition, p.422.

[美] 利昂·莱德曼、迪克·泰雷西：《上帝粒子：假如宇宙是答案，究竟什么是问题》，米绪军、古宏伟、赵建辉、陈宏伟译，上海科技教育出版社 2003 年版，第 422 页。

beautiful blueprint in the mind of a scientist who studies the laws of the operation of things, in which people accept and acknowledge the greatest and most profound truth in the world, and also frankly admit their own defects and deficiencies. But at the same time people are extremely excited to welcome a fully new era of human. By that time, not only has there been enough phenomena and evidences in the spirituality and spiritual world of human, but even the scientific community has also recognized a certain cognition and conclusion that has been doubted by many people for thousands of years --- we are a kind of creature, which such giants in the scientific world as Newton and Einstein, etc., did not deny such conclusion. [1] Such conclusion answers the most basic question in the human world --- where do we come from and where do we go?

物运行规律的科学家心中的一幅美好的蓝图，在那里面人们接受承认了人世间最伟大、最深奥的事实真相，也坦然承认自己的缺陷和不足，但与此同时，人们也会带着极度兴奋的心情去迎接全新的人类大纪元。到那时，不仅是人类的灵性和精神世界出现了足够多的现象和证据，就连科学界也认同了，千百年来某个被不少人一直怀疑的认知结论——我们是受造之物，牛顿和爱因斯坦这些科学界的巨匠，也并没有否认这样的结论。这个结论回答了人类世界最基本的问题，那就是我们究竟从哪里来，要到哪里去。

---

① Wikipedia, Isaac Newton, Wikipedia the Free Encyclopedia, https://en.wikipedia.org/wiki/Isaac_Newton#cite_ref-tiner_126-0. Wikipedia, Albert Einstein, Wikipedia the Free Encyclopedia, https://en.wikipedia.org/wiki/Albert_Einstein#Political_and_religious_views.

The understanding and answer to this question represent the main attribute of one's belief. If you believe that people were created and not evolved from lower creatures, then your behavior and life will have obvious traces of self-restraint, and you will not indulge your own selfish desires and evil deeds. Because you believe that the end of human physical life does not mean eternal death, and that another form of life energy will continue after that. You want that process to become like what you are told by the revelation from God or your subconsciousness. You will choose to persist in patience, overcome the harsh environment and the sufferings of life to obey the guidance from a certain force in the dark, and to go through the limited life course under such guidance, and then quietly enter another world, and continue your life in a new form of energy.

If you believe that humans

对于这个问题的理解与回答，代表着一个人信仰的主要属性。如果你相信人是被创造出来的，而非由低等生物进化而来。那么你的言行和生活，就会带有很明显的自我约束的痕迹，你不会放纵自己的私欲和恶行。因为你相信，人类肉体生命的终结并不意味着永远的死亡，另一种形式的生命能量会在那之后继续进行，你想让那个过程变得如同你得到的启示或是潜意识告诉你的那样。你会选择坚持忍耐，克服恶劣环境和人生的苦难，去服从冥冥之中某种力量给你的指引，并在其指引下走完有限的生命历程，然后安静地进入另一个世界，并以一种全新的能量形式继续你的生命。

如果你相信人是由低等生

evolved from lower creatures, humans are a kind of animal, and should constantly satisfy their desires and pursue all kinds of happiness, then your life state will be completely different. The most obvious difference is that you will seldom care about the situation and feelings of others. Because you think those things have nothing to do with you, and only to satisfy yourself is the most correct thing. The end of life means that everything is over. No matter to what extent you are satisfied and how much you have gained, they can only be achieved during the process of your limited life. If people hold such understanding and viewpoint, they will easily become greedy and fearless. You will make use of every opportunity to satisfy your endless desires and needs, even by means harming or hurting others. Because such people do not believe that they will enter another world after their death, and they are not afraid that the punishment after death is true,

物进化而来，人就是动物的一种，应该不断地满足自己的欲望，追求各种快乐。那么你的生活状态就会完全不同，最明显的不同就是，你会很少去关心别人的境况和感受，因为你认为那些和你无关，只有满足自己才是最正确的事情。生命的终结，就意味着所有的一切都结束了，你满足了多少，收获了多少，都只能在有限的生命过程中才能实现，如果抱着这样的认知和观点，人们就会很容易变得贪婪，且无所畏惧。你会利用各种机会去满足自己无穷尽的欲望要求，哪怕通过伤害他人的方式手段也在所不惜，因为这样的人不相信，人死后还会有另一个世界，他们不害怕死后的惩罚会是真实的，或者说他们不害怕"地狱"，准确地说应该是他们不相信"地狱"。

or to say, they are not afraid of "hell." To be precise, it should be said that they don't believe there will be the "hell."

Perhaps one has never thought about the boring and tough question of "Where do I come from and where do I go?" But this does not imply that he/she can completely abandon the guidance and restraint from a certain voice or idea in the heart (brain). Deep in his/her consciousness, he/she may still believe that people are with spirituality (a kind of energy different from tangible matter) and even everything is spiritual. Nothing is incidental or accidental. Behind the seemingly complex and chaotic world, there is a mysterious power that dominates and control it.

But no matter how people consider such most basic questions of mankind, one's cognition and attitude towards such questions will become his/her belief --- some cognitions or conclusions that explain the world and mankind for

或许一个人根本就不曾想过"我从哪里来，要到哪里去"这样枯燥且困难的问题，但这并不代表他（她）能够完全摒弃，心（大脑）中某种声音或意念对他（她）的指引和约束。在他（她）的意识深处，很有可能仍然在相信人是有灵性的（一种不同于有形物质的能量），甚至万物都是有灵性的。每一件事情都不是偶然的，看似繁杂混乱的世间万象，其背后都有神秘力量在主宰和操控。

但无论人们如何对待这个人类最基本的问题，一个人对这个问题的认识和态度，都将成为他（她）的信仰——一些为自己解释世界和人类的认知或结论。

oneself.

Belief and Religion

Belief is a cognition or conclusion with which people explain the world and the mankind. The basic content of belief usually covers a most basic question --- where do we humans come from, and where do we go in the end on earth? Besides, belief can also tell people why one often feels unsatisfactory and painful, how to get happiness, etc.

Why do we feel sad and fearful when we see injustice, cruelty or deceit, but we feel happy physically and mentally when we feel love? As if the integration of our bodies and another part of existence constitutes the whole of life. With the death and decay of a body, does one really disappear completely? With these endless while difficult-to-answer questions, people can always find certain scriptures (doctrines) at right time and place. And among

信仰与宗教

信仰是人们解释世界和人类的认知或结论。信仰的基本内容往往都要涵盖一个最基本的问题——我们人类究竟从哪里来，最后我们要到哪里去。另外，信仰还能告诉人们，为什么一个人会常常感到不如意和痛苦，究竟怎样才能得到幸福等等。

为什么我们看到不公义、残暴和欺诈时会感到难过恐惧，当感受到爱意时却会身心愉悦，仿佛我们的肉体和另一部分存在的融合才构成了生命的全部。随着肉体的死亡和腐朽，一个人就真的完全消失了吗？带着这些无穷无尽且难以解答的问题，人们总能在适当的时间和地点，发现某些经典（宗教教义），不管是佛家、道家，还是伊斯兰教和基督教，在其核心教义当中都有对上述问题的解答和描述。找到了经典上的答案，人

their core doctrines, there are all answers and descriptions of the above questions, whether in Buddhism, Taoism, Islam or Christianity. Having found the answer in the scriptures, people stop being fearful gradually. People with beliefs gradually calmed themselves down through religion and begin to communicate with certain mysterious force, and herewith their spiritual pain is accordingly reduced. So, the function of belief is mainly that it can eliminate people's mental pain and point out the direction and ultimate meaning of life for those who believe in it.

Then, what is religion? We can say that religion is a way of belief in which people, with doubts in their mind, seek the answers they want. After finding or approaching the answer you want, stick to and practice your belief constantly through repeated practice of the rituals and patterns required by such answer, and expect for the final promise that

们开始慢慢地不再恐惧了，有信仰的人们通过宗教，逐渐让自己平静下来，开始同某种神秘力量进行交流，精神方面的痛苦也相应地随之减弱。所以，信仰的作用主要在于它可以消除人们的精神痛苦，为信它的人指明生命的方向和终极意义。

那宗教是什么呢？我们可以说，宗教是信仰的一种方式，人们带着心中的疑惑去寻求想要的答案。在找到或接近想要的答案后，通过反复实践这种答案所要求的礼仪式样，去不断坚守和践行自己的信仰，并且期待着自己心中信仰蓝图之中那最后属于自己的允诺，无论何种礼仪式样，这份允诺基本上都会和喜乐幸福有关。而

belongs to yourself in the blueprint of the belief in your heart. Such promise is basically related to joy and happiness no matter which kind of ritual or pattern it is. Religion in the common sense is the general term for the answers to people's doubts and the rituals and patterns required by it. The essence of religion is people's beliefs, which are people's cognitions or conclusions about a series of difficult-to-answer questions. People strengthen such cognitions and conclusions through religious activities.

Religion is to belief like cup is to water. The cup is religion, and the water is belief. We hold the cup in our hands, but what our dry heart's desire is not the cup but the water in the cup.

通常意义上的宗教，就是这些给人们解疑释惑的答案及其所要求的礼仪式样的总称。宗教的背后其实质是人的信仰，是人们对于自身一系列难以回答的问题的认知或结论，人们通过宗教活动来强化这样的认知和结论。

宗教对于信仰来讲，就像是水杯和水的关系。杯子是宗教，水是信仰，我们手中握着水杯，但干涸的心想要的却不是杯子，而是杯子里的水。

Belief vs. Science

信仰与科学

Belief is a cognition or conclusion formed by people in explaining the world and the human. It was naturally produced

信仰是人们在解释这个世界和人类自身的过程中形成的认知或结论，是人们为了追求理性和消除痛苦而自然产生的。

by people to pursue rationality and eliminate pain. It can also be said that the more rational or painful one is, the stronger strength one will have to seek belief. Many people want to know: Why we were born and what for we live? Why there are mental and physical pains, Will people be painful for a lifetime, or we'll all obtain happiness after sticking to kindness, patience and dedication?

With such questions, people started their own path of belief. Initially, they seek belief by imagination or spiritual exploration. But gradually a considerable number of people will verify the questions and answers in their mind in more rational ways. They analyze and verify the origin and laws of this world step by step in their own ways. In other words, they try to explain the world where we live with human wisdom, and solve all our troubles and problems with human abilities. Such a person saw an apple fall from a tree. He

也可以说，人有多么理性或者多么痛苦，他就会有多大的力量去寻求信仰。有很多人想要知道，一个人活着究竟是怎么回事，为什么会有精神和肉体上的痛苦，人会痛苦一辈子吗，还是坚守良善，忍耐付出之后，我们都会得到幸福快乐。

带着这样的问题，人们开始了自己的信仰之路。起初都是通过想象或精神探索去寻求信仰，但慢慢的有相当数量的人，会用较为理性的方式去求证心中的问题和答案。他们用自己的方法一步一步地分析验证这个世界的本源和规律，换句话说，他们试图用人类的智慧解释我们所生存的这个世界，用人类自身的能力去解决我们所有的麻烦和问题。苹果从树上掉下来，被这样的人看到，他没有简单地解释为这是上帝的安排，那个苹果就是要在那个时候落在那个地方，而是开始理性的思索，他开始用"为什么"去

did not simply explain that it was arranged by God to fall there and then. Instead, he began to think rationally and explore the doubts by asking "why". [1] It is exactly such rational "why" that allows people to find a fully new way to seek belief, which is usually called "scientific research" as it respects rationality, analysis and verification. Those people who solve problems by scientific research completely differ from those religious people who explain the world using religious doctrines and subjective feelings. Most scientific researchers do not deny that it is God who created the world, but they also do not rule out the possibility that God does not exist at all. They just carry out research and analysis that can satisfy their needs and are logical in rational ways, and answer and solve many doubts in the process of mankind's search for belief with

探究疑惑。正是这个理性的"为什么",让人们找到了全新的方式去寻求信仰,这种全新的方式因为推崇理性和分析论证,通常被人们称作"科学研究"。通过科学研究解决处理问题的人们,完全不同于用宗教教义和主观感受来解释世界的宗教人士,大部分科学研究者不否认是上帝创造了这个世界,但他们也不排除上帝根本就不存在的可能性。他们只是在用理性的方法,进行能满足需求且合乎逻辑的研究分析,用科学的结论来回答解决人类寻求信仰过程中的诸多疑惑。历史上曾有科学家,用自己的方法研究得出人类是从某种生物进化而来,而不是由上帝创造出来的。这样的结论,至今仍有相当数量的人不持异议。也有科学家用自己的理论,试图证明上帝是不存在的,因为他认为宇宙和人类并不需要由上帝来创造。从这个角度看去,我们可以说,科学其实是在证明宗教的真伪,

---

[1] Amanda Gefter, Newton's apple: The real story, NewScientist, https://www.newscientist.com/blogs/culturelab/2010/01/newtons-apple-the-real-story.html.

scientific conclusions. In history, there were scientists who studied in their own ways and found that humans evolved from certain creature and were not created by God. [1] This is a conclusion to which a considerable number of people do not object up to now. Also, there is a scientist who tried to prove that God does not exist using their own theories as he believed that the universe and the mankind do not need God to create them. [2] From this perspective, it can be said that science is actually proving religion is true or false. And the purpose of scientific research is also to satisfy human needs for belief. Cognitions and conclusions told by a belief can enable one to be linked to the powerful energy needed in overcoming difficulties

科学研究的目的也是为了满足人类对信仰的需求。信仰告诉人们的认知和结论，可以让一个人在克服困境和苦难时连接到所需要的强大能量，用科学的方式寻求信仰，也正是人们理性探索某些问题认知结论的过程。宗教是信仰的一种方式，与其相对应，科学也是人类满足信仰需求的有效方法，两者都是人类信仰的载体和平台。

[1] *The Origin of Species*, by Darwin [Britain], translated by Zhou Jianren, Ye Duzhuang, and Fang Zongxi, the Commercial Press, 1997 edition, p.525.

[英] 达尔文：《物种起源》，周建人、叶笃庄、方宗熙译，商务印书馆 1997 年版，第 525 页。

[2] *The Grand Design,* by Hawking, Leonard Mlodinow [Britain], translated by Wu Zhongchao, Hu'nan Science and Technology Press, 2011 edition, p.153.

[英] 霍金、蒙洛迪诺：《大设计》，吴忠超译，湖南科学技术出版社 2011 年版，第 153 页。

and sufferings. Seeking belief in a scientific way is also a process of people rationally exploring certain cognitions and conclusions to questions. Religion is a way of belief. Correspondingly, science is also an effective way for humans to satisfy the needs for belief. The two both are the carriers and platforms of human beliefs.

The relationship between science and belief is like that between religion and belief. What people are really interested in is not science itself, instead, they want to figure out what they want to understand through science just like through religion --- why are this world and we humans are like this? Are what religious doctrines tell us true or not?

Religion vs. Science

Humans seek belief to satisfy their inner curiosities and desires. The cognitions and conclusions that belief tells people can satisfy such curiosities and desires of

类似于宗教与信仰，科学与信仰的关系也是一样的。人们真正感兴趣的并不是科学本身，而是像通过宗教那样，来透过科学弄清楚自己想要明白的问题——这个世界和我们人类为什么会是这个样子，宗教教义告诉我们的是真的吗？

宗教与科学

人类寻求信仰是为了满足自己内心深处的好奇和欲望，信仰告诉人们的认知结论，可以让人类的这些好奇和欲望得到满足。信仰就像是一块硬币，

humans. Belief is like a coin. When people find belief, it will be like getting a coin that can satisfy their spiritual needs. Such coin will allow people to understand the answers to the questions they desire --- whether we were created by God or evolved from a certain kind of lower creature? Besides, we still have other countless questions that need such coin to answer. For example, when I open my eyes, who is the one smiling to me, feeding me, loving and protecting me? Why do I feel love in my heart? And why I feel happy only when there is love. . .

Such innate thirst for knowledge of human is the bud of belief, and people gradually formed their own beliefs in satisfying such thirst for knowledge. There are many scriptures (e.g. the Bible, Quran, Buddhist scriptures, myths legends, etc.) and various theories handed down about belief in the human world. The main reason is that humans chose different methods to solve problems in

人们找到了信仰，就像是得到了一块能够满足心灵需求的硬币。这块硬币会让人们明白自己所渴慕的问题答案——我们是上帝创造出来的，或者我们是从某种低等生物进化而来的。另外，我们还有其他多到数不清的问题，都需要这枚硬币来解答。比如，当我睁开眼睛，冲着我微笑，喂养我、爱护我的人是谁，为什么我的心中会有爱的感觉，为什么有爱才会感到幸福…

人类与生俱来的这种求知欲，便是信仰的萌芽，人们在满足这种求知欲的过程中逐渐形成自己的信仰。关于信仰人类世界流传下来的有很多经典（比如圣经、古兰经、佛家经典、神话传说等），还有各种各样的学说，主要原因就在于人类在寻求信仰的过程中，选择了不同的方式来解决问题。这些方法总的来说，可以归为两大类，它们就像是信仰这枚硬币的两

seeking belief. In general, such methods can be divided into two categories, and they are like the two sides of the coin of "belief". One side is that human discover and reveal the internal laws of the natural world and the human world through their own wisdom, research and analysis. So this side of the coin of belief is called "science" as such method advocates rationality; while the other side is that people explain the doubts for themselves through the intuition and induction gained from authoritative scriptures passed on by word of mouth or revelation from the unknown world. Such method can be called perceptual method or religious method, which constitutes the other side of the coin of belief --- religion.

Religion and science are two different methods that human use in trying to answer the doubts they are born with. There are many differences between the two, and even they are completely

面。一边是人类通过自身的智慧和研究分析，去发现揭示自然界和人类世界的内部规律，这类方法因其倡导理性，所以硬币的这一面就叫做——科学；在硬币的另一边，人们透过口舌相传的权威经典所得到的直觉和感应，或者通过未知世界的启示，来给自己解疑释惑，这类方法可以称作感性的方法或者宗教的方法，这些构成了信仰硬币的另一面——宗教。

宗教与科学是人类在试图解答与生俱来的那些疑惑过程中，所使用的不同方法。宗教与科学有很多不同之处，甚至在某些方面它们还是格格不入的，但这些并没有影响到两种方法

incompatible in some aspects. But these don't affect the consistency of the ultimate goal of the two methods --- they are both to explain the curiosities and desires deep in human heart. It is in satisfying their such own unique thirst for knowledge that human gradually formed their own beliefs with the cognitions and conclusions drawn by them. The two methods have often drawn different conclusions on certain issues. But so far there is not yet sufficient evidence in the human world to prove that the cognitions and conclusions drawn by the two methods are completely contrary to each other.

"Difficulties" in Science

Science is a field that explores the origin and laws of the world, where a lot of highly rational human wisdom is gathered. But a phenomenon that is very difficult to explain arises right here at such a place full of logical reasoning,

在终极目标上的一致性——它们都是为了解释人类内心深处的好奇和欲望，人类也正是在满足自身特有的这种求知欲的过程中，用所得出的认知和结论来慢慢形成自己的信仰。尽管这两种方法在很多时候，就某些问题曾得出过不同的结论，但迄今为止，人类世界还没有足够充分的证据，来证明这两种方法所得出的认知结论，是完全背道而驰的。

界的"难题"

科学界是一个探究世界本源与规律的领域，在这里汇集了很多高度理性的人类智慧。但正是这样一个充满逻辑推理和分析论证的地方，却出现了十分难以解释的现象，几乎成为科学界的难题——绝大多数的

analysis and verification, and it almost becomes a difficulty in science --- most famous scientists have their religious beliefs. Although a considerable number of them are constantly try to explore and verify the origin and laws of all things in the universe using the scientific computing tools and theoretical models mastered by them, and try to negate the perceptual and uncertain predictive conclusions that religion has left on such issues. Regrettably, no one in the scientific community has been able to thoroughly deny the basis for existence and the doctrinal system of religion logically and rationally so far.

According to the survey data published by a religious publication, in the first half of the 20th century, totaling 639 people won the Nobel Prize which is the highest award of the academic community in human society. But only 21 of whom did not have religious beliefs or with low

著名科学家都相信宗教。尽管他们当中有相当数量的人，在不断努力用自己掌握的科学计算工具和理论模型去探究论证宇宙万物的本源及规律，并试图否定宗教在这些问题上给人们留下的感性且不确定的预言性结论。但遗憾的是，科学界至今还没有人能够从逻辑和理性的角度，彻底否定宗教的存在根基和教义体系。

某宗教刊物公布的调查数字显示，人类社会在20世纪前半页，共评选出学术界的最高奖项——诺贝尔奖639人，其中不信宗教或是宗教意识淡薄的获奖者只有21人，而信仰各种宗教的却有618人。这样的数据告诉我们20世纪前半页人类社会的600余位学术精英当中，

religious consciousness. Whereas 618 of whom had their own beliefs of various religions. [1] Such data tells us that around 97% of the over 600 academic elites in human society in the first half of the 20th century believed that humans themselves are not the masters of the world, and that humans cannot obtain happiness by themselves. Or to say, humans cannot get salvation by themselves. If people want to obtain what they truly want and realize the ultimate meaning of life, they have to obey the specific target who they believe in their hearts --- an existence of energy that differ from the objective matters that humans can directly perceive --- which people usually call "God", "Lord", Allah, or Buddha, etc.

For the conclusions drawn from the above data, another two

有大约97%是相信人类自身并不是世界的主宰，相信人类无法仅仅依靠自己，获得幸福和快乐。或者说是人类无法仅靠自己得到救赎，人们要想获得自己真正想要的东西，实现生命的终极意义，必须要顺从自己心中信奉的特定对象——一种不同于人类所能直接感知的客观物质的能量存在，人们通常称其为神、主、真主或是佛等等。

对于上述数字得出的结论，另外两位人类历史上的科学巨

[1] *A Brief Analysis of the Nobelists' Beliefs,* by Wen Dao, published in the Chinese Data Journal Database, http://www.cqvip.com/read/read.aspx?id=12312889#, access time: 17: 07 Mar 7, 2017.

文刀：《诺贝尔奖得主信仰小考》，载中文数据期刊数据库，http://www.cqvip.com/read/read.aspx?id=12312889#，访问时间：2017年3月7日17：07。

giant scientists in human history --- Newton and Einstein --- can also exemplify that.

Newton believed that God controls the movement of the sun, planets, and comets, and that is God who established the laws of all tings of the universe.[①] And Einstein put religion at a very lofty level. He once said, "I am of the opinion that all the finer speculations in the realm of science spring from a deep religious feeling, and that without such feelings they would not be fruitful."[②] "A person who is religiously enlightened appears to me to be one who has, to the best of his ability, liberated himself from the fetters of his selfish desires and is preoccupied with thoughts, feelings, and aspirations to which he clings because of their superpersonal value." "Science without religion is lame, religion

匠牛顿和爱因斯坦，也可以作为例证来说明。

牛顿认为上帝支配着太阳、行星和彗星的运行，他相信是上帝定下了宇宙万物之间的规律。而爱因斯坦则把宗教放在很崇高的位置上，他曾说'很难在造诣较深的科学家中间找到一个没有自己宗教感情的人。''在我看来，一个人信仰宗教，他就摆脱了自私的欲望，全神贯注追求崇高的思想、感情和志向。''科学离开宗教就像瘸子，宗教离开科学就像瞎子'他还说过他不相信人格化的上帝。也就是说，他没有否认非人格化的上帝是存在的（上帝不具有人的模样和特征，上帝以不同于人类的生存方式客观存在）。

① Wikipedia, General Scholium, Wikipedia the Free Encyclopedia, https://en.wikipedia.org/wiki/General_Scholium.

② The Collected Papers of Albert Einstein (Volume 1), the Commercial Press, 1994 Edition, p.283.
《爱因斯坦文集》（第1卷），商务印书馆1994年版，第283页。

without science is blind." [1] He also said that he does not believe in a personalized God. [2] That is, he did not deny that there is an impersonal God (God does not own the appearance and features of human, and God exists objectively in a way of living different from human).

These examples show that the giant scientists have also continuously drawn the reasonableness of religion in human society in earnestly and rationally exploring and analyzing the laws of the universe. Although such result obviously violates the scientific spirit of challenging authority, respecting facts, and rational reasoning, it is an unchangeable fact.

这些说明，科学巨匠们在认真理性地探究分析宇宙规律的过程中，也不断地得出人类社会宗教的合理性，尽管这一结果明显违背了挑战权威、尊重事实、理性推理的科学精神，但却是一个无法改变的事实。

---

[1] *Albert Einstein,* Shaanxi Normal University Press, 2010 edition, p.87-88.

《爱因斯坦自述》，陕西师大出版社 2010 年版，第 87-88 页。

[2] Wikipedia, Albert Einstein, Wikipedia the Free Encyclopedia, https://en.wikipedia.org/wiki/Albert_Einstein#Political_and_religious_views.

Ancient and Mysterious Legend

In the many ancient scriptures that have been handed down in human society for a long time, there are myths and legends whose authenticity humans cannot verify or deny, but they are, like prophecies, constantly verifying the development and changes of the human world.

In ancient China, there was a prophecy book named *The Military Prophecies of China* [1], which predicted the history of China for thousands of years after the author wrote the book using illustrations and text annotations. Some people say that what is said

古老而神秘的传说

在人类社会流传已久的许多经典古书当中，有人类无法证实也无法否认其真实性的神话传说，但这些传说却像预言一般，在不断地验证着人类世界的发展变迁。

在中国古代，有一本名叫《推背图》的预言书，书中用插图和文字注释的方式，预言了作者著书之后几千年的中国历史。有人说书中所言与其后发生的历史事件，只是偶然巧合，不足为奇，但也有人认为并非那么简单。其中，最为引人关

[1] *The Military Prophecies of China,* by Li Chunfeng, Yuan Tiangang [the Tang Dynasty, China], published in Baidu Encyclopedia, http://baike.baidu.com/link?url=iEmu0wYWQOEokQcoPu YCYoBWHiY4iUqv9rfbHZt4GkDnLZqQzF0AZYnJObxonA55yGeXk92mSAFJZs3mMdwc OJvmcC2Sczu_vq4c5PrywhII9FVr3A1zGEyO3MO9RJ9E, access time: 19:03 Mar 7, 2017.

（唐）李淳风、袁天罡：《推背图》，载百度百科，http://baike.baidu.com/link?url=iEmu0 wYWQOEokQcoPuYCYoBWHiY4iUqv9rfbHZt4GkDnLZqQzF0AZYnJObxonA55yGeXk9 2mSAFJZs3mMdwcOJvmcC2Sczu_vq4c5PrywhII9FVr3A1zGEyO3MO9RJ9E，访问时间：2017 年 3 月 7 日 19：03。

in the book and the subsequent historical events just coincide and it is not surprising. But some other people think that it is not that simple. Among them, the most eye-catching prophecy is that a saint was to come into being, he/she would make the human world harmonious and "one world, one family". [1]

There is one more scripture widely circulated in both the East and the West --- the *Bible*, which also predicted that the human world would eventually enter the doomsday. The savior Messiah would save people in the world and lead mankind to establish a new world and create a new era. [2]

注的预言则是一位圣人将要出现, 他（她）会使人类世界和谐, 迎来"天下一家"。

还有一本在东西方都广为流传的经典——《圣经》, 也同样预言了人类世界最终要进入末世, 救世主弥赛亚将拯救世人, 引领人类建立新世界, 开创新纪元。在伊斯兰教的经典中, 同样有与此类似的预言和论断。佛家的经典也有末法时代, 到那时弥勒佛要下凡拯救

---

① *The Military Prophecies of China*, by Li Chunfeng, Yuan Tiangang [the Tang Dynasty, China], published in Baidu Encyclopedia, http://baike.baidu.com/link?url=iEmu0wYWQOEokQcoPu YCYoBWHiY4iUqv9rfbHZt4GkDnLZqQzF0AZYnJObxonA55yGeXk92mSAFJZs3mMdwc OJvmcC2Sczu_vq4c5PrywhII9FVr3A1zGEyO3MO9RJ9E, access time: 19:03 Mar 7, 2017.

（唐）李淳风、袁天罡:《推背图》, 载百度百科, http://baike.baidu.com/link?url=iEmu0 wYWQOEokQcoPuYCYoBWHiY4iUqv9rfbHZt4GkDnLZqQzF0AZYnJObxonA55yGeXk9 2mSAFJZs3mMdwcOJvmcC2Sczu_vq4c5PrywhII9FVr3A1zGEyO3MO9RJ9E, 访问时间: 2017 年 3 月 7 日 19: 03。

② *Bible*, National Committee of Three-Self Patriotic Movement, the Protestant Churches in China (National TSPM), China Christian Council (CCC), 2009 edition, (Isaiah 9:6, 9:7, 11, 11:2, 11:3, 11:4, 11:5) p.667, p.669~670.

《圣经》, 中国基督教三自爱国运动委员会、中国基督教协会 2009 年版,（赛9: 6、9: 7、11、11: 2、11: 3、11: 4、11: 5）第 667 页、第 669-670 页。

In the Islamic scripture, there are similar prophecies and judgments. [1] Also, in the Buddhist scripture, an era of the end of Dharma was depicted, when Maitreya Buddha would come down to the earth to save people in this world and lead mankind get out of sufferings. [2] There are still many other ancient books with similar contents, e.g. *Poem on Plum Blossom, the Quick Prediction Method of Zhuge Liang,* etc., and the degree of similarity of some of the prophecies in these books is also astonishing.

If there are multiple prophecies with the same content within a

世人，带领人类脱离苦海。记载有相似内容的古文书籍还有不少，诸如梅花诗、马前课等等，并且这些书中某些预言的内容相似度也让人感到惊讶。

如果说，一个民族聚集的区域或是一个国家的范围之内，

---

[1] Sunan of Abu Dawud, by Mahdi, published in Baidu Encyclopedia, http://baike.baidu.com/link?url=2KeXP2Ul1sLoUmT3e4mU5El2xzsbzdspthoM2MxKIAdqCk0Xp9CjhYUOdBYuB5fCCY9OWhd4rpEokQqb9BfrAiZi--WGuRP1idcX0tFfHHIOsftkbUVEEz3ThRQEPNS4, access time: 19:20 Mar 7, 2017

艾布达吾德圣训：马赫迪，载百度百科，http://baike.baidu.com/link?url=2KeXP2Ul1sLoUmT3e4mU5El2xzsbzdspthoM2MxKIAdqCk0Xp9CjhYUOdBYuB5fCCY9OWhd4rpEokQqb9BfrAiZi--WGuRP1idcX0tFfHHIOsftkbUVEEz3ThRQEPNS4, 访问时间：2017年3月7日19：20。

[2] The Transformation from the Pure Land of Maitreya to the Pure Land of Amita", by Shi Guangming, published in Masters' Lecture on Buddhist Knowledge, edited by editorial department of Knowledge of Literature and History, Zhonghua Book Company, 2016 edition, p.232-233.

施光明："从弥勒净土到阿弥陀净土嬗变"，载《文史知识》编辑部编：《名家讲佛教知识》，中华书局2016年版，第232-233页。

region where an ethnic group gathers or a country, it can be understood and interpreted as that such prophecies originated from the same place or even the same person. So such prophecies are unreliable, and the truth will prove its absurdity. But from the above description, it can obviously be seen that such a doomsday and such a savior who would save people in this world is not only a prediction that appeared within a region or country, but is also almost a voice from all mankind. Where do these cognitions and conclusions come from on earth? Each has its own respective explanations in the religious community. But the results are quite similar --- humans would be redeemed by a great man, who is an "ordinary person" that can connect with the mysterious power of the unknown world. Some people call him/her "saint", some people call him/her "Messiah, Jesus", and others call him/her "Buddha Maitreya"... No matter

出现了多个同样内容的预言，我们可以理解解释为，这种预言是源自同一个地方，甚至同一个人，所以这样的预言是不可靠的，事实真相会证明它的荒谬性。但通过上面的描述，可以很明显地看出，这样的末世和拯救世人的伟大人物，不仅仅是一个地区或一个国家范围内出现的预言，它几乎是来自全人类的声音。这样的认知和结论究竟从哪里来，宗教界各有各的解释，但结果却非常相似——人类要被一位伟人救赎，他（她）是能够连接未知世界神秘力量的"普通人"，有叫他（她）"圣人"的，也有叫他（她）"弥赛亚、耶稣"的，还有叫他（她）"弥勒佛"的…，无论人们如何解释他（她）的到来，最终他（她）都要来拯救世人，引领人类走出末世的灾难。

how people explain his/her advent, he/she would eventually come to save people in this world, and lead mankind to get out of the disaster of the doomsday.

Discovery of "God Particle"

Two famous physicists once made a bet. One said that it is impossible for a certain particle in physics to be found in reality, or that such particle does not exist at all. While the other believed that such particle would ultimately be proved by science and technology to exist objectively. Their bet for this is $USD100 and the result is that the former lost the $USD100.[1] As scientists announced that they had discovered such particle at a global top physics experiment center

"上帝粒子"的发现

曾经有两位非常有名的物理学家打过一个赌，一位说物理学中某种粒子在现实层面不可能被发现，或者说这种粒子是根本不存在的，另一位认为这种粒子最终将被科学技术证明，它是客观存在的，他们的赌注是 100 美金，他们打赌的结果是，前者输掉了这 100 美金。因为 2012 年 7 月 4 日，在一个世界顶级的物理学实验中心，科学家们宣布他们发现了这种粒子。该实验中心 CMS 实验组发言人称"实验结果综合

---

[1] *Hawking Admits That He Likes betting As He Lost $100 This Year Due to Nobel Prize"*, published in International News, China News Network , http://www.chinanews.com/gj/2013/11-13/5496233.shtml, access time: 19:26, Mar 7, 2017.

中国新闻网：《霍金承认喜欢打赌 因今年诺贝尔奖输掉 100 美元》，载中国新闻网国际新闻，http://www.chinanews.com/gj/2013/11-13/5496233.shtml，访问时间：2017 年 3 月 7 日 19:26。

on Jul 4th, 2012. A spokesperson for the CMS experimental group of the experimental center said, "After the experimental results are combined, the error exceeds 5 standard errors, namely the confidence coefficient is 99.99994%. According to the precedents of the top quark, this means the particle is discovered!" [1] The two physicists who predicted the existence of such mysterious particle were also awarded the Nobel Prize, the world's highest award in physics in 2013 in recognition of their "theoretical discovery of a mechanism that helps us understand the origin of the mass of subatomic particles. Which has been confirmed by the elementary particles in the predictions recently discovered in the experiments carried out with Large Hadron Colliders

起来后, 超出误差 5 个标准误差, 即 99.99994% 的可信度, 按顶夸克的前例, 这就是发现粒子! " 预言这种神秘粒子存在的两位物理学家, 也在 2013 年被授予物理学世界级最高奖项——诺贝尔奖, 以表彰他们 "理论性发现了一种机制, 有助于我们理解亚原子粒子质量的起源, 最近欧洲大型强子对撞机 ATLAS 和 CMS 实验所发现的预测中的基本粒子对其进行了确认。" 这种粒子还以其中一位物理学家的名字进行命名——Higgs bosons, 又叫做 "希格斯玻色子"。

[1] *CERN Announces the Discovery of God Particles,* cnBeta, published in Network CBN News, China Broadcasting, http://www.cnr.cn/gundong/201207/t20120704_510111540.shtml, access time: 19: 33 Mar 7, 2017.

cnBeta:《欧洲核子研究中心宣布发现上帝粒子》, 载中国广播网央广快讯, http://www.cnr.cn/gundong/201207/t20120704_510111540.shtml, 访问时间: 2017 年 3 月 7 日 19:33。

ATLAS and CMS in Europe."[1] And such particle is also named after one of the physicists --- Higgs bosons, also known as "Higgs bosons particle."

What are the features and functions of such mysterious particle? In layman's terms, above all, it's invisible and intangible but exists objectively. Moreover, only by combining with it will the matters in the natural world have mass. Finally, its advent has fulfilled many physicists' previous predictions about the standard physics model of particles, who believed that such model still lacks a kind of particle. Only when such particle is discovered can the previous standard model play a role to explain various mysteries of the material world. So, some people call such particle discovered by humans "God particle".

These fruits of scientific research

这种神秘的粒子，究竟有什么特征和作用呢？通俗的讲，首先它看不见、也摸不着，但却客观存在。并且，自然世界的物质，只有和它结合之后，才会有质量。最后，它的出现应验了不少物理学家之前对粒子标准物理学模型的预言，他们认为这个模型当中还缺少一种粒子，只有发现这种粒子，之前的标准模型才能发挥作用，去解释物质世界的种种奥秘。因此，也有人称这种被人类发现的粒子为"上帝粒子"。

这些科学研究的成果，对

---

[1] *Nobel Prize Winners in Physics for 2013 Announced,* by Mei Jin and Zhang Xiao, published in Sciencenet News, http://news.sciencenet.cn/htmlnews/2013/10/283493.shtm?id=283493, access time: 19:40 on Mar 7, 2017.

梅进、张笑：《2013 年诺贝尔物理学奖揭晓》，载科学网新闻，http://news.sciencenet.cn/htmlnews/2013/10/283493.shtm?id=283493，访问时间：2017 年 3 月 7 日 19：40。

are also of great significance to the beliefs of mankind. It is like gleamingly portraying a scene on this coin of human beliefs --- it is extremely likely that there is still an unknown world that we can't see but is full of power in the universe that we see with our naked eyes.

Human "Spirit" Exist or Not?

Now that scientific research has drawn a blueprint for human to yearn for, we can continue to explore the mysteries of life and nature along the direction guided by science.

The scientific research on "God particle" shows that all matters with mass have such particle field in it; otherwise such matters would not have had mass. [1] Then, how about us

于人类的信仰来说，同样具有非常重大的意义。它就像是在人类信仰这块硬币之上，隐隐地刻画出一个景象——在我们肉眼所见的宇宙之中，极其可能还有一个我们看不见，但却充满力量的未知世界一直存在。

人的"灵魂"是否存在

既然科学研究给人类描绘出了一幅让人憧憬想象的蓝图，那我们就可以沿着科学指引的方向，继续探索生命和自然界的奥秘。

科学界对"上帝粒子"的研究说明，凡是有质量的物质，其中都有这种粒子场的存在，否则这种物质就不会有质量。那么我们人呢，在我们身体内是不是也有一个可以赋予

---

[1] *Nobel Prize Winners in Physics for 2013 Announced,* by Mei Jin and Zhang Xiao, published in Sciencenet News, http://news.sciencenet.cn/htmlnews/2013/10/283493.shtml?id=283493, access time: 19:40 on Mar 7, 2017.

梅进、张笑：《2013 年诺贝尔物理学奖揭晓》，载科学网新闻 http://news.sciencenet.cn/htmlnews/2013/10/283493.shtml?id=283493，访问时间：2017 年 3 月 7 日 19:40。

human, is there a force field in our bodies that can give us life and spirituality, which make us be with mass? If this force field exists, does it have anything to do with the spiritual world that has been talked about in the human world for thousands of years? For these questions, currently scientific research cannot yet give us accurate answers, but the religious doctrines of mankind clearly tell us that humans are with spirit, human bodies will decay and become massless, but human spirit will not die but subsist --- either to be tried or to undergo the retribution of a causal cycle.

There is such a saying in the Bible that the spirits (souls) are divided into two categories: one from gods while the other from devils.[①] Once one is controlled by the spirit from devils (evil spirit),

我们生命和灵性——让我们变得有质量的力场呢？如果存在这个力场，那么它和人类世界几千年来一直传说的灵魂世界，有什么关系吗？对于这些问题，虽然科学研究目前还不能给我们准确的答案，但人类的宗教教义却清楚地告诉我们，人都是有灵魂的，人的肉体会腐朽，会变得没有质量，可人的灵魂不会消亡，还要继续存在下去，或是接受审判，或是经历因果循环的报应。

在圣经里有这样的说法，灵（魂）有出于神和鬼魔之分。鬼魔（邪恶）之灵一旦控制了一个人，这个人就会作恶多端、不知羞耻，也常常表现得无所畏惧，专做伤害他人、欺诈暴

---

① *Bible,* National Committee of Three-Self Patriotic Movement, the Protestant Churches in China (National TSPM), China Christian Council (CCC), 2009 edition, (John 1: 4, 4:2, 4:3, 4:6, 4:13, Revelation 16:14) p.270, p.286.

《圣经》，中国基督教三自爱国运动委员会、中国基督教协会 2009 年版，(约翰一书 4、4:2、4:3、4:6、4:13 启示录 16:14) 第 270 页、第 286 页。

he/she will be evil, shameless, and often unscrupulous, specializing in harming others, deceiving and inhuman things. But the spirit (soul) from gods will guide people to consciously suppress the evil of human nature, show love everywhere, obey authority, obey rules, and refrain from committing deeds that violate their conscience (the laws from the unknown world to mankind). When one feels that he/she has done something "bad" (thing that violates the conscience), he/she will feel painful in his/her heart, and even sometimes such pain will drive people to end their lives. Why do humans feel painful after violating their conscience? This is also a question that science cannot accurately answer. But we can get revelation on this question in religious doctrines --- this punishment imposed upon people who violate the laws from the unknown world, or violate the rules of the spiritual world. "Destiny" we often mentioned means that nothing

虐的事情。但出于神的灵（魂），会引导人们自觉抑制人性之恶，处处显现爱心，服从权威，遵守规则，不做违背良心（来自人类未知世界的律法）的事情。当一个人感觉做了"亏心事"（违背良心的事）的时候，他（她）的内心就会感到痛苦，甚至有时这种痛苦会驱使人们终结自己的生命。人类在违背良心之后，为什么会感到痛苦，这也是一个科学无法给出准确答案的问题。不过这个问题在宗教教义当中，我们却可以得到启示——这是因为人触犯了来自未知世界的律法，或者说违反了灵魂世界的规则，而受到的惩罚。所谓的"宿命"，也就是没有什么事情是无缘无故发生的，人类世界的一切都是在某种力量的安排下，按照既定的却看不见的模式在运行。

happens for no reason. Everything in the human world is operating as per an established but invisible pattern under the arrangement of a certain force.

Then, does human "soul" exist? The religious world's conclusion that people have a "soul" is definitely beyond doubt, and up to now the scientific community has not only failed to deny the existence of "soul", but also discovered a particle field similar to the "soul world". But meanwhile, those who strongly deny the existence of "soul" are also insisting that there is no convincing evidence to verify the existence of human "soul", so it does not exist.

If "Spirit" Didn't Exist

What corresponds to the human "soul" is "body" that includes tangible matters e.g. bones, blood, etc. If the soul does not exist, we humans will only have such body

那么，人的"灵魂"存在吗？宗教界对于人有"灵魂"的结论，肯定而不容质疑，并且科学界至今不但未能否认"灵魂"的存在,还发现了类似"灵魂世界"的粒子场。不过与此同时，极力否认"灵魂"存在的人们也在坚持认为，根本就没有让人信服的证据来证实人类"灵魂"的存在，所以它是不存在的。

假如"灵魂"是不存在的

与人的"灵魂"相对应的，是包括骨骼、血液等有形物质在内的"肉体"，如果灵魂是不存在的，那么我们人类就只剩下这样的肉体了。所有的生命

left. All life phenomena can only be interpreted as the functions of the body. All human emotions and thinking activities, including joy, anger, sorrow, and happiness, are derived from the body itself and without other functioning factors.

If so, God, Allah, Buddha, etc., who are closely related to the human soul world should not exist. And, some people spare no effort to prove that such a conclusion is correct and unquestionable. A world-renowned physicist once tried to prove that God doesn't exist. He wrote in one of his books: "Due to laws like gravity, the universe can create itself out of nothing. Spontaneous creation is the reason why physical things exist instead of nothing there, why the universe exists, and why we exist. No need to pray to ask God to light the fuse to make the universe run. "[1] In other words ---

现象就只能解释为肉体的机能，包括喜、怒、哀、乐在内的全部人类情感和思维活动，都是源自肉体本身，没有其他方面的作用因素。

这样和人的灵魂世界密切相关的上帝、真主、佛等就应该也不存在，并且也有人不遗余力地想要证明这样的结论是正确和毋庸质疑的。有一位世界知名的物理学者，试图用自己的理论证明，神灵是不存在的。在他的一本书中这样写道，"因为存在像引力那样的定律，宇宙能够从无之中把自己创生出来。自发创生是存在实在之物而非一无所有，为什么宇宙存在，为什么我们存在的原因。不必要祈求上帝点燃导火索使宇宙运行。"换句话说——他认为宇宙不是神灵创造的。

---

[1] The Grand Design, by Hawking, Leonard Mlodinow [Britain], translated by Wu Zhongchao, Hu' nan Science and Technology Press, 2011 edition, p.153.

[英]霍金、蒙洛迪诺:《大设计》, 吴忠超译, 湖南科学技术出版社 2011 年版, 第 153 页。

he believes that the universe was not created by God.

If such kinds of invisible energy as souls and gods do not exist, the world would be running naturally simply as per its own laws (discovered and summarized by human scientific research). Then, there will be no way to judge the evil and goodness of human nature. Body function has nothing to do with "right or wrong". It is determined by the laws of nature or physics. You have to eat when hungry, and you have to drink when thirsty..., all desires must be satisfied. Because body function is determined by its own natural attributes and laws. There is no conscience or morality, nor laws from the unknown world. The expansion and satisfaction of the body function (expansion of desire) should be a very natural thing, and "value judgment of advantages vs. disadvantages and correct vs. incorrect" like what "spirit" does shouldn't and cannot be there.

如果灵魂和神灵这些看不见的能量都是不存在的，这个世界仅仅是按照自身的规律（被人类的科学研究所发现和总结）在自然运行。那么关于人性的邪恶与善良，便无从评判了。肉体的机能无所谓对错，这是由自然的、或是物理学的规律所决定的，饿了要吃，渴了要喝…凡是欲望都要满足才行，因为肉体的机能是由它自身的自然属性和规律所决定，没有什么良心道德，也没有来自未知世界的律法，肉体机能的扩张（欲望的膨胀）和满足应是一件很自然的事情，不应该也不可能出现类似"灵魂"所为的"利弊对错的价值评判"。

If the above is true, the world where we live will definitely be in constant conflict and chaos. Because there is a truth that almost all humans understand --- there natural defects in human nature. If people blindly satisfy their own desires and needs, it will inevitably affect or harm the interests of their compatriots. Moreover, cruelty and ruthlessness caused by hatred of human cannot be overcome by themselves.

Also, there is a very strange phenomenon that confuses people who do not believe in souls and gods, that is, humans will feel "painful" --- an invisible and intangible feeling that still may arise even all his/her physical desires are satisfied. Such pain can even make him/her commit suicide. If only the body constitutes human life, or the body is the whole of life, when human desires are satisfied, people should be normal. But often human pain will not diminish or fade simply because their physical desires are

如果真的如上所述，那我们身处的这个世界，一定会冲突不止，混乱不堪。因为有一个道理几乎所有的人类都明白——人性存在天然的缺陷，人们一味地满足自己的欲望需求，必定会影响伤害到同胞的利益，并且人类由仇恨而导致的凶残暴虐，依靠自身也是无法克服的。

另外，还有一个很奇怪的现象，会让不相信灵魂和神灵的人们感到困惑，那就是人类会"痛苦"——一种看不见、摸不着的，即便满足了他（她）肉体的所有欲望需求，也仍然可能出现的感觉，这种感觉甚至会让人难受到驱使自己终结生命。如果只是肉体组成了人的生命，或者说肉体即是生命的全部，那么当人的欲望得到满足时，人们应该正常无异才对，可在很多时候，人类的痛苦丝毫不会因为肉体欲望的满足而消减衰退。这便是在假定灵魂和神灵不存在的前提下，人类

satisfied. This is something that humans cannot explain under the assumption that souls and gods do not exist.

无法解释的事情。

"Spirit" in Religious Doctrines

Currently, the science, technology and principles that humans have studied and mastered cannot yet explain what human "soul" is. But the most cutting-edge physical discoveries are likely to point out the direction for us. With the inner doubts about "soul", people will think more deeply about who we are, where we come from, and where we go. Deciphering the mystery of soul may mean that the development and changes of the human world will enter a fully new era from then on. Belief is a cognition and conclusion that people draw in solving their own doubts. So, the cognition on "soul" is also an important content of human belief, and "soul" has been recorded in

宗教教义中的"灵魂"

人类所研究掌握的科学技术与原理，目前还不能解释人类的"灵魂"是什么，不过最前沿的物理科学发现，却很有可能已经为我们指明了方向。带着对于"灵魂"的内心疑惑，人们会在更深层次上思考，我们究竟是谁，我们从哪里来，要到哪里去。破译了灵魂之谜，就可能意味着人类世界的发展变迁，将从那时开始进入一个全新的时代。信仰是人们在给自己解疑释惑的过程中得出的认知和结论，因此关于"灵魂"的认知，也是人类信仰的重要内容，并且"灵魂"在各种宗教教义当中都有不同形式的记载。

different forms in various religious doctrines.

In the Bible, there are records and descriptions like this: "Then the Lord God formed man from the dust of the ground and breathed the breath of life into his nostrils, and the man became a living being" (Genesis 2:7); "When Jesus therefore had received the vinegar, he said, It is finished: and he bowed his head, and gave up the ghost." (John 19:30); Stephen said before his death: "Lord Jesus, take my spirit." (Acts 7:59); "And the dust goes back to the earth as it was, and the spirit goes back to God who gave it." (Ecclesiastes 12:7); Jesus said: "And fear not them which kill the body, but are not able to kill the soul" (Matthew 10:28). [1]

In the *Quran*, there is such a sentence: "And they ask you (O

圣经上有这样的记载和描述：在创 2:7 说："耶和华神用地上的尘土造人，将生气吹在他鼻孔里，他就成了有灵的活人"。在约 19:30 说："将灵魂交付神了。"在徒 7:59 司提反临死前也说："求主耶稣接收我的灵魂。"在传 12:7 说："尘土仍归于地，灵仍归于赐灵的神。"在太 10:28 耶稣说："那杀身体不能杀灵魂的，不要怕他们。"

在古兰经里有这样的句子：他们问你精神是什么？你

---

[1] *Bible*, National Committee of Three-Self Patriotic Movement, the Protestant Churches in China (National TSPM), China Christian Council (CCC), 2009 edition, (Genesis 2:7, John 19:30, Acts 7:59, Ecclesiastes 12:7, Matthew 10:28) p.2, p.130, p.142, p.650, p.12.

《圣经》，中国基督教三自爱国运动委员会、中国基督教协会 2009 年版，（创 2:7、约 19:30、徒 7:59、传 12:7、太 10:28）第 2 页、第 130 页、第 142 页、第 650 页、第 12 页。

Muhammad SAW) concerning the Ruh (the Spirit); Say: "The Ruh (the Spirit): it is one of the things, the knowledge of which is only with my Lord. And of knowledge, you (mankind) have been given only a little. "(Quran 17:85) "It is Allāh Who takes away the souls (Wafat) at the time of their death, and those that die not during their sleep. He keeps those (souls) for which He has ordained death and sends the rest for a term appointed. Verily, in this are signs for people who think deeply." (Quran 39:42) [①]

Regarding the human "soul", there are also other descriptions and records in various religious theories that humans believe in. The forms are different, but there is one thing in common, that is, most doctrines or theories among them believe that there exists dematerialized "soul" which is more important in human and can influence and control the physical

说:"精神是我的主的机密。"你们只获得很少的知识。(古兰经 17:85)人们到了死亡的时候,真主将他们的灵魂取去;尚未到死期的人们,当他们睡眠的时候,真主也将他们的灵魂取去。他已判决其死亡者,他扣留他们的灵魂;他未判决其死亡者,便将他们的灵魂放回,至一定期。对于能思维的民众,此中确有许多迹象。(古兰经 39:42)

关于人的"灵魂",在人类信奉的各种宗教理论当中还有其他的描述和记载,虽然形式各异,但有一点却十分相似,那就是它们当中绝大部分的教义或理论,均认为人类除了有形的物质化肉体,还有更重要的,可以影响控制肉体的非物质化的"灵魂"存在。

---

① *Quran*, translated by Ma Jian, China Social Sciences Press, 1981 edition, p.218-219, p.356-357.
《古兰经》,马坚译,中国社会科学出版社 1981 年版,第 218-219、356-357 页。

body in addition to the tangible materialized body.

"Prophecies" Are True or Not?

The technologies and equipment that mankind has invented and mastered by scientific research institutes can now predict many things accurately. For example, people can predict future weather conditions using pictures transmitted by space satellites; people can accurately calculate the specific time of sunrise at a certain time and place using relevant technology and calendar knowledge; people can detect the sex of the fetus in a pregnant woman's body using ultrasound equipment. . . There are many predictions like this, and they all have a common feature, that is, they can make people know exactly what is going to happen.

Perhaps a considerable number of people will hold a view like this: the above phenomena

"预言"是真的吗

人类通过科学研究所发明掌握的技术和仪器设备，现在已经可以较为准确的预言很多事情。比如，人们可以通过太空卫星传送的图片，来预测未来的天气情况；人们可以用相关的科技和历法知识，精确计算出某时某地日出的具体时刻；人们可以借助超声波设备，探测孕妇体内胎儿的性别…诸如此类的预言还有很多，它们都有一个共同的特征，就是可以让人们准确地知道，将要发生的事情是什么。

或许相当数量的人会持有这样的观点，上面这些现象不能称作是预言，它们是人类发

cannot be called prophecies. They are the inevitable results determined by the scientific laws discovered by mankind. While prophecies should be subjective judgments with a dark religious color and often appear very mysterious. Those who hold such view will strictly distinguish scientific laws from various "prophecy" systems, and treat religious "prophecies" cautiously and skeptically.

What are the religious prophecies, and have they been fulfilled? Are there any connections among different religious prophecies? With doubts and curiosities about the unknown world, most humans have extraordinary attention and enthusiasm for religious prophecies. The following are the prophecies recorded in some religious scriptures:

Bible: "And the heaven was open; and I saw a white horse, and he who was seated on it was named Certain and True; and he

现的科学规律所决定的必然结果，而预言应是带有浓重宗教色彩的主观论断，常常会显得很神秘。持这种观点的人，会把科学规律同各种"预言"体系严格区分开来，并以审慎质疑的态度去对待宗教"预言"。

宗教预言都有什么呢，它们应验过吗？不同的宗教预言之间有什么联系吗？带着对未知世界的疑惑和好奇，绝大多数人类都对宗教预言有着非同一般的关注与热情，下面是一些宗教经典中记载的预言内容：

圣经《启示录》"19:11 我观看，见天开了。有一匹白马，骑在马上的称为诚信真实，他审判、争战都按着公义。""19:

is judging and making war in righteousness." (Revelation 19:11) "and his name is The Word of God." (Revelation 19:13) "And out of his mouth comes a sharp sword, with which he overcomes the nations" (Revelation 19:15) "And on his robe and on his leg is a name, KING OF KINGS, AND LORD OF LORDS." (Revelation 19:16) "I am Alpha and Omega, the beginning and the end, the first and the last." (Revelation 22:13)

Sunan of Abu Dawud of Islam: "The Prophet said: The Mahdi will be of my stock, and will have a broad forehead a prominent nose. He will fill the earth will equity and justice as it was filled with oppression and tyranny, and he will rule for seven years."

In Buddhism, there is a prophecy that the blooming of the udumbara flower once every 3,000 per Sāsanā Sakaraj (the Buddhist calendar) symbolizes the rebirth of the Cakkavatti (Chakravartin), Tathāgata. Dīrgha Āgama: "Even

13 他的名称为神之道。"19:15 有利剑从他口中出来，可以击杀列国。""19:16 在他衣服和大腿上，有名写着说：万王之王，万主之主。""22:13 我是阿拉法，我是俄梅戛；我是首先的，我是末后的；我是初，我是终。"

伊斯兰教《艾布达吾德圣训》"先知穆罕默德说，救世者麦海迪出自我的宗室，他额宽鼻高，在位期间世间充满公道，如以前充满不义一样。"

佛家预言佛历三千年时代，优昙花开就象征着转轮圣王如来出世，《长阿含经》："如来时时出世，如优昙钵花，时一现耳。"《法华经·文句四上》："优昙花者,此言灵瑞。三千年一现，现则金轮王出。"

in countless millions of kalpas it is difficult to come upon and meet a Tathagata. It is as difficult as seeing an udumbara flower, which blooms very rarely." Lotus Sutra·Dharmapāda (vol. IV 1H): "Only very rarely do the Buddha Tathāgatas teach such a True Dharma as this, as rarely as the uḍumbara flower blooms."

Seeing these prophecies, most people can't help but look forward to such things. Although they cannot be explained by scientific knowledge, humans are all waiting for such a moment due to their own insurmountable pain and fear. Although there is no direct and clear evidence to verify them, different religious doctrines have given extremely similar prophecies. Are these all just accidental coincidences?

Decisive "Faith"

Everyone understands that "faith" is crucial to one's success in doing things. Although something

看到这些预言，大多数人都会情不自禁地期盼这样的事情。尽管无法用科学知识去解释，但人类由于自身难以克服的痛苦和恐惧，都在不约而同地等待这样的时刻到来。尽管没有直接明了的证据证实，但不同的宗教教义却给出了极为相似的预言，难道这些都只是偶然巧合？

举足轻重的"信心"

人们都明白，"信心"对于一个人做事的成功与否至关重要。虽然是看似不可能的事情，

may seem impossible, as long as there is faith, it is possible to attain the goal ultimately. One thing is not difficult to do, but if the person who does it loses the faith, then in all likelihood, the thing will fail, failing to attain the intended goal. As for "faith", no normal adult will not know what it is. Most people will describe faith as a feeling --- a state of mind of people to attain their goals via actions or inactions, which is accompanied with what they say and do.

How does science explain such feeling? The knowledge and laws that humans currently master can only tell us that this is a human psychological phenomenon. When people further explore what faith is with scientific rationality and logic, science can no longer answer the question instead. Does faith have a shape? Is it a matter that exists objectively? What is the difference between all kinds of visible and tangible substances and it? And what is the human will, is it the same as faith? Such

但只要有信心，最终就有可能实现目标。一件事情做起来不难，可做事者丧失了信心，那么十有八九这件事就会失败，达不到预期目的。对于"信心"，没有哪个正常的成年人会不知其为何物。绝大多数人都会把信心描述成一种感觉，一种伴随人们说话做事，让人通过作为或不作为实现目标的心理状态。

科学是如何解释这种感觉的呢？人类目前所掌握的知识和规律，只能告诉我们，这是一种人类的心理现象。当人们按照科学的理性和逻辑，进一步考证信心究竟是什么的时候，科学反倒无法回答了。信心有形状吗，它是一种客观存在的物质吗，我们看得见、摸得着的各类物质和它有什么区别呢，人的意志又是什么，意志和信心长的一样吗…这一连串的问题，都会让科学无从着手，解释乏力。

a series of questions make it impossible for science to answer, and the explanations drawn by science will be unconvincing.

But one thing is certain anyway, that is, whether humans or the scientific knowledge they master agree that human faith is an existence instead of out of thin air. Then, where does faith come from? Is it inborn? Maybe yes, maybe no. As people sometimes have the feeling of faith, but sometimes they can't find it at all. Does faith come from the unknown world of mankind? Do human life and it belong to another dimension that we have not yet discovered? With such doubts, let's read the scriptures:

In Bible, "And when these words came to the ears of Jesus he was surprised, and said to those who came after him, Truly I say to you, I have not seen such great faith, no, not in Israel." (Matthew 8:10) "Make a test of yourselves, if you are in the faith; make certain of yourselves. Or are you

但不管怎样,有一点是肯定的,那就是无论人类自身还是人类所掌握的科学知识,都认可人类的信心是一种存在,它不是凭空捏造出来的。那么信心究竟是从哪里来的呢?是人们与生俱来的吗,好像是,又好像不是。因为有信心的感觉,人们有时会有,有时却怎么找也找不到。信心是来自人类的未知世界吗,它和人类的生命是不是同属于我们未曾探明的另一个空间呢?带着这些疑问,让我们来翻阅一下经典:

《圣经》太 8:10 耶稣听见就希奇,对跟从的人说:"我实在告诉你们:这么大的信心,就是在以色列中,我也没有遇见过。"林后 13:5 你们总要自己省察有信心没有,也要自己试验。岂不知,你们若不是可弃绝的,就有耶稣基督在你们心里吗?帖后 3:2 也叫我们脱离无理恶

not conscious in yourselves that Jesus Christ is in you, if you are truly Christ's? "(Corinthians 13:5) "And that we may be made free from foolish and evil men; for not all have faith." (Thessalonians 3:2)

With the descriptions and explanations of faith in the scriptures, as for our knowledge of faith, we have more comprehension than just relying on science. Faith does exist for us humans, and it probably comes from the unknown world of us. They just exist like "God particles", and play a huge and inestimable magical role to us humans.

What Faith Is?

To human, faith is very important and direct. If one speaks and does things with faith, it implies that his/her behaviors appear to be "confident" --- a sense of self-confidence that what he/she has said will be fulfilled and what he/she has done will succeed. Such faith is first manifested as an inner

人的手，因为人不都是有信心的。

凭借经典对信心的描述和解释，我们对信心的认识，就比仅靠科学有了更多的体会。信心对于我们人类来说，的确是存在的，并且很有可能来自我们未知的世界，它们就像"上帝粒子"一样存在着，对我们人类发挥着巨大、不可估量的神奇作用。

信心是什么

信心对于人类来说，它的作用十分重要和直接。一个人如果说话做事有信心，那就意味着这个人的言行会显得很有"底气"——一种说过的话一定会兑现，做过的事必会实现目标的自我信任感。这种信任感首先表现为一种内在的感觉，而后在其巨大的驱动作用下，让

feeling, and then, under its huge driving force, one who has it will behave differently from others, and he/she will have a strong infecting power (influence on others), which will make people around him/her pay attention to and follow him/her unconsciously.

Then, what is faith on earth? Is it something like air? It is a substance invisible and intangible but indispensable like air or just a psychological phenomenon of humans derived from the functions of human organs that everybody has as explained by scientific theories (No matter what people say or do is fulfilled or not, it doesn't matter whether you have faith or not. Everyone will succeed as long as they work hard)? If one fails to attain his/her goal when doing something, it's not because he/she has no faith, but because he/she hasn't made enough efforts or has no objective conditions. Even if he/she has strong faith, it will not help.

Thinking scientifically and

拥有它的人在说话行事时表现地与众不同，并且会有很强的感染力（对他人的影响力），这种影响力会让周围的人不知不觉地关注他（她）、跟随他（她）。

那么信心究竟是什么呢？它是像空气一样的东西吗？是我们看不见、摸不着，却像空气一样不可或缺的物质；还是如同科学理论解释的那样，信心只是人类的一种心理现象，源自人体器官的功能，人人都会有，无论人们说话做事应验成功与否，有没有信心无关紧要，只要努力付出，每个人都会成功。一个人做事没有达成目标，不是因为他（她）没有信心，而是自身努力和客观条件尚不具备，即便信心再强大，也会无济于事。

按照科学的逻辑思维方法，

logically, the above reasoning and viewpoints are very strict and there is no unreasonableness. If one cannot lift a stone that exceeds his/her weight, can he/she move it simply because he/she owns greater faith? Scientifically and logically, his/her failure to lift such a stone is due to objective reasons --- his/her muscle contraction ability instead of faith cannot lift the weight of the stone. There is no causal relationship between faith and ability to move a stone.

In such case, let's make a scientific assumption: assuming that humans have to own energy from an unknown field to succeed in doing something, such energy has to be faith that is invisible and intangible but can be clearly perceived by people. When more and more such energy is concentrated on a person, his/her ability will become stronger and stronger, so that he/she can predict what will happen and can accomplish whatever he/she wants to do. Some people will definitely

上述推理和观点，非常严密没有不合理之处，一个人搬不起一块超过其体重的巨石，难道会因为他（她）有了更大的信心，就可以搬起来吗？按照科学的逻辑，他（她）搬不起这样的石头，是因为客观原因——他（她）的肌肉收缩能力无法擎起石头的重量，而不是信心，信心和搬起石头，两者之间没有因果关系。

这时让我们做一个科学式的假设，假设我们人类说话做事，如果想要应验成功，都必须拥有来自身外某个未知领域的能量，这种能量就是看不见、摸不着，但会被人们清晰感知到的信心。当这种能量越来越多地汇聚在一个人身上的时候，这个人的能力便会越来越强大，以至于他（她）可以预言将要发生的事情，可以完成任何他（她）想做的事情。有些人一定会说，这完全是空想，是主观猜测，根本没有任何证据来证明。但科学的精神是不要迷信

say that this is totally fantasy and a subjective guess, no evidence to prove it. But the scientific spirit is not to be obsessed in any unproven authoritative conclusions. Then, now that there is not enough evidence to prove that such a hypothesis is incorrect, why should we deny its existence? Before "God particle" was discovered, some people judged that it does not exist, but now it does exist. With scientific philosophy and thinking, we humans should carefully verify and cautiously doubt them, not easily affirming or denying anything before there is evidence for it. In a severe earthquake, a thin and weak mother even unexpectedly moved a 0.2kg concrete slab to save her son in the ruins. Is this possible without muscle strength and faith? [1]

任何未经证实的权威结论，那么在没有足够的证据证明这样的假设是错误的，为什么就要否定它的存在呢？"上帝粒子"在没有发现之前，不是也有人论断它是不存在的，但现在它真的出现了。带着科学的理念和思维，我们人类应该小心地求证，谨慎地怀疑，没有证据之前不要轻易肯定或否定什么东西。大地震之中，一位瘦弱的母亲为了拯救废墟中的儿子，居然挪动了 200 斤重的水泥板，只有肌肉的力量，没有信心，可能吗？

---

[1] A Thin and Weak Mother Removed A Prefabricated Slab Alone to Rescue Her Crushed Son", by Xi Qinling, published in Sohu News, http://news.sohu.com/20130421/n373420709.shtml, access time: 20: 16 Mar 7, 2017.

席秦岭：《瘦弱母亲独自挪开 200 多斤预制板 救出被压儿子》，载搜狐新闻，http://news.sohu.com/20130421/n373420709.shtml，访问时间：2017 年 3 月 7 日 20:16。

What is faith on earth? We humans should calm down and feel it with our heart before answering it --- this is the truly wise and scientific way.

Faith Leads to Hope

For human faith, now we cannot describe it rationally and objectively, nor have evidence to prove what faith is on earth and where it exists. Perceptually, human faith is an invisible and intangible dematerialized energy. Although faith does not have materialized forms and features, such energy can indeed play a huge role imperceptibly and affect or even change the trace of human life. As human hearts will be filled with hope once they have faith.

What is hope? This is another difficulty --- an object that we cannot describe and explain accurately. Scientifically, hope seems not to exist, as hope is as invisible and intangible as faith. But hope and faith are both, like

信心究竟是什么，我们人类应该冷静一些，用心感受一下，然后再做回答，才是真正明智和科学的做法。

有了信心就会收获希望

对于人类的信心，我们目前无法理性客观地描述，也没有证据证实信心究竟是什么，它存在于什么地方。感性地说，人类的信心是一种看不见、摸不着的非物质化能量。虽然信心没有物质化的形态和特征，但这种能量的确可以发挥潜移默化的巨大作用，可以影响甚至是改变人类生命的轨迹。因为，一旦人类有了信心，希望便会充满人的心灵。

希望是什么，这又是一个难题，是一个我们无法准确描述解释的对象。从科学的角度来看，希望好像是不存在的，因为希望同信心一样看不见、摸不着，但希望和信心却也好像空气一样，对于人类不可或缺。无论

air, indispensable to mankind. Whatever you do, say or expect, they will all become torment without faith and hope. When one has faith, he/she will be filled with a sense of strength --- a feeling that drives you to say, do and wait patiently for good things to happen. Such positive and exciting feeling is hope. And hope is a feeling that faith brings to people. Hope will prompt you to do something that even you yourself feel incredible. If a patient has faith, there will be hope of healing in his/her heart. Faith and hope will make a patient feel energized, so that he/she can actively cooperate with the doctor in treatment, actively change bad living habits and temperament, and make himself/herself become optimistic and broad-minded. In most cases, such patients will get better soon. As to whether one's physical illness can be cured, however, it should be described like this: it can be cured as long as he/she has faith and hope.

你做什么，说什么，期盼什么，没有了信心和希望，它们都会变成让人痛苦的事情。当一个人有了信心，他（她）就会被充满力量感，一种驱使你去说、去做、去耐心等待好事情发生的感觉，这种让人积极振奋的感觉就是希望，希望是信心带给人们的感觉，希望会促使你做成你自己都觉得不可思议的事情。一位病人有了信心，他（她）的心中便会有让疾病痊愈的希望，信心和希望会让病人感到有力量，从而积极配合医生治疗，主动改变不良的生活习惯和性格脾气，让自己变得乐观豁达。大多数情况下，这样的病人都会很快有所好转。不过一个人躯体之上的病痛，究竟能不能痊愈，应该这样描述，有了信心和希望，就有可能治愈。但如果病人没有信心和希望，无法得到信心希望的指引和支撑，而只剩下药物和医疗措施时，哪怕付出再高昂的医疗成本，病人也仍然不会痊愈，因为他们总会有这样那样不舒服的感觉萦绕心头，甚至出现病痛越医治越严重的现象。

However, if a patient does not have faith and hope, and cannot be guided and supported by hope and faith, and only medicines and medical measures are left for him/her, the patient will not be cured even if a high cost of medical treatment is paid as they will always feel all kinds of malaises one way or another, and even the longer he/she gets treated, the more severe his/her illness will be.

In the process of a patient's recovery, the invisible and intangible faith and hope of mankind plays an immeasurable role imperceptibly. Faith and hope are like intimate twins. With faith, as long as you don't give up, there will surely be hope. Where does faith come from? The scientific theories of mankind cannot yet accurately explain it. But the hope that people feel, as well as one's inner strength that comes with hope both come from faith.

在病人康复的过程中，人类看不见、摸不着的信心和希望，发挥了不可估量的潜在作用。信心和希望就像是一对亲密的孪生兄弟，信心有了，只要你不舍弃它，就一定会有希望。信心从何而来，人类的科学理论目前还不能准确解释，但人们感受到的希望，以及伴随希望而出现的一个人的内在力量，却都是因着信心而来。

Upon Faith and Hope

For a person, whatever he/she wants to do, in addition to necessary physical work, some inner feelings (hope) are also required in order to succeed in something. Where do such feelings come from? Currently the scientific knowledge we master cannot describe it objectively. It is also unclear they are whether a formless dematerialized existence, or come with an energy unknown to the mankind. The scientific community has no evidence to prove their existence, so they tend to agree that human inner feelings are not an objective existence, and they are just human psychological phenomena, or functions of human organs.

But such feelings that all normal people can perceive clearly impress people so greatly deeply under certain circumstances. If you ask an athlete who won the championship of a top sports event

有了信心和希望以后

对于一个人来说，无论他（她）要做什么事情，除了付出必需的肢体劳动以外，还要有内心里的一些感觉（希望），才能最终促成这些事情的成功。这些感觉是怎么来的，我们掌握的科学知识，目前还无法进行客观描述，也不清楚人类的这些内心感觉，究竟是不是不具有形态的非物质化存在，或者是一种人类未知的能量所带来的。科学界没有证据来证明他们的存在，所以倾向于认同人类的内心感觉不是一种客观存在，它们只是人的心理现象，或者称作人体器官的功能。

但这些所有正常人都可以清晰体会到的感觉，在特定的环境下，给人们留下的印象却是那么的强烈和深刻。一位获得人类社会顶级体育赛事冠军的运动员，你若问他（她）是

in human society how he/she peaked this sport, the answer will probably be perseverance --- stick to a certain feeling in the heart, and constantly motivate himself/herself with such inner feeling to break through and transcend himself/herself until succeed. Not just participants in sports activities need such feelings to motivate themselves to overcome difficulties and exercise thousands of times, in almost all fields of labor creation in human society, such invisible and intangible inner feelings (hope) are imperceptibly driving people to continuously achieve success and attain their goals.

According to the interpretation of religious doctrines, human faith comes from a certain energy (humans call such energy Lord, God, Allah, Buddha, etc.). Those who have faith will perceive the beautiful vision of the future and then burst out their own strength to carry out repeated physical or intellectual exercises and work as

如何攀登上这项运动的巅峰，答案多半是坚持，坚守心中的某种感觉，并用这种内在的感觉激励自己不断突破超越，直至成功。不光是体育竞技活动的参与者，需要这些感觉来激励自己克服困难，去成千上万遍的重复练习，在人类社会几乎所有的劳动创造领域，这种看不见、摸不着的内在感觉（希望），都在潜移默化地驱使人们不断取得成功，实现心中的目标。

按照宗教教义的解释，人类的信心源自某种能量（人类称这种能量为神、上帝、安拉、佛等），有了信心的人，只要继续相信这是来自造物主的恩赐，他们就会感知到未来的美好愿景，进而迸发出自身的力量去进行肢体或智能方面的重复练习与劳动付出。在信心的指引下，人们会朝着心中的目标和方向，

long as they continue to believe that this is a gift from the Creator. With the guidance of faith, people will persevere toward their goals and directions unhesitatingly until they ultimately succeed and enter the beautiful vision promised by the Creator via human faith.

When people have faith and believe that such an indescribable dematerialized existence is an objective energy beneficial to them, they will obtain a positive and excited feeling, which is called hope. Hope can make beautiful visions and pictures present in human hearts, and stimulate their own energy, which will be extremely powerful when being driven by faith and hope. Faith, hope, and the energy that burst out of people themselves will enable those who own them to achieve something that others think incredible or even impossible. When one's faith, hope, and his/her own energy is naturally fused together and show a strong force outwards, their fusion becomes

义无反顾的坚持努力下去，直至取得最后的成功，走进造物主透过人的信心所应许的美好愿景之中。

当人们有了信心，且相信这种不可名状的非物质化存在，是一种对自己有益的客观能量时，就会获得积极振奋的感觉，这种感觉叫做希望。希望可以让人类在心中呈现出美好的愿景和图画，并激发出人类自身的能量，这种能量在信心和希望的驱使下是极其强大的。信心、希望以及人们自身迸发出的能量，会让拥有他们的人，做出让其他人觉得不可思议、甚至是不可能的事情。当一个人的信心、希望和自身的能量很自然地融合在一起，并对外展现出强大力量时，他们的融合体就是人的意志力，人们也常常把做出丰功伟绩的人，称作是具有惊人意志力的人。

the human willpower. People often call those who have made great achievements as people with astonishing willpower.

How Faith Comes?

Belief is a cognition and conclusion with which humans answer their doubts. Such cognitions and conclusions explain to people the basic issues that all humans urgently concern about, e.g. where we come from, where we go, and how we can avoid pain, etc.. People with beliefs will stick to such cognitions and conclusions, resist temptation in their own lives, and strive to obey the implicit rules embedded in people's hearts by faith--- morality and conscience, and wait for the ultimate moment of happiness. In this process, people with beliefs, or people with answers in their hearts, often have a feeling --- a sense of trust that the vision they believe in is sure to happen, which seems to come from an objective

信心是怎么来的

信仰是人类满足自己内心疑惑的认知和结论，这些认知结论给人们解释了，诸如我们从哪里来，要到哪里去，怎样才能不让自己感到痛苦…等所有人类迫切关心的基本问题。有信仰的人们会坚守这些认知结论，在自己的生命历程中抵御诱惑，努力遵守信仰埋植在人们心中的隐性规则——道义和良知，并等待最后的幸福时刻。在这个过程中，有信仰的人们，或者说是心中有答案的人们，便常常会有一种感觉，一种所相信的愿景必定要发生的信任感，而人们的这种感觉好像来源于一种客观存在，这种存在的名字叫做——信心。

existence --- faith.

As long as you believe in certain cognitions and conclusions (or as long as you have faith), you will have faith in your heart. But "faith" mentioned here will vary depending on one's belief. If one believes that humans are a kind of creature, and that there exists a world of gods in the universe where we live, most people who hold this belief will have awe to them in their hearts. People who hold such belief will naturally be embedded in their hearts with rules (morality and conscience), some inner and intangible consciousness that can restrain people's souls and behaviors --- what they can do and what they cannot do, how can people get happiness and how can they get painful? These matters which seem hard to have accurate answers will all become clear because of belief.

If one does not believe that a world of gods exists in this universe, but believes that human life is only a comprehensive

只要你相信某些认知和结论（或者说只要你有信仰），你的心中就会有信心，只不过这里的信心，会随着一个人信仰的不同而不同。如果一个人相信人类是受造之物，我们所生存的宇宙当中还有神灵世界的存在，那么绝大部分持有这种信仰的人们心中都会怀有敬畏之心。持有这种信仰的人们的心中，会被很自然地埋下规则（道义和良知），一些内在的、无形的、却可以约束人们心灵和行为的意识——什么样的事情可以做，什么样的事情不能做，怎么样可以让人得到幸福快乐，怎么样会使人痛苦。这些看似很难有准确答案的事情，都会因为有了信仰而清晰可鉴。

如果一个人不相信这个宇宙之中有神灵世界的存在，而是相信人的生命只是肉体组织和各种人体器官机能的综合反

reflection of physical tissues and various human organ functions, he/she will also show faith in his daily behaviors. In many cases, such faith will make people who hold it fearless. They will want to conquer the nature bravely. But they have no awe to the nature but the desire to conquer it in their hearts. And there are no rules and taboos to restrain themselves in their hearts. The faith mentioned here should also be an existence. But such faith obviously differs from that mentioned above. In spite of the difference, the biggest similarity between the two is that such different existences can both drive people's souls and behaviors.

In our human society, there are also other beliefs and lots of cognitions and conclusions that explain the doubts in human hearts. Such cognitions and conclusions are believed to bring us faith. But different cognitions and conclusions will bring people completely different faiths accordingly. We can basically

映，那么这个人在平日的言行中，也会表现的有信心。这种信心在很多时候，会让持有这种信仰的人们变得无所畏惧，他们会很勇敢地想要征服大自然，但他们的心中没有敬畏感，取代敬畏感的是他们的征服欲望，在他们的心中也没有约束自己的规则和禁忌。这里的信心也应该是一种存在，但这样的信心明显不同于上面的信心。虽然不同，但信心之间最大的相似之处在于，这些不同的存在都可以驱使人的心灵和行为。

在我们人类社会，还有其他类型的信仰，还有很多解释人类内心疑惑的认知和结论，相信这些认知结论都会引来信心，但不同的认知结论也会带给人们完全不同的信心。我们基本可以确认一点，那就是只要你有信仰，你就会有信心，或者说，只要你相信，你就会有信心。

confirm one thing, that is, as long as you have a belief, you will have faith, or to say, as long as you believe, you will have faith.

Faith & "Positive/Negative Energy"

As the history of human society entered the 21st century, advanced science and abundant information have made mankind more address threats and difficulties from nature with ease. But meanwhile, a lot of conflicts and issues that originated from humans themselves and make people helpless have arisen too. Such things that make humans painful are not due to the lack of natural resources and the failure of humans to satisfy their basic physiological needs, but due to the cruelty, tyranny and indifference of humans which make people feel fearful and lonely from deep their hearts and unable to be happy.

To abuse a cute kitten to death, and then place it next to

信心与"正负能量"

当人类社会的历史车轮驶入二十一世纪，科学的发达与资讯的丰富，使得人类在应对来自大自然的威胁和困难时，显得越发游刃有余。但与此同时，也出现了很多源自人类自身，且让人束手无策的矛盾和问题。这些让人类痛苦不已的事情，不是因为自然资源的匮乏和人类基本生理需求无法得到满足，而是因为人类自身的残忍、暴虐和冷漠，让人们从内心深处感到恐惧孤独，无法快乐。

把可爱的小猫虐待致死，然后放在母猫的身边…偷盗轿车

its mother... [1] To steal a car but strangle a baby to death after finding it in the car and then bury it in snow... [2] To cruelly gouge out a little child's eyes... [3] To chopped at innocent kids with knife to take revenge... [4] To mutilate elderly and children and force them to beg... [5] To battle against

后发现车内有婴孩，便将其掐死埋藏于雪堆…残忍地挖出幼童的眼睛…为了复仇，将手中的砍刀砍向无辜的儿童…为了钱财，残害老人小孩，迫使他们乞讨…因为信仰不同，便互相征战，涂炭生灵，将同胞处决…

---

[1] *Someone Abused a Kitten to Death and Then Put It Next to Its Mother and Scolded by Passers-by for His Inhumanity,* published in Highlights, xilu.com, http://shizheng.xilu.com/20140104/1000150000502158.html, access time: 23:08 Mar 7, 2017.
西陆网:《虐猫后将尸体放回母猫身边 路人怒骂人性何在》，载西陆网要闻，http://shizheng.xilu.com/20140104/1000150000502158.html，访问时间: 2017 年 3 月 7 日 23: 08。

[2] *The Criminal of the Case of Car Theft and Infanticide Was Executed on Nov 22nd, 2013,* published in "the Rule of Law" column, Xinhuanet, http://news.xinhuanet.com/legal/2013-11-22/c_118259457.htm, access time: 16:03 Mar 07, 2017.
新华网:《长春盗车杀婴案罪犯 22 日被执行死刑》，载新华网法治，http://news.xinhuanet.com/legal/2013-11-22/c_118259457.htm，访问时间: 2017 年 3 月 7 日 16: 03。

[3] *A 6-year-old Boy Had His Eyes Gouged out and Were Thrown away at the Scene of Crime,* Shanxi TV, published in Sina News Video, http://hebei.sina.com.cn/video/news/2013-08-27/15136436.html , access time: 23:13, Mar 7, 2017.
山西电视台:《6 岁男孩被挖掉双眼 眼珠被遗弃案发现场》，载新浪网新闻视频，http://hebei.sina.com.cn/video/news/2013-08-27/15136436.html，访问时间: 2017 年 3 月 7 日 23: 13。

[4] *A Jiangsu Man Chopped at Little Children with A Knife and Claimed to Be Revenge, with One Killed and One Injured,* by Liu Qingxiang, published in Tencent News, http://news.qq.com/a/20141105/022017.htm, access time: 23:16 Mar 7, 2017.
刘清香:《江苏男子持刀砍伤幼童致一死一伤 自称系报复》，载腾讯新闻，http://news.qq.com/a/20141105/022017.htm，访问时间: 2017 年 3 月 7 日 23:16。

[5] *Revealed: Dongguan Beggars Cruelly Mutilated Elderly and Children and Forced Them to Beg,* published in Phoenix Satellite TV, Guangzhou, http://gz.ifeng.com/zaobanche/detail_2014_03/18/1999361_1.shtml, visit time: 23:20 Mar 7, 2017.
凤凰卫视:《东莞丐帮揭秘: 东莞丐帮残忍将老人小孩致残 逼其乞讨》，载凤凰广州，http://gz.ifeng.com/zaobanche/detail_2014_03/18/1999361_1.shtml，访问时间: 2017 年 3 月 7 日 23:20。

each other, kill the creatures, and execute compatriots because of different beliefs... [1]

There are still many such cases, and each scene will make the human mind convulsed and painful and unable to self-control. What on earth have caused such a tragic tear in the human world? What has blinded the human soul and buried hatred and indifference deeply in their hearts? People explored the causes for all of these relying on science and rationality but failed to get the answer, unable to explain such human tragedies.

People who feel painful begin to think it over in pain, and begin to distinguish and mark different kinds of energy leading to different behaviors of people, and name these kinds of energy that they have felt differently. So far, there are mainly two kinds of energy that humans feel. One is the

这样的事例还有很多，每一幕都会让人类的心灵，抽搐痛苦，不能自已。究竟是什么让人类世界出现了如此悲惨的撕裂，是什么蒙蔽了人类的心灵，将仇恨与冷漠深深地埋植在他们心底，人们依靠科学和理性去发掘这一切的原因，却找不到答案，无法解释这些人间悲剧。

感到痛苦的人开始在痛苦中沉重地思考，也开始去区分标记导致人们言行作为出现差异的不同能量，并给他们感觉到的能量冠以不同的名称。迄今为止，人类感知到的这些能量主要有两种，一种可以使人们感到轻松，充满力量感，满足快乐，会让人留下泪水，获得

---

[1] *Jordanian Pilot Hostage Burnt Alive by ISIS*, Dailymail.com, published in China.com, http://news.china.com/hd/11127798/20150204/19275718.html, access time: 23:31 Mar 7, 2017.

每日邮报：《IS 对被俘约旦飞行员人质执行火刑处决》，载 China.com，http://news.china.com/hd/11127798/20150204/19275718.html，访问时间：2017 年 3 月 7 日 23:31。

energy that can make people feel relaxed, full of strength, satisfied and happy, which will make people tear and feel happiness, and such energy that brings people such feelings is marked by people as positive energy; the other is the energy that makes people feel nervous, depressed, angry, suspicious, which will accumulate hatred, instigate violence, and make people feel painful, and such energy is marked by people as negative energy.

We can try to understand such kinds of energy as faith, which is explained above. It is because humans believe in certain cognitions and conclusions that they get the energy of faith linked to such cognitive conclusions accordingly. As beliefs as well cognitions and conclusions people believe in differ, people will get different kinds of energy: the energy that makes people happy and comfortable is positive energy; while the energy that makes people jealous, angry, hateful, cruel and

幸福感,人们把给人带来这些感觉的能量标记为正能量;把那些让人感到紧张、压抑、生气猜疑、积聚仇恨、挑唆暴力,让人觉得痛苦的能量标记为负能量。

我们可以试着把这些能量理解成上面所阐述的信心,人类都是因为相信了某些认知结论,而相应得到这些认知结论所连接的信心能量。因为信仰和相信的认知结论不同,人们便会获得不同的能量,让人开心舒适的那种就是正能量,让人嫉妒愤怒,心生仇恨,并变得残忍暴虐的就是负能量。正能量和负能量在人类身上,都表现为信心,他们是某种形式的存在,是由于人们相信的认知结论不同,而得到的迥然不同的信心能量。

tyrannical is negative energy. Positive energy and negative energy are both manifested as faith in humans. They exist in certain forms and are completely different kinds of energy of faith obtained due to different cognitions and conclusions people believe in.

Believe in That Feeling and You Can Get "Positive Energy"

Each of us will leave some feelings and impressions on the people around us. Some people make people feel happy and comfortable, while others make people feel nervous, angry, or even afraid or fearful. Why is there such a difference? So far, we have not drawn a convincing conclusion to explain such a phenomenon in human society, even rapidly-changing modern science and technology do not help.

Since it is an inconclusive question, we might assume the answer to this question relying

相信那种感觉 就能 得到"正能量"

我们每一个人都会给自己接触交往的人，留下一些感觉和印象。有的人让人觉得心里喜悦、舒服，而有的人却让人感到紧张、生气，甚至是害怕恐惧。为什么会有这样的差别，人类社会发展至今，我们还没有得出令人信服的结论来解释这样的现象，即便是日新月异的现代科学技术也无能无力。

既然是没有定论的问题，那我们不妨凭借科学的精神和理性的逻辑思维，来假定这个问题

on scientific spirit and rational logical thinking: those who make people feel happy and comfortable own positive energy --- an existence like "God particle". Positive energy is an energy that is invisible and intangible but exists objectively and affects the mankind and the world. Such energy directly functions on those who own it in the form of "faith". It will make people's faces full of smiles, make their hearts full of joys, and make them enthusiastic, kind, simple while being wise. Moreover, such energy can also be spread, allowing more and more people to feel it, believe in its existence and then own it. In terms of the form, those who initially own it will gradually become welcome to many people and will have more and more friends as they interact with others. More and more people will trust them and behave more like them --- they all value human qualities that make people happy e.g. kindness, integrity, fraternity, etc.

的答案：让人觉得喜悦、舒服的人身上，拥有的是正能量——一种类似于"上帝粒子"的存在，正能量是一种看不见、摸不着，但却客观存在并且影响着人类和世界的能量。这种能量以"信心"的方式，直接作用于拥有它的人们，它会让人们脸上洋溢笑容，心中充满喜悦和热情，善良纯朴而不失智慧。并且这种能量还可以传播，让越来越多的人们感受到它，相信它的存在,进而拥有它。从形式上看，就是起初拥有它的人，随着和别人的交往，慢慢地受到许多人的欢迎，朋友越来越多，相信他的人越来越多，说话做事也和他越来越具有相似性——他们都看重善良、诚信和博爱等让人喜悦的人类品质。

Those who own positive energy bring others a unique feeling. What they own in their body is a positive energy that makes people happy and comfortable, and which decides everything of the people who own it. Also, positive energy can help those who own it avoid disasters and over-interaction with people with negative energy; and avoid negative energy in a restrained and tolerant way in case of conflicts with it to protect the positive energy against invasion and assimilation by negative energy.

But the biggest problem with the above hypothetical reasoning is that current science and technology of human society cannot yet prove whether its content truly exists and works or not. What people can prove with their own senses is that people who are full of positive energy firmly believe in a certain feeling or state in their hearts. They will actively strengthen their behaviors that can match such feeling, and

身上拥有正能量的人，给别人的感觉是特别的，他们身上拥有的是一种让人喜悦舒服的能量，这种能量主宰着拥有它的人们的一切。并且正能量还可以让拥有它的人避开灾祸，避免和带有负能量的人深度交集，在与负能量发生冲突时，用克制宽容的方式绕开它，保护身上的正能量不被负能量侵袭和同化。

但是上面的假设推理存在的最大问题是——以目前人类社会的科学技术还无法证实其内容，是真实存在且发生作用的。人们用自身的感官所能证明的，仅是充满正能量的人们，心中都对人的某种感觉或状态深信不疑，他们会主动强化自己身上能够和这种感觉相匹配的言行，并不断地去努力"做好人，做好事"。

try hard to "be a good person and do good deeds."

Even if with just the proof by the senses, we can draw such a conclusion to some extent --- one can get positive energy in the form of "faith" and show a powerful force that makes people happy as long as he/she has faith in positive energy (or maybe such person doesn't realize what he/she believes in is positive energy) and believes in the feeling brought by certain conclusions to him/her. Although such assumption and reasoning sound a bit like fantasy and guess, they are more scientific and rational than denying them directly without evidence.

How "Negative Energy" Comes?

According to the what-if reasoning in the previous section, those who often feel angry, jealous and fearful should have "negative energy", which totally differ from positive energy. Such energy is

即便仅是感官的证明，我们也可以从一定程度上得出这样的结论——只要一个人有对正能量的信仰（也可能这个人并未意识到自己信奉的是正能量），相信某些认知结论带给自己的感觉，他（她）就能以"信心"的方式得到正能量，从而表现出让人喜悦的强大力量。尽管这样的假设和推理，听起来有些像幻想和猜测，但也比在没有证据的前提下，直接否定它要科学理性的多。

"负能量"是怎么来的？

按照上一节的假设和推理，常常感觉生气愤怒、嫉妒和恐惧的人们身上，应该是带有完全不同于正向能量的"负能量"。这种能量同样也是类似于"上帝粒子"的存在，和"正能量"

also an existence similar to "God particle", what's common between "positive energy" and it is that it also affects and controls all aspects of a person.

Walking on the street, if two persons with positive energy collide unintentionally, they may both say "sorry" to each other friendly, and then help each other up, kindly solve each other's material losses. The result is that both persons leave there smoothly. If two persons with negative energy collide, the situation can become terrible. First, one of them may scold loudly "Are you blind?" or even more unbearable words, and then the other will scold back, and then the conflict will escalate, which may result in violent injuries and even life-threatening dangers. These are normal and reasonable analyses with no exaggeration. But if a person with positive energy and a person with negative energy collide, the result may change. The reason for such change is the strength of the

相似的是，它也会影响控制一个人的方方面面。

走在大街上，如果两个拥有正能量的人无意相撞，两人可能都会友好的道一声对不起，然后互相帮扶，善意地解决彼此的物质损失问题，最后结果是双方顺畅地离开那里。如果是两个拥有负能量的人相撞冲突，情况就可能变得非常糟糕。首先，会有大声的叫骂"眼瞎了"或是更加不能入耳的话语，进而对方也开始叫骂，然后冲突升级，出现暴力伤害甚至是生命危险，这些是正常合理的分析，没有夸张的手法。但如果情况是一个拥有正能量，另外一个拥有负能量，这样的两个人相撞，结果就会存在变化的可能。变化的原因，就在于两人身上正能量和负能量的强弱不同，很强的正能量会始终采取克制宽容的方式，来避免负能量的侵袭（负能量会让人失去理智），并在适当的时候，采取有力的防卫措施，避免损失

positive energy and the negative energy of the two persons differ. Positive energy strong enough will always avoid the invasion of negative energy in a restrained and tolerant way (negative energy will cause people to lose their minds), and take effective defensive measures, when appropriate, to avoid greater losses, deter the negative energy, thereby forcing the negative energy to compromise to solve the conflicts and issues. However, if the positive energy in such person involved is not strong enough, once he/she encounters negative energy that is stronger, he/she will soon become impulsive and angry, no longer restrained and tolerant, no longer believe in human goodness, thus making the positive energy in himself/herself leave quickly. And then, the negative energy will take advantage of it and dominate them to solve the issue with instinct. The outcome will be a bloody ending, just like the second scenarios we've analyzed above.

扩大，有力的震慑负能量，从而迫使负能量让步，使矛盾问题得到解决。可是如果当事人身上的正能量不够强大，这时一旦遇到更强的负能量，很快拥有正能量的人就会变得冲动、愤怒，不再克制宽容，不再相信人的善良，从而使自己身上的正能量迅速离开，负能量会乘虚而入主导双方用本能解决问题，事情的结局就会回到刚才第二种情况分析的那样，很可能血腥收场。

According to the above assumptions and reasoning, now that positive energy is so important to human social order, then, how does negative energy come? Does it also come from faith? Currently we have no direct evidence yet to prove it. What we can perceive is that the negative energy that makes people feel angry, jealous and fearful, or people with negative energy don't believe in human goodness and affection. Their hearts are often full of hatred. And such state causes them to give negative explanations when encountering conflicts and issues --- one with negative energy will think that the other party is full of hostility and is not a good person, and that there are many bad people in the world (one with positive energy will think that everyone has defects and should be tolerated and forgiven, and that everyone wants to be a good person though no one is perfect), and that hatred and violent attack are the best solution for conflicts, otherwise

按照上面的假设和推理，既然正能量对于人类社会秩序如此重要，那么负能量又是怎么来的呢？它也是因信而来的吗？我们目前仍然没有直接证据来证实，我们能够感知的是，让人们感到生气愤怒、嫉妒恐惧的负能量或是拥有负能量的人们，都不相信人类的善良和情感，他们的心中常常充满了仇恨，这样的状态导致他们在遇到矛盾问题时，会作出消极的解释——负能量会认为对方充满敌意，不是好人，并且这个世界上有很多坏人（正能量会认为每个人都有缺陷，应该宽容谅解，虽然人无完人，但人人都想做好人），认为仇恨和暴力攻击才是解决冲突的最好办法，否则自己就会受到损失和伤害。但让他们无法明白的是，当他们这样做了以后，自己的损失却更大，或是心灵或是肉体都会有痛苦感。而那些拥有正能量的人们，没有选择暴力伤害解决矛盾冲突，最后除去物质和肉体上的损失以外，他们的心灵不会痛苦。原因就在于，和拥有正能量的人们不一

himself/herself will suffer loss and injury or hurt. But what makes them unable to understand is that their loss becomes even greater, or feel painful mentally and physically at the same time when after doing so. Those with positive energy do not choose to solve conflicts with violence. At last, except for material and physical losses, their souls will not suffer. Because people with negative energy --- unlike those with positive energy --- do not believe that positive energy will bring people benefits. Instead, they believe that negative energy will bring them what they want, and they continually strengthen their behaviors that match the feeling caused by negative energy. In the end, they will also be led to pain by negative energy in this way --- a state of trauma to the soul.

Why People "Suffer"?

Physical wounds can bleed, and are sometimes painful; severe

样——拥有负能量的人不相信正能量会给人带来益处，他们相信负能量会给他们想要的，他们因着相信负能量带来的感觉，而不断强化与那种感觉相匹配的言行，最终他们也会被负能量通过这种方式引向痛苦——一种心灵的创伤状态。

人为什么会"痛苦"

肉体上的创伤会流血，有时会很痛，严重的肉体创伤可以

physical wounds can endanger human life. The pain of the human soul may, however, result in suicide although it will not bleed. Furthermore, such miserable ending not only results in suicide sometimes, but also hurts innocent people as nowhere for them to vent their pains. So, it can also be said that the pain of the human soul is far more unbearable than the trauma of the body.

Abuse --- a behavior that makes most people painful --- is common seen among those whose souls are painful. Hurting themselves, others, innocent vulnerable groups, and even weak and cute animals... are all their ways to alleviate pain. Such people also deserve the sympathy and attention of their human compatriots while being condemned and punished by the society although they behave terribly. Why our compatriots are so painful that they even choose to mutilate or kill the weak and innocent lives? Why they cannot

危害到人的生命。但人类心灵的痛苦，虽不会流血，却可能导致生命的自我终结，并且这种痛苦的结局有时候不仅是自我结束生命，还会因为自己的痛苦无处宣泄而伤害无辜。因此也可以说，人类心灵的痛苦，远比肉体的创伤更让人难以承受。

虐待——这样一种让多数人感到难过的行为，在心灵痛苦的人群当中却是司空见惯。伤害自己、他人、无辜的弱势群体，甚至是弱小可爱的动物…都是他们减轻痛苦的方式途径。尽管这样的人行径恶劣，但在遭受社会谴责惩罚的同时，他们也应该得到人类同胞的同情和关注。为什么我们的同胞会如此痛苦，以致于让他们选择残害弱小无辜者的生命，为什么他们的心中感觉不到，人类因为爱或被爱而激发出的美好情感，进而愉快地与他人分享交流，彰显出更多的人性之美。这里问题的根源就在于，他们

feel in their hearts that humans can share and communicate with others happily and show their beauty of human nature by virtue of the good affections stimulated by love or being loved. The root cause of the issue here is that there is lingering pain in their hearts. Then where does their pain come from?

One with positive energy rejects harm. He/she will not harm himself/herself and others easily. In case of conflicts, he/she will always seek mutually beneficial win-win solutions, creating a harmonious and pleasant interpersonal atmosphere. So there is seldom pain in their hearts. But when one begins not to believe in positive energy, he/she will be gradually attacked by negative energy. The positive energy in him/her will become weaker and weaker as he/she do not believe it so that the positive energy in him/her at last cannot control his/her behaviors. Due to the loss of guidance of positive energy,

心中有挥之不去的痛苦，那么这些痛苦又是从哪里来的呢？

一个拥有正能量的人，是排斥伤害的，他（她）不会轻易伤害自己和他人，遇到矛盾冲突时他们总是寻求互利双赢的问题解决方案，营造出和谐愉快的人际关系氛围，因此他们的心中很少有痛苦的感觉。不过当一个人开始不相信正能量之后，他（她）就会慢慢地被负能量侵袭，因为不相信，他（她）身上的正能量会越来越弱，以至于最后正能量无法控制影响他（她）的言行。因为失去了正能量的指引，人们开始无节制地顺从自己的本性和欲望，他们的心中会因此出现痛苦感。引导怂恿人们肆意满足本性欲望的就是负能量，负能量可以让人屈服于自己的本性欲望，

people begin to uncontrollably follow their own nature and desires, and they will feel pain in their hearts because of this. It is negative energy that guides and instigates people to arbitrarily satisfy their nature and desires. It can make people yield to their own nature and desires and do all kinds of evil deeds that hurt others and themselves.

If people can persist in believing in positive energy, and adhere to their belief in positive energy no matter how tough the situation is, the negative energy won't be able to take advantage of the emptiness to confuse people, and control and affect their behaviors. People will have messages instructed by positive energy in their hearts --- which words we can say and which things we can do; and which we can't say and do. People who firmly believe in positive energy will clearly perceive such rules and bottom lines in their hearts, which are usually called "morality" or

做出伤人害己的种种恶行。

如果人们能够坚持相信正能量，再苦再难，也要坚守对正能量的信仰，那么负能量就不能趁虚而入，无法蛊惑人心，控制影响人们的言语行为。人们的心中会拥有正能量给人们的讯息——哪些话、哪些事我们可以说、可以做，哪些我们不可以。坚守正能量的人们心中，都会清晰地感知到这些规则和底线，通常它们也会被称作是——道义或良知，一个人违背道义良知去说话做事，便是他（她）会觉得痛苦的根源。人类的道义或良知源自正能量，相信正能量的人们都能感知到，并且会努力自觉地遵守它们。遵守道义良知的人们，不论身

"conscience". One's behavior against morality and conscience is the root cause of his/her pain. Human morality or conscience stems from positive energy, and which people who believe in positive energy can perceive and will strive to obey consciously. People who obey morality and conscience, regardless of their status, being poor or rich, have a feature in common, that is, they will not feel painful for long, nor will they hurt their lives easily.

One Hypothesis, One Belief

Human belief is a spiritual issue, and it cannot yet be proved and deduced using scientific and visualized. And our belief is also invisible and intangible. But some concepts about human beliefs can be drawn through what-if analysis reasoning: statically, belief refers to the cognitions or conclusions that people draw in explaining the world and the mankind itself;

份地位、贫穷或富有，都会具有一个相似的特征，那就是他们不会感到长久的痛苦，也不会轻易伤害生命。

一个假设 一种信仰

人的信仰属于精神层面的问题，目前还无法用科学直观的资料数据来证实和演绎，我们看不见也摸不着我们信仰的对象。但经过理性的假设分析推理，可以得出关于人类信仰的一些概念——从静态角度讲，信仰是指人们在解释世界和人类自身的过程中得出的认知或结论；从动态的过程来看，信仰是人们对上述认知结论的信

dynamically, belief is people's believing in, and compliance with the foregoing cognitions and conclusions.

We can make a hypothesis: assuming that the following content holds --- human life comprises two parts: one is visible and tangible body; and the other is invisible and intangible dematerialized existence, which is also called "spirit". The two parts are closely integrated in a way that humans have not yet understood up to now. Their combination and interaction have constructed a variety of life phenomena, and burst energy out of human life. And, in the universe where we live, there are also very powerful spirit-like dematerialized existences, and the energy formed by which is sufficient to control our entire mankind. Between spirit and such dematerialized existences, there will be communication and energy transmission, and such kinds of energy can dominate human

奉和遵守。

我们可以做出一个假设，假设下面这些内容是成立的——人类的生命是由两部分组成的，一部分是看得见的、有形的肉体，一部分是看不见的、无形的非物质化存在，这种存在又叫做灵魂。两者以某种人类迄今还未洞悉的方式紧密结合着，他们的结合与互动，构筑了千姿百态的生命现象，迸发出人类的生命能量。并且在我们所生存的宇宙之中，还有十分强大的类似灵魂的非物质化存在，这些非物质化存在所形成的能量足以控制我们整个人类。在灵魂和这些非物质化存在之间，会有沟通和能量的输送，这些能量可以主宰人的生命。在灵魂和这些非物质化存在的沟通过程中，人类的信仰——也就是人们所信奉和遵守的认知结论，起到了链接点的作用——你相信什么，你就会链接到什么样的能量以及输送能量的非物质化存在。这些能量在和人类灵

lives. In communication between spirit and such dematerialized existences, human beliefs, namely the cognitions and conclusions that people believe in and obey, serve as the linking point --- you will be linked to what you believe and transmit such kind of dematerialized existences. Such kinds of energy will bring different feelings to people in the interaction with human spirit. We can divide these kinds of energy into two categories by inner feeling: one is the positive energy --- energy that makes people kind and enthusiastic, and happy; the other is negative energy --- energy that makes people angry, hateful, jealous, and painful, and can satisfy people's desires without happiness.

If the conclusion described above holds, our belief in, and obeyance of this conclusion will become a belief. Those who choose to believe in the conclusion of such hypothesis and uphold positive energy will link their

魂的交流互动中，会给人们带来不同的感受，依据内在感受的不同，我们可以把这些能量分为两大类：一类是正向的能量——让人们善良热情、幸福快乐的能量；一类是负向的能量——让人们愤怒、仇恨、嫉妒、痛苦的能量，一种能让人满足欲望，却不会幸福快乐的能量。

如果上面描述的结论是成立的，我们对这个结论的信奉和遵守便成为一种信仰。选择相信这个假设的结论，并崇尚正能量（正向的能量）的人，会因为信念（相信正能量会让自己幸福快乐）使自己的灵魂

spiritual life to the existence that emits positive energy by virtue of belief (believing that positive energy will make themselves happy), and then deliver their physical life to be under its control (the energy of such existence is so powerful that it can control human thoughts, consciousness and behaviors as long as people believe that such existence will make them happy, and are willing to give all their desires and claims to it for control). In opposite cases, people's spirit and body may be linked to negative energy and be controlled by it.

Different Beliefs and Their Respective Kinds of Energy

Everyone living in this world will face the issue of belief. What is belief, in a layman's words, it is as to what you believe, or what the truth in your heart is, and you are willing to believe in and obey such cognitions and conclusions.

生命链接到发出正能量的存在，进而将自己的肉体生命也交其主宰（这种存在的能量十分强大，以至于可以控制人类的想法意识和言语行为，只要人们相信这种存在会让自己幸福，愿意将自己的欲望要求全部交其掌管）。相反的情况下，人们的灵魂和肉体则有可能链接到负向的能量，并进而被其控制。

不同的信仰和能量

生活在这个世界上的每一个人，都会遇到信仰问题。什么是信仰，简单通俗地说，就是你相信什么，或你心中的事实真相是什么，并且你也愿意心甘情愿的信奉和遵守这样的认知结论。

You can believe that God created everything, and God controls everything. God has arranged everything of you. All you need to do is to believe in and obey the conscience and morality inspired by God.

You can believe that humans evolved in some way from lower level creatures. There is no mystery about humans and nature. It is simply the principle of "the survival of the fittest". Mankind does not have to believe in or follow conscience and morality. It is a matter of course for people to satisfy their desires and needs. And, there will be no doomsday trial and salvation at all.

Also, you don't have to think about what you need to believe, what you should do, just follow your heart. It's contentment being alive and happy, no matter Genesis or Evolutionism.

Believe it or not, as a person, he/she will have some doubts deep in his/her heart that he/she cannot answer, "Where do I come from,

你可以相信是上帝创造了一切，是上帝在掌控着一切，有关于你的一切，上帝也已安排妥当，你需要做的只是信奉遵守上帝默示给你的良知和道义就行了。

你可以相信人是由低等生物通过某种方式进化而来，人与自然没有什么奥秘可言，优胜劣汰，适者生存而已。人类无须信奉遵守良知和道义，满足人的欲望需求，是天经地义的事情，也根本不会有什么末日审判与救赎。

你还可以不去考虑你需要相信什么，你应该做的，只是顺从你内心的指引就好。不管是创世论还是进化论，活着并且幸福快乐就是满足。

不管信与不信，做为一个人，他（她）的内心深处都会有一些自己无法解答的疑惑，"我从哪里来，要到哪里去，为什

where I go, why I desire happiness, and how can I be happy...?" With such doubts, believe it or not, whether think actively or accept it passively, people have to face the issue of belief. As everyone wants happiness, and belief is the only way that leads people to happiness.

With belief, there will be faith, and then hope. Faith and hope can stimulate the tremendous energy of humans. Together, they are human willpower. The strength of willpower determines whether one can succeed or not.

During the course of human belief, the cognitions and conclusions you believe in or not function as linking points, which allow one to be linked to energy similar to "God particle" in the unknown world. Such energy can, by feeling given by such energy, be divided into "positive energy" and "negative energy". Such energy linked to humans is all manifested as human faith. Because of the difference of

么我会渴慕幸福，我该怎样才能幸福…"带着这些疑惑，不论你信或是不信，主动思考还是被动接受，人都要面对信仰的难题。因为人人想要幸福，而信仰是人们通往幸福的必经之路。

有了信仰，就会有信心，有了信心，便会有希望，信心和希望能激发出人类自身的巨大能量，他们融合在一起就是人类的意志力，意志力的强弱则决定着一个人的成功与否。

在人类信仰的过程中，信或不信的认知结论，充当了链接点的作用，它们可以让一个人连接到未知世界中类似"上帝粒子"一样的能量。根据这些能量给人的感觉不同，他们被区分为"正能量"和"负能量"。连接到人类的这些能量，都表现为人的信心，但因为"正负"不同，信心也会随之显示迥然不同的方向，信心带来的希望也会展现出完全不一样的内容。更重要的是，信心、希望及其

"positive or negative", however, faith will also indicate completely different directions, and the hope brought by faith will also indicate completely different content. More importantly, the willpower formed by faith, hope and the energy stimulated by them will also reflect the huge difference between "positive energy" and "negative energy". Such willpowers of different directions and goals bring people either beneficial results or painful harms.

What Authority Is?

What is authority? Few people go deep into this issue. But everyone can perceive whether there exists authority around them. Generally \, when people perceive the existence of authority, they will focus on certain people or objects. Because such people and objects give people a strong feeling that they carry or convey certain energy, and which can make people willingly surrender

激发出的能量所形成的意志力，也会体现出"正能量"和"负能量"的巨大差异，这些不同方向和目标的意志力，给人们带来的将是有益的结果，或是让人痛苦的伤害。

权威是什么

权威是什么，很少人去深究这个问题，但每个人都能感知到自己的周围是否存在权威。通常情况下，当人们感知到权威存在的时候，会把注意力集中在某些人或是物品上，因为这些人和物，给了人们很强烈的感觉——他们承载传递了某种能量，而这些能量可以让人们心甘情愿地交出自己的原始权利，放弃原本属于自己的自由。这些能量的载体可以是教

their original rights and give up the freedom belonged to them. Carriers of such energy can be pope, priest, or Bible, Quran, Buddhist scriptures, etc. What they say and do, or what is recorded in the scriptures has a great effect and influence on most people who believe in them. The relationship between them is like the Pope and Catholics.

But such people and things are not the authority in people's hearts. The authority in one's heart should essentially be a certain energy carried and conveyed by such people and things, which may be a dematerialized existence like "God particle". What does it mean when one perceives the existence of authority? Imagine that there is a person you admire very much, who is a highly respected person in your eyes, would you want to hear his opinions when you encounter confusions and difficulties? In your eyes, he/she is a benchmark character as well as the incarnation of authority. His/her recognition

皇、牧师或者是圣经、古兰经、佛经等，他们所说所做的，或者是经文记载下来的内容，对于大多数相信他们的人具有非常大的作用和影响力，其中的关系就好比罗马教皇与天主教徒一样。

但这些人和物，还不是人们心中的权威。一个人心中的权威，实质上应该是这些人和物所承载传递的某种能量，这些能量可能是像"上帝粒子"一样的非物质化存在。当一个人感知到了权威的存在，会意味着什么呢？试想一下，有一位你非常敬佩的人，是你眼中德高望重的人物，在你遇到困惑和难题的时候，你会不会想听到他的观点意见？你眼中的他（她），是一个标杆式的人物，也是权威的化身，他（她）对你的认可，意味着你的做法正确合理，你对他（她）的自觉服从，也意味着你相信的某些认知结论在

of you means that your actions are correct and reasonable. And your conscious obedience to him/her also means certain cognitions and conclusions you believe are better interpreted by him/her. In other words, one's obedience to authority means that he/she has followed his/her belief. You will gain energy of faith by believing in and obeying authority, and then do what you want; and, obeying real authority will also make people feel at ease and stay away from pain. If a person violates the implication or requirement of authority, it means that he/she has violated his/her belief. He/she will drive his/her conscience uneasy and self-condemn. What is the human conscience? Conscience is the implication or requirement of an authority to humans that one perceives (links) via his/her own belief; it can also be said that conscience is the "law" that authority puts in human hearts.

The science and technology currently mastered by mankind

他（她）的身上得到了更好地诠释，换句话说，一个人对权威的服从，也就意味着他（她）遵从了自己的信仰。你会因为相信和服从权威得到信心能量，进而做成你想做的事情，并且顺从真正的权威，也会让人觉得心安理得，远离痛苦。如果一个人违背了权威的默示或要求，就说明他（她）违背了自己的信仰，这个人会良心不安，会自我谴责。人的良心是什么？良心是一个人通过自己的信仰感知（连接）到的权威对人类的默示或要求，也可以说，良心就是权威放在人类心中的"律法"。

人类目前掌握的科学技术，还不足以完全破译权威（人类信

cannot yet completely decipher which kind of existence authority (a certain energy that humans believe in, which is also called Lord, God, Allah, Buddha, etc.) is on earth. But the latest fruits from the natural science community have inspired people. The discovery of God's particle allows people to make such an assumption: authority is the ultimate goal of human beliefs, or to say, what the cognitions and conclusions that people believe (beliefs) link is a vast unknown field of mankind, where the energy has been inspiring mankind in different ways to let people gain faith, hope and strength via belief. If such a hypothesis holds, it can demonstrate that the scriptures, myths and legends handed down in human society are not illusory but all come from this unknown field of mankind. Authority is what people are linked to via faith which they think is the strongest energy. And, due to individual differences among humans, people

服的某种能量，这些能量也被人们称做神、真主、佛等）究竟是何种形式的存在。但自然科学界的最新成果却给了人们启示，上帝粒子的发现，让人们完全可以做出这样的假设——权威是人类信仰的终极目标，或者说人们相信的认知结论（信仰）所连接到的，是一片浩瀚的人类未知领域，这里的能量千百年来，一直在用不同的方式和方法，给人类以启示，让人们通过信仰获取信心、希望和力量。这样的假设如果成立，就可以说明人类社会流传下来的经典和神话传说，并非虚无缥缈，而是全部来自这片人类未知的领域。权威就是人们通过信仰连接到的，他们认为是最强的能量，并且因为人类的个体差异，拥有不同信仰的人们会连接到不同的能量那里，信奉其为自己的权威。

with different beliefs will be linked to different kinds of energy and believe in them as their own authority.

The Role of Authority

If one perceives authority around him/her, people will be very pious and obedient in front of authority no matter such authority is reflected in some people or in other forms of carriers e.g. scriptures, as the faith, hope, and strength in people all come from the authority they believe in. Belief in, and obedience to authority means that energy of faith can be obtained from authority; while violating the implication or requirement of authority means punishment will be imposed from authority. Now, we still analyze such likelihood by hypothetical reasoning.

Assuming that each of us humans has an existence similar to "God particle", or we can call such existence "spirit". The

权威的作用

一个人如果感知到自己的周围存在权威，那么不管这种权威是体现在某些人身上，还是在经典书籍等其他形式的载体之上。在权威面前人们都会表现的十分虔诚和顺服，因为人身上的信心、希望和力量，都来自自己所信奉的权威。信服权威意味着可以从权威那里得到信心能量，而违背权威的默示或要求，则意味着要接受来自权威的惩罚。下面，我们仍然使用假设推理的方法来分析说明这样的可能性。

假定我们人类每个人的身上都有一种类似"上帝粒子"的存在，或者我们可以把这种存在称作"灵魂"。人的灵魂是

human spirit is an energy, which is the driving force of one's life and determines all the desires and needs of such person (human original rights). As discussed in Chapter I hereof, everyone has the freedom to behave at will. Freedom mentioned here is one's original right. Different people want to own different rights or freedoms --- some people want this, while some want that. We also assume the source of such difference is the existence in an unknown way in us --- spirit. There are big differences between different kinds of spirit. There will be conflicts among people with different kinds of spirit when they are together --- fighting, scrambling, hurting each other and other cruelties and atrocities in human society are all caused by people's various desires, namely unrestrained human original rights. And such human right will not easily yield due to the restraints of external forces, as the power of one's spirit is endless. On the

一种能量，这种能量是一个人的生命原动力，它决定着人的全部欲望需求（人的原始权利）。正如本文第一篇章中论述的那样，每个人都有按照自己意愿去做的自由，这里的自由便是一个人的原始权利。不同的人会想拥有不同的权利或自由——有的人想这样，有的人想那样。这种差异性的根源，我们也假定是来自我们身上未知方式的存在——灵魂。不同的灵魂会有很大的差异性，具有不同灵魂的人们在一起时就会出现矛盾冲突——争斗、拼抢、彼此伤害等人类社会的残酷和暴行，无不因人的各种欲望而起，也就是不加约束的人的原始权利导致。并且人类的这种权利不会因为外在力量的制约而轻易屈服，因为一个人灵魂的力量是无穷尽的，表面上一个人迫于恐惧可能屈服于某些力量，但是一旦遇到适当机会，他（她）是一定会奋起反击的。我们也可以说，一个人的灵魂是不可征服的，灵魂的这种特性，决定了人类社会的秩序，很难实现长久和谐的稳定。因为每个

surface, one may yield to certain forces due to fear. But he/she will surely rise up to fight back once there is appropriate chance. We can also say that one's spirit is unconquerable. Such feature of spirit determines that it's tough for the order of human society to achieve long-term harmony and stability. Because everyone's original rights cannot be restrained due to the unconquerablility of their own spirit. The peer-to-peer war depicted in Leviathan is not a joke.

However, the above situation will become quite different due to the intervention of a certain energy, which is much stronger than human spirit, and the power of which is that it can make human spirit feel painful. When people perceive such energy and regard it as authority, they will willingly restrain their original rights, thus consciously accepting the guidance and requirements of authority. Also, authority will give the believers faith (energy), hope

人的原始权利都因着各自灵魂的不可征服而无法约束，所以《利维坦》当中的每一个人对每一个人的战争，并不是戏言。

不过，上述境况会因为某种能量的介入而变得大不相同，这种能量比人的灵魂要强大的多，这种能量的强大之处在于其可以让人的灵魂感到痛苦。人们感知到这种能量，且视之为权威时，便会心甘情愿地将自己的原始权利约束起来，从而自觉接受权威的指引和要求，权威也会以未知的方式给信奉的人们信心（能量）、希望和力量。在这个过程中，连接灵魂和权威的是人的信仰——对某些认知结论的遵守和信奉。权

and strength in unknown ways. In this process, what links spirit and authority is human belief --- obeying and believing in certain cognitions and conclusions. The authority's guidance to the believers is achieved through implied rules, which are imprinted in human spirit by authority in an intangible way --- and such rules are called human "conscience".

Although there is no direct evidence to prove such hypothetical reasoning, we should not deny it categorically without evidence. In the visible universe, there also exists an invisible dimension similar to "God particle". We can still imagine and believe that authority from such dimension is of great importance to everything in human society. Of which, for us humans, the biggest role of authority is to allow people to consciously restrict their original rights by way of rules (conscience) so as to make it possible for the human social order to be harmonious and stable.

威对信徒的指引是通过默示的规则来实现的，这种规则被权威以无形的方式印记在人的灵魂之中——这些规则被称作是人类的"良心"。

这样的假设推理虽然没有直接证据来证实，但我们也不应该在没有证据的情况下就断然否认，在看得见的宇宙之中，还存在一个看不见的，类似"上帝粒子"一样存在的未知空间。我们仍然可以想象并相信，来自这个空间的权威对于人类社会的一切都十分的重要，其中对于我们人类来说，权威最大的作用就是可以用规则（良心）的方式让人们自觉约束自己的原始权利，从而使人类社会秩序的和谐稳定具备可能性。

"Positive Energy"

Many people are pursuing a state of life -- a state in which people feel happy. As stated in the United States Declaration of Independence --- everyone has the right to pursue happiness (freedom). [1] How to be happy is an eternal topic in human society. No one does not want to be happy. No matter what you have, whether it is power, money, reputation or status, it cannot be directly equated with happiness. The feeling of happiness is related to one's spirit, belief, and even the authority he/she believes in.

For anyone who is happy, most of the people around him/her will describe the feeling he/she brings to others using a very special word, that is,

"正能量"

很多人都在追求一种生命的状态，一种让人感到幸福快乐的状态。正如某个国家的独立宣言所言——每个人都有追求幸福的权利（自由）。怎么样才能幸福快乐，是人类社会一个永恒的话题。没有人不想得到幸福快乐，不管你拥有什么，是权力、金钱还是名誉地位，都不能直接等同于幸福快乐，幸福快乐的感觉和一个人的灵魂有关，和一个人的信仰有关，更和一个人所信奉的权威有关。

但凡幸福快乐的人，其身边的人们大多会用一个很特别的词汇来形容他们给人带来的感觉，那就是这些人的身上充满了"正能量"。那"正能量"

[1] *United States Declaration of Independence,* by Thomas Jefferson, etc. published in https://en.wikipedia.org/wiki/United_States_Declaration_of_Independence Access time: 00:12 Mar 8, 2017.
杰弗逊等:《美国独立宣言全文及译文》，载华中大法律网，http://law.hust.edu.cn/Law2008/ShowArticle.asp?ArticleID=495，访问时间：2017 年 3 月 8 日 00:12。

such person is full of "positive energy". So what is "positive energy" on earth? Currently clear interpretation cannot yet be found in the scientific knowledge and religious doctrines mastered by the mankind. Also, it is very difficult to answer such question directly and clearly. But we can first feel what "positive energy" brings to people. People who are considered to be with "positive energy" usually like smiling and are easy-going. They are friendly, helpful and don't lose their temper easily. Except in extreme circumstances, they don't use words or body to hurt others; they don't care much about the gains and losses of material benefits; they are often grateful and conscientious, and treat their relatives and friends attentively.

It can make people feel relaxed and happy to interact with such people. When interacting with people with "positive energy", you will rarely feel nervous, angry, suspicious and alert. You usually

究竟是什么呢？目前人类掌握的科学知识和宗教教义中并无明白解释，想要直接清楚地回答这样的问题难度也很大。不过我们可以先来感受下"正能量"都给人们带来了什么，身上被认为有"正能量"的人们，通常都是喜欢微笑，容易相处的，他们对人友善，乐于助人，不轻易发脾气，除非极端情况，不会用言语或肢体去伤害他人，他们不太与人计较物质利益的得失，常常感恩尽责，用心对待身边的亲人朋友。

和这样的人交往，可以让人们获得一种轻松愉悦的感觉。和拥有"正能量"的人交往，你很少会有紧张、生气、猜疑和戒备的心理，你通常都会觉得对于他（她）你有一种发自内

feel that you have a kind of trust and relaxation to him/her from your heart. Such feeling may start with his/her smile or first words for you, you will trust and respect him/her, and you will be willing to cooperate and communicate with him/her, co-work and co-study with him/her to create value. Such people have a natural attraction, which will make more and more people to gather around them, sharing happiness and relieving sorrow. Over time, the people who interacted with such people seem to have "positive energy". Their wordings, doings, as well as mentality and temperament share something in common, and the reason for this is that they all own "positive energy".

An elderly sanitation worker found the wallet of a young college student and contacted the owner actively. Before the owner came, such old man kept waiting where he found it. He waited in spite of the rain until the young college student came.

心的信任和放松，这种感觉或许从你看到他（她）的微笑时起，或者从他（她）和你说的第一句话开始，你就会相信尊重他（她），你会愿意和他（她）合作沟通，一起工作学习，共同创造价值。这样的人身上有一种自然的吸引力，会让越来越多的人聚拢在他们的周围，分享快乐，化解忧愁。久而久之，和这些人交往的人们似乎都拥有了"正能量"，他们的说话做事与心态气质，都有了某种相似性，原因就是他们都拥有了"正能量"。

一位年长的环卫工人，捡到了年轻大学生的钱包，并主动联系了失主。在失主到来之前，这位老人坚持等候在原地，尽管天空在下雨，但他一直等到年轻大学生的到来。看到站在雨中等候的老人，丢钱包的姑娘哭了，哭的不能自已。这时，

Seeing the old man standing in the rain waiting, the girl who lost her purse couldn't help crying [1] . In such case, the feeling this old man gives people is that he is full of "positive energy". And, from then on, the "positive energy" in the old man would also affect the girl who lost her wallet. She will also help others just like this old man does. Because she has once been affected and influenced by "positive energy".

Anyone who feels "positive energy" is basically willing to actively get their words, behaviors and thoughts subject to the influence of "positive energy" and believe and obey the guidance and requirements given by "positive energy", and thereby gets happiness. It can also be said that most humans are willing to believe

这位老人给人的感觉就是他被"正能量"充满，并且从那以后，老人身上的"正能量"也会影响到丢钱包的姑娘，她也会像老人一样去帮助别人，因为她曾经受到过"正能量"的作用和影响。

凡是感受到"正能量"的人们，基本上都愿意把自己的言行和思想，主动置于"正能量"的影响作用之下，愿意相信服从"正能量"给他们的指引和要求，并藉此得到幸福快乐。也可以说绝大多数的人类，都愿意相信"正能量"，相信"正能量"可以给人幸福，并且认为"正能量"才是人类所处时

---

[1] *A Sanitation Worker Who Found A Purse Waited for 2 Hours in the Rain and Moved the Owner to Tears,* dzwww.com/-Qilu Evening News, published in Sina News Center, http://news.sina.com.cn/s/2010-05-18/070620293147.shtml , access time: 23:33, Mar 7, 2017.

大众网 - 齐鲁晚报：《环卫工捡钱包雨中苦等两小时 失主感动落泪》，载新浪新闻中心，http://news.sina.com.cn/s/2010-05-18/070620293147.shtml，访问时间：2017 年 3 月 7 日23：33。

in "positive energy", believe that "positive energy" can bring people happiness, and that it is "positive energy" that is the most powerful energy in the time and space in which humans live. So, "positive energy" is the authority that people who pursue happiness believe in.

"Love" Brought by "Positive Energy"

Those who pursue happiness often enjoy the pleasant feeling brought to them by "positive energy". They regard such energy as their authority, and believe in and obey the guidance and implication of "positive energy". Under the "shepherding" of "positive energy", they are often with joy and peace. And, over time, those who truly believe in and own "positive energy" will get to have a feeling in their hearts --- a wonderful feeling benefiting others and themselves at the same time and making people pleasant both physically and mentally ---

空之中最强大的能量。因此，"正能量"就是追求幸福快乐的人们所信奉的权威。

"正能量"带来的"爱"

追求幸福快乐的人们常常享受"正能量"带给他们的愉悦感觉，他们视这种能量为自己的权威，相信并顺从"正能量"对他们的指引和默示。在"正能量"的"牧养"下，他们常常喜乐平安，并且随着时间的推移，真正相信并拥有"正能量"的人们，心中会滋生出一种感觉，一种益人利己，让人身心愉悦的奇妙感觉，人们常常把这种感觉叫做"爱"。有了"爱"，一个人距离生命的终极目标——幸福也就不远了。

people usually call such feeling "love". With "love", one will not be far away from the ultimate goal of life --- happiness.

Then, how does "love" feel like? We humans cannot accurately describe it in words. But we can truly perceive the magic of "love".

"Love" will make you smile from the heart, let you learn how to be kind, how to be strong, let you tolerate and forgive, and abandon hatred, while being able to protect the truth and defend justice wisely and bravely, firmly believing and obeying the revelation and guidance of "positive energy".

"Love" is magical and wonderful. No matter how much trauma you encounter, as long as you still can feel "love", you can quickly recover. Though sometimes the physical injury may not recover, "love" can definitely make your trauma of heart (spirit damage) be as good as ever.

Also, "love" maintains the intimacy among humans. None of

那"爱"的感觉是什么样子的呢？我们人类无法用语言准确地描述它，但我们可以真真切切地感知到"爱"的神奇。

"爱"会让你发自内心地去微笑，让你学会如何善良，懂得怎样坚强，让你包容宽恕，摒弃仇恨，但却能智慧勇敢地保护真相，捍卫公义，坚定地相信服从"正能量"的启示与指引。

"爱"是神奇而美妙的，无论你遭遇多大的创伤，只要你还有"爱"的感觉，你都能很快地恢复痊愈，虽然有时肉体的伤害可能无法还原，但"爱"一定可以让你的心灵伤口（灵魂伤害）完好如初。

"爱"还维持了人类的亲密关系，父母子女的亲情，人和

the affection between parents and children, friendship among people, and the love between male and female, is not promoted by "love." Only when love is often felt by people can various relationships among people be harmonious for long and can humans multiply and thrive.

"Love" can solve all conflicts and disputes in human society. As for human hatred and resentment, if violence is used to control violence, people will fall into a vicious circle of revenge for grievance. Because the human spirit is unconquerable. Due to the original rights, everyone will want to conquer and eliminate each other, resulting in endless mutual harm. But once both parties of the hatred feel "love", it won't be far away from peace any more.

The significance and role of "love" to humans are far more than those described in the several situations above. But no matter what form of "love" is presented, it is a wonderful feeling brought by

人的友情，异性的爱情，无不由"爱"促成。常常感受到爱，人与人之间的各种关系才能长久和谐，人类才得以繁衍生息。

"爱"可以化解人类社会当中的所有矛盾和纠纷，人类的仇恨怨气，如果以暴制暴，将会冤冤相报无时了，因为人的灵魂是不可征服的，每个人的原始权利会想要不断地征服对方、消灭对方，以致出现无穷无尽的彼此伤害。可是一旦仇恨的双方感受到了"爱"，化干戈为玉帛便不再遥远。

"爱"对于人类的意义作用，远非上面描述的几种情形所能涵盖，但无论以何种形式呈现出来的"爱"，都是"正能量"带给人类的奇妙感受。因此，我们也可以说"正能量"最大的

"positive energy" to humans. So, we can also say that the biggest feature of "positive energy" is "love", or "positive energy" means "love" for humans --- a kind of "love" that allows people to experience happiness in the end.

特征就是"爱",或者说"正能量"对于人类来说就意味着"爱",一种能让人最终体验到幸福快乐的"爱"。

Loving People Are Kind

有爱的人是善良的

Those who believe in "positive energy" and regard it as authority can link themselves to "positive energy" via such belief, and willingly follow the revelation and guidance of "positive energy" to him/her. "Positive energy" will guide people's spirit in the form of conscience and morality, and then regulate and restrain people's words and deeds lest people commit evil deeds that harm others. From a perspective of human, we can say that it is a feeling of "love" that gives us guidance, and let us protect ourselves and not do evil. For us humans, it is "positive energy"

相信"正能量"并视其为权威的人们,可以通过这种信仰,把自己连接到"正能量"那里,自愿遵从"正能量"对他(她)的启示和指引。"正能量"会以良心道德的方式,引导人的灵魂,进而规制约束人的言行,使人们不去做伤害他人的恶行。从人的角度来看,我们可以说,是一种"爱"的感觉给了我们指引,让我们保守自我,不去行恶。在这里对于我们人类,是"正能量"带给了我们"爱",一个人有了"爱"的感觉,也就预示着他(她)拥有了"正能量"。

that brings us "love". If one feels "love", it indicates that he/she has owned "positive energy".

Then, what are loving people like? What loving people usually think of is others' benefits and interests, and are unwilling to cause inconvenience and troubles to others; they care about others and those in need, do not care about personal material losses, and only wish their relatives and friends to be happy and healthy.

A little child was crushed by a car, and a dozen of passers-by ignored him/her, passing by coldly and indifferently. [①] Such behavior, in terms of human rights, people do have no obligation to help such little child, nor is there anyone or any authority that can force them to do so. Because people have not surrendered such freedom to others, and hence it's their right

那么有爱的人，是什么样子的呢？有爱的人心中想的常常是他人的利益和好处，不愿意给别人带来不便和麻烦，关心他人和需要帮助的人群，不计较个人的物质损失，只愿亲人朋友幸福安康。

一位幼童被汽车碾压，路过的十几位路人，都漠然视之，冷冷的走过，无动于衷。这样的行为，从人的权利角度来看，人们的确没有义务去做救助幼童的事情，也没有人或是权力机构能够强迫他们这样做，因为人们并没有交出这样的自由给他人，冷漠也是他们的权利，纯粹的人类原始权利，决定了这些人无需因此而受到社会的

① *A Crushed Little Girl Was Ignored by 18 passers-by But Saved by A Scavenger,* by Zhang Shuling, published in Tencent News, http://news.qq.com/a/20111017/000066.htm, access time: 23:35 Mar 7, 2017.

张淑玲：《18 名路人见死不救 拾荒阿姨救起遭碾压女童》，载腾讯新闻，http://news.qq.com/a/20111017/000066.htm，访问时间：2017 年 3 月 7 日 23:35。

to be indifferent. Purely original human rights determine that such people shall not be punished by the society for this. But obviously, their behavior cannot be called kind behavior. Because there is no trace of "love" or "positive energy" in their such behavior. It can also be inferred from another direction that such people do not believe in "positive energy". Because people who believe in "positive energy" as their authority will have a power to force them to help such little child when encountering similar situations. Whatever the result will be, people who believe in positive energy and those with love in their hearts will choose to stop to do something for such little child, regardless of whether there is still hope for the child to survive. Even if just a phone call or an appeal is enough to proves that there is love and belief in positive energy in his/her heart. But in the end, someone with love and positive energy in her heart appeared. No matter what she

惩罚。但他们的行为显然，不能被称作是善良的，因为他们的行为中，丝毫找不到"爱"的感觉，或是"正能量"的痕迹。也就可以从另一个方向，推出这些人并不相信"正能量"，因为信奉"正能量"为权威的人们，遇到类似情景时，会有一种力量迫使他们去救助这位幼童，无论结果如何，相信正能量的人、心中有爱的人都会选择停下来，然后为这位幼童做点什么，不管幼童是否还有生还的希望，哪怕仅仅只是一个电话，一声呼喊，就足以证明他（她）的心中有爱，有对正能量的信仰。不过最后，心中有爱、拥有正能量的人出现了，不管她是做什么工作的，不管她的身份，我们可以非常肯定地说，她拥有正能量，有爱，并且充满了爱带给她的力量，她的生命也是幸福快乐的。

does, no matter what her identity is, we can say with certainty that she has positive energy, love, and is full of power brought to her by love. Also, her life is happy.

Such people may sometimes worry and fear in their heart that they will cause trouble to themselves by doing good deeds, but "positive energy" gives them their conscience and morality, which allows them to overcome their worries eventually and help those who they believe need help wisely and bravery. Because "positive energy" is guiding people who believe in it as authority to do good deeds and promote goodness, so that people can often remember the goodness of others and always consider the interests of others.

这样的人，虽然有时心里也会担忧和恐惧，会害怕因做好事而给自己带来麻烦，但"正能量"给他们的良心道义，可以让他们最终克服忧虑，智慧勇敢地去救助他们认为需要救助的人们。因为"正能量"在引导信奉其为权威的人们去做善事，弘扬善良，让人们常常记得别人的好处，时时为他人的利益着想。

Loving People Are Honest

有爱的人是诚实的

Loving people, due to their kindness, always think about the interests of others. They don't care about personal gains or

有爱的人因为善良，心里总是想着别人的利益，不太计较个人得失，总有自己的无所谓，够用合适就行，从不贪多求大。

losses. They always stick to an it-doesn't-matter attitude and easily get satisfied and don't expect too much. What they think and what they say always keep consistent. They won't lie and conceal the truth unless doing so will harm others, for example, doctors and relatives conceal their conditions from the patient in order not to undermine the their faith and courage.

An honest person brings us a feeling of reliability. Interacting with an honest person will make people feel relaxed and trusting in the heart. There are defects in human nature, which determines that what people first consider is how to seek advantages and avoid disadvantages instead of keeping promises, honesty and trustworthiness. Due to the defects in human nature, it's not easy to be honest. One picked up some valuables of others on the side of the road. But he/she is very poor and is in urgent need of living support. In such case, Human

他们心里想的和说的做的都是一样的，除非为了不伤害别人，他们才会撒谎隐瞒真相，比如医生和家属为了不打击病人的信心勇气，而对病人隐瞒病情。

一个诚实的人，给人的感觉是可靠的，和诚实的人交往，会让人们从心底觉得放松和信任。人的本性是有缺陷的，这些缺陷决定人们首先考虑的是如何趋利避害，而不是恪守承诺，诚实守信。因为人性存在缺陷，所以诚实不是一件容易的事情。一个人在路边捡到了别人的贵重财物，而这个人又非常贫穷，急需生活资助。这时人的本性会让他产生占有这些财物的欲望冲动，可绝大多数人心中都有的良知道义，却告诉他这是他人财物，私自侵吞属不义之举。诚实的人会克服私欲，顺从良心道义的指引，

nature will cause him to have the desire to possess these assets. But most people have a conscience in their hearts, and tell him/her that this is another person's assets and it is unjust to embezzle them privately. An honest person will overcome selfish desires, follow the guidance of conscience and morality, look for the owner or wait for the owner to come, so as to impress people with the precious character of returning money found and win the trust and respect of others.

Why do honest people actively overcome the defects in human nature and the temptation of selfish desires, and choose to be honest and trustworthy? Because dishonesty means to conceal the truth, consequently the owner may never be able to retrieve his/her belongings, perhaps that is what he/she needs to save his/her life. If so, it will cause others to be harmed or even fall into a very miserable situation. Loving people will never want to see that

寻找失主或是等待失主的到来，从而给人留下拾金不昧的宝贵品格，赢得别人的信任和尊重。

为什么诚实的人，会主动克服人性的缺陷和私欲的诱惑，而选择诚实守信呢？因为不诚实就意味着要隐瞒事实真相，失主或许就永远无法找回属于自己的财物，或许那正是他用来救命的东西。如果是这样的话，就会导致别人受到损害，甚至陷入非常悲惨的境地。心中有爱的人，绝不愿意看到，因为自己的言行而使他人利益受损、伤心痛苦，爱带来的良心和道义，会让他们选择诚实，不去欺骗伤害他人。

their own words and deeds make others suffer losses of interests, sadness and pain. The conscience and morality brought by love will make them choose to be honest and not deceive and harm others.

Loving People Are Just

What is the justice of human society, usually what people think is fair and just can be just. Fairness is the balance of the interests of social members, while justice means that in no cases shall any social member suffer discrimination and prejudice to their character and treatment. But fairness and justice are not equal to absolute average and equal quantity. Most people in modern society can accept fairness and justice in a substantial sense and oppose absolute egalitarianism.

A hardworking and simple but very poor mother is giving pancakes to hungry children. Although she herself is also very hungry, she is reluctant to let

有爱的人是公义的

何为人类社会的公义，通常人们认为公平正义的，就称得上公义。公平是社会成员的利益所得均衡，正义则是无论处于何种条件和环境之下，社会成员所受到的人格待遇都不会有歧视和偏见。但是公平正义并不等同于绝对平均和数量相等，现代社会大多数人们可以接受，实质意义上的公平正义，反对绝对化的平均主义。

一位勤劳朴实但却十分贫穷的母亲，正在烙饼给饥肠辘辘的孩子们吃。尽管她也很饿，但她舍不得让自己先吃，她要先在三个孩子当中分配这少的可

herself eat first. She had to first distribute the pitiful pancakes among the three children. The youngest kid is yet very little, and his body is developing. He looks short and weak and looks pitiful due to frequent hunger. Anyway, the mother can't bear to let him be hungry; the second child is usually the most obedient and sensible. He is the smartest of the three. His mother likes him very much and should get him full too; the eldest child often helps the mother to carry water, fetch and chop firewood, and do all kinds of housework at home, she should give him pancakes to get him full. But the pancakes made by the mother are not enough for all the three to eat. If to let one or two children eat, they can basically get full. But together with the mother, there are four in total who need food, it's far from enough and they can only share the food.

How should these pancakes be divided in a fair way? Is it fair to allocate the same size of

怜的烙饼。最小的孩子，年龄尚幼，身体正在发育，由于常常吃不饱肚子，显得矮小瘦弱，看起来让人怜惜。不管怎么说，妈妈都不忍心让他吃不饱；老二孩子平时最听话，也很懂事，是三个孩子当中最聪明的一个，很让妈妈喜欢，也应该让他吃饱；老大孩子经常帮助妈妈挑水、砍柴，平时家里的各样家务活，老大没有不帮妈妈去做的，这次的烙饼也应该让他吃饱。可是这位母亲能做出的烙饼，是不够三个孩子都吃饱的，如果让一个孩子或是两个孩子吃，他们还差不多能吃饱，可加上这位母亲一共有四个人要吃，就远远不够了，只能分着吃。

这些饼该怎样分才是公平的呢？每个人都分到一样大小的烙饼是公平的吗？不是，很显

pancake to each of them? No. Obviously the portion everyone needs differs. If to divide that way, possibly the youngest child can't finish it but the others don't have enough. It should be divided according to the actual situation of each child, and this will be fair and just. The youngest child, with the smallest appetite, should not take the biggest piece, but he is developing, cannot let him be hungry; The second child is smart and promising and should eat more; The eldest child often work and should eat more to get energy. According to their respective usual food intake and the number of pancakes, the mother allocates the pancakes to the three children. The youngest will not feel hungry and the eldest and the second feel still a little bit hungry after eating their pancakes. But there are no pancakes left for the mother herself to eat as she has distributed them all to the children. She will manage to use wild vegetables or otherwise to satisfy her hunger.

然每个人需要的份量都不一样，如果那样分，有可能是最小的孩子吃不完，其他的却不够吃。应该按照每个人的实际情况来分，才是公平正义的。小孩子食量小，不应拿最大块的，但他正在发育长身体，不应该让他饿肚子，老二聪慧有前途应该多吃，老大经常干活需要力气也要多吃，根据他们平时的食量和烙饼数量，母亲把饼分到三个孩子手中，最小的拿到的饼可以吃的感觉不饿，老大和老二吃完了各自的饼，仍有一点不够，但却不至于饿肚子。至于这位母亲自己呢，已经没有烙饼可吃了，因为她把它们全都分给了孩子们。她会去想办法，用野菜或是其他食物来充饥。

In such case, the mother's such deed embodies fairness and justice. The reason why she can do so is that she is a loving person. Her kindness allows her not only to appropriately satisfy each child's need to show fairness by balanced pancake distribution, but also she did not ignore any of them because of the differences among them. She did not treat her children differently because of the inability to help her with housework or lack of intelligence, doing so manifests justice. The reason why fairness and justice can still be manifested in such a poverty-stricken condition does not lie in whether the goods to be allocated is full or not but whether there is love in her. Only love that represents positive energy can bring people fairness and justice.

Loving People Are Diligent and Brave

When one has a feeling of love, he/she will often consider

在这样的情况下，这位母亲的做法就体现出了公平和正义，她之所以能做到这一点，就是因为她是一个充满爱的人，她的善良让她不仅适当地满足了每一个孩子的需要，均衡地分配烙饼显示出公平，并且她也没有因为三个孩子的不同，而忽略其中任何一个，她没有因为不能帮她做家务或不够聪慧等原因去差别化对待她的孩子，公义也因此显现。究其原因，如此窘迫，还能体现公平正义，不在于所分之物是否充盈，而在于是否有爱在身，只有代表正能量的爱才会给人们带来公平正义。

有爱的人是勤劳勇敢的

一个人拥有爱的感觉，心中便会常常顾及他人的利益和

the interests and feelings of others. They would rather ignore the benefits they deserve, hoping that their relatives and friends, and even strangers can live peacefully. Such people often have gratitude and joy in their hearts. They don't need very good things for their own use. As long as they have them, they will be satisfied. They will hardly compete with others because they are short of materials.

Such people often work tirelessly for the happiness of others in exchange for the materials necessary to make others and themselves happy. In order to let her son can learn useful knowledge and skills so that in the future he can create value and become self-reliant, and let her husband develop his with peace of mind so as to make life better and better, a mother gets up very early every day to cook for her son, send him to school, and then go home to clean the house, wash clothes, buy vegetables and cook,

感受，他们宁可忽略自己应得的好处，也希望身边的亲人朋友，甚至陌生人能够安然祥和。这样的人心中常常怀着感恩和喜乐，自己用的东西不需要很好，只要有他们便会满足，几乎不会因为物质匮乏而与人争夺计较。

这样的人为了他人的幸福快乐，常常不辞劳苦，终日劳作，以换取让他人和自己幸福快乐所必需的物资。一位母亲为了儿子能够学到有用的知识本领，将来可以创造价值，自强自立，为了丈夫能够安心开拓事业，让生活越来越好。每天都早早起床去给儿子做饭，送孩子去学校，然后回家打扫卫生，洗涤衣物，买菜做饭，整理家居。终日操劳受累，但她的心里却从未觉得苦、觉得累，反倒是常常在丈夫和儿子的努力进步之中感受到喜悦和甜蜜。因为她有爱，这种强大的能量使得

and tidy up the home furniture. She toils and all day long, but she never feels hard or tired in her heart. Instead, she often feels joy and sweetness from the hard work and progress of her husband and son. Due to the love in her heart, such powerful energy makes her feel happy for what she has paid for love and affection even if she works hard all day long.

For the sake of love, loving people often work painstakingly without regard to personal gains and losses and without complaints. Because in their view, they are worth it no matter how hard she works as long as people around them can be happy. Her son grows up healthily and happily, and her husband's career becomes prosperous, both can bring her comfort and rewards. Although many women are proud of wearing famous brands and paying attention to pomp, she still has the courage to walk on the street beside others without makeup and with simple clothes.

她即便是终日辛勤劳作，也不会觉得苦累，反而是为爱付出而感到幸福快乐。

有爱的人为了爱，常常不计个人得失，不辞劳苦地努力付出，且毫无怨言。因为在他们看来，只要身边的人能够幸福快乐，自己无论怎样辛苦都值得。儿子能够健康快乐地成长，丈夫事业蒸蒸日上，都能让她得到安慰和回报。尽管很多的女人们都以穿名牌、讲排场为荣，但她仍然有勇气素颜无状、衣着简朴地与别人一同走在大街上。她不会在意眼下生活的拮据和紧张，她的心中有爱带给她的憧憬和希望，不会因为一时的物质匮乏而抛弃信心、丢掉爱。她身上的爱让她变得勇敢而坚强，不再畏惧世俗的偏见，敢于为了爱坚持去做心

She will not care about the current financial difficulties in life, she owns the longing and hope in her heart that love brings her, and will not abandon her faith and love due to temporary material shortage. The love in her makes her brave and strong, no longer afraid of worldly prejudices, dare to persist in doing what she deems right for love, dare to guard the happiness of the loved ones of her for love, and dare to defend the affection and love that she has already owned. These are all precious gifts brought by the love that she believes in to her. It is love that makes her hardworking and brave and work hard with her dedication and courage in exchange for happiness.

Loving People Are Modest and Obedient to Rules

There is a narrative in the Bible about Cain and Abel. They both were Adam's children. Cain

里认为正确的事情，敢于为了爱去坚守所爱之人的幸福快乐，敢于捍卫已经拥有的亲情与爱情。这些都是她相信的爱，带给她的宝贵礼物，是爱让她勤劳勇敢，用自己的付出和勇气去努力换取幸福快乐。

有爱的人是谦逊守规则的

圣经当中有一段叙述，是关于该隐和亚伯的故事，他们是亚当的两个孩子，该隐是大

is elder while Abel is younger. Whenever Cain offered sacrifices to God, he was always jealous. Because he felt that God was not pleased with his sacrifices but Abel's sacrifices. So in a conflict with Abel, Cain's jealousy turned into hatred, and killed his younger brother. To punish Cain, God expelled him from the Garden of Eden. [1]

Judging from the biblical records, it is the first murder in human history that Cain killed Abel. Abel did not make a mistake, he caused his elder brother to be jealous simply because his sacrifice made God more pleased and finally caused to himself a scourge. What Cain did made people see the defect or evil in human nature --- one can't see that others are better than himself/herself. If others are better than himself/herself, he/she will

的，亚伯是小的。每逢给上帝献祭，该隐总是心生妒嫉，因为他觉得上帝并不喜悦他的祭物，亚伯的祭物更让上帝欢喜。于是在一次和亚伯的冲突之中，该隐心中的嫉妒变为仇恨，将自己的弟弟杀害，上帝为了惩罚该隐，便将他逐出伊甸园。

从圣经的记载来看，该隐杀死亚伯算得上人类历史上第一起凶杀案，亚伯并未犯错，只不过他的祭物更让上帝喜悦，便召来了哥哥的嫉妒，最终酿成杀身之祸。该隐的所作所为让人们看到了人性的缺陷，或者说是人性之恶——见不得别人的状况比自己好，如果别人的好过自己的，人的心中便会难过，这种反应人人都会有，只是程度有所差异。但拥有不同信仰的人在这种反应之后，会有不同的表现和作为。相信正

[1] *Bible*, National Committee of Three-Self Patriotic Movement of the Protestant Churches in China (National TSPM), China Christian Council (CCC), 2009 edition, (Genesis 4:14, 4:16) p.4.

《圣经》，中国基督教三自爱国运动委员会、中国基督教协会 2009 年版，（创 4: 14, 4: 16）第 4 页。

feel sad. This is a reaction that everyone has; simply the degree of sadness differs. But people with different beliefs will behave and act differently after such reaction. Those who believe in positive energy regard such difference as the motivation and pressure for their advancement and struggle, and alleviate the sadness in their hearts with their own efforts because they have love in their heart and are unwilling to hate others. Such person often gives others a feeling of modesty, that is, he/she will make his/her words and deeds seem inferior to those of others. A modest person often talks about others' goodness and try not to accuse others of their badness. But they admit about their own defects although sometimes it is not the case. But their attitude is just not to hurt the self-esteem of others, not making others feel sad due to his/her own superiority. In order not to make others feel unhappy and hurt, a loving person choose not to show off or show

能量的人们，因为有爱，不愿意去仇恨他人，便将这种差异视为自己前进奋斗的动力和压力，用自己的努力来缓解冲淡心中的难过。这样的人往往给他人谦逊的感觉，就是他（她）的言行会表现地让别人觉得不如自己的，谦逊的人常说别人的好，尽量避免指责别人的不好，但却坦诚自己的不足，尽管有时事实上并非如此。但他们的态度，只是为了不伤害他人的自尊，不让他人因为自己的优越而心生难过。为了不让他人感到不悦和受到伤害，有爱的人选择不张扬、不炫耀，从不说自己的才是最好的。尽管他们的初衷是为了不伤害他人，但也正是这种方式使得谦逊的人因此而避开喜欢妒嫉之人的仇恨，是爱让他们轻松躲开了人性之恶的攻击。

off, and never say that he/she is the best. Although their original intention is not to hurt others, it is precisely in this way that makes modest people avoid the hatred from people who like jealousy. It is love that allows them to easily escape from the attacks of the evil in human nature.

A remarkable feature of loving people is that they are unwilling to make others sad, let alone to hurt the spirit or body of others. Due to the inherent defects of humans' original rights, when one claims all his/her desires, that is, when he/she wants to realize all his/her original rights, he will inevitably infringe the legitimate rights and interests of others. For stable order of human society, and to make the legitimate rights of every social member effectively secured, people who gather together for production and life exercise self-restraint by transferring some of their unreasonable original rights, and give up unreasonable

有爱的人，很大的一个特征就是不愿意让别人难过，更不愿意去伤害他人的心灵或是肉体。由于人的原始权利具有先天的缺陷，当一个人主张自己所有的欲望要求时，也就是自己的全部原始权利都要实现时，就不可避免地要侵害他人的正当权益。为了人类社会的秩序稳定，让每一位社会成员的正当权利都能得到有效保障，汇聚在一起生产生活的人们便通过让渡部分不合理原始权利的方式，进行自我约束，主动放弃不合理的原始权利，以避免自己的不当欲望和要求侵害他人权益，破坏社会秩序。社会成员进行自我约束的具体方法，便是用某种方式制定大家都需遵守的契约规则，比如不

original rights lest their own improper desires and needs from infringing the rights and interests of others and disrupting social order. A specific way for social members to exercise self-restraint is to formulate contract rules that everyone must obey in some way, e.g. not allowing theft, murder, rape, etc. Such behaviors will seriously hurt the legitimate rights and interests of social members. It is exactly because the perpetrator of such behaviors cause harm to others due to the exercise of his/her own barbaric and improper original rights that social members shall restrain or prohibit such behaviors or incidents. With rules available, loving people will firmly support such contract rules. Because such rules can better protect the interests of social members against infringement --- this goal is also what loving people pursue unremittingly. So, loving people like a contractual society with rules and order. They reject a jungle society where they

许偷盗、杀人、强奸等等。这些行为都会深深伤害社会成员的正当权益，而行为的实施者正是因为行使了自己野蛮不正当的原始权利而给他人带来伤害，所以社会成员要用规则来约束或禁止这些行为事件的发生。有了规则以后，有爱的人们会坚定地拥护这些契约规则，因为这样的规则可以更好地保护社会成员的利益不受侵害，而这一目标也是有爱之人所不懈追求的。因此，有爱的人喜欢有规则秩序的契约社会，排斥各行其是、肆意妄为的丛林社会，为了不伤害他人，保护自身正当权益，他们也会成为最愿意遵守规则契约的一群人。

do whatever they want in their own way. In order not to harm others and protect their legitimate rights and interests, they will also become a group of people who are most willing to obey the rules and contracts.

Loving People Are Often Touched by Love

Loving people often feel that they are full of positive energy, and that they are surrounded by people and things that are good to them. In the trivial of daily life, loving people can always discover the precious qualities and goodness of humans. When they truly feel the love and warmth brought to them by positive energy, they will actively get themselves affected and touched very naturally --- such feeling of being touched by positive energy is called "moving" or "touching", which will make people pure, willing to dedicate, and unhesitating.

Such touching will happen

有爱的人常常因爱 而感动

有爱的人，心中时常感到自己被正能量充盈，觉得周围都是对自己好的人和事。在日常生活的细碎点滴当中，有爱的人总可以发现人类的可贵品质和善意好处，当他们真的感受到正能量带给他们的爱意和温暖时，会极其自然地被影响和触动——这种被正能量影响触动的感觉就叫做"感动"，"感动"会让人变得纯粹、情愿付出、义无反顾。

这种感动会发生在，被他

when being helped by others, when seeing the true love in human nature, when the wicked becomes conscientious, and when everyone jointly try their best to guard love together. . . In many occasions, people can be moved. The reason, through analysis, may be that the positive energy in the touched person meets stronger positive energy of the same kind and then interact with each other to form resonance, and finally get people moved. According to such what-if analysis, it can be said that the reason why humans are touched is that the positive energy that people believe in is at work.

Loving people are often touched by love. One's moving is usually manifested as an inner touch. If such touch goes very deep, it will trigger a physiological reaction --- people's eyes will shed tears when being touched. However, people will also shed tears due to pain when they are hurt and feel painful. Such tears can indirectly prove that there is

人帮助之时；会发生在看到人性真爱之时；会发生在恶人良心发现之时；会发生在众人齐心协力为爱坚守之时…在很多的时间场合，人们都可以被感动，分析其中的原因很有可能是被感动者自己身上的正能量遇到了与其一样的更强大的正能量，彼此互相作用，形成共鸣，最后让人感动。按照这样的假设分析，我们也可以说，人类之所以会被感动，就是因为人们信奉的正能量在发挥作用的缘故。

有爱的人常常因爱而感动，一个人的感动通常表现为一种内在的触动，如果这种触动很深，就会引发生理上的反应——人们的眼睛会因为感动流出泪水。不过在人们受到伤害，感到痛苦的时侯，也会因为痛苦留下眼泪。这些泪水可以间接证明，人类的身上有我们看不到但却可以感知到的能量驻留。当这种能量被来自外部的正能

invisible but perceivable energy in humans. When such energy is filled and strengthened by external positive energy, we will be touched in some way. Also, when such energy is weakened or destroyed by external force, we will be shocked. In the former, we are moved to tears as we feel a stronger positive energy, and which will make us feel full of strength. In the latter, we are shocked by weakening and destruction of the positive energy in us and shed tears nervously, fearfully and painfully. In such case, if we cannot be linked to stronger positive energy that we need to strengthen our belief, the original positive energy in us may leave due to the wavering of our beliefs. When positive energy leaves, we will be affected or even controlled by negative energy. If there is no stronger positive energy to expel such negative energy, one will no longer be touched after he/she is controlled by negative energy.

量充盈、加强的时候，我们会有某种方式的触动，当这种能量被来自外部的作用力破坏、削弱的时候，我们也会被触动。在前一种情况下，我们因为感受到了更强大的正能量而感动地流泪，并且这种正能量也会让我们充满力量感。在后一种情况下，我们因为身上的正能量遭到破坏削弱而触动，会紧张、恐惧而痛苦地流泪，这时如果我们无法连接到我们需要的更强大的正能量，来坚固自己的信仰，我们身上原有的正能量，就有可能因为我们信念的动摇而离开，正能量离开之时我们会被负能量影响，甚至是控制。一个人被负能量控制以后，如果没有更强大的正能量来驱走这些负能量，他（她）便不再会有感动。

Loveless People Often Fear

Due to the inherent defects of humans, people will infringe or harm the legitimate rights and interests of others if they speak and act at will following their own instincts and desires. If human life comprised only the body, humans may never be aware that their words and deeds will easily infringe the legitimate rights and interests of others; humans will think that it's just to satisfy their own desires and needs, never need to feel guilty.

But strangely, most humans have a keen sense to right and wrong as well as kind and evil. People usually have a self-judgment as to whether what they said or did is right or wrong. Human desires are endless, and correspondingly it becomes endless to satisfy oneself. However, most people will delimit a boundary for themselves in

无爱的人常常恐惧

人类由于先天的缺陷，如果顺着自己的本能欲望随意说话行事，多数情况下都会侵犯或者伤害到他人的正当权益。假如人的生命只有肉体构成，可能人类永远不会觉察到自己的言行会轻易侵犯他人的正当权益，人类会认为满足自己的欲望需求是天经地义的，永远无需愧疚。

但奇怪的是，绝大多数人类对是非善恶都有着敏锐的感觉，自己说过的话，做过的事，人们通常都有是非对错的自我评判。人的欲望是无穷尽的，满足自己也因此而变得漫无止境，可是往往大多数人在满足无穷尽的欲望过程中都能给自己划定一个边界，这是什么原因造成的呢？是因为每个人的身上都有一个"印记"，这个"印

satisfying their endless desires. What caused them to do so? It's because everyone has a "mark" in their body, and which is what people often call "conscience". Conscience will directly let one know whether his/her words and deeds are correct or not. To simplify, those which violate their conscience are wrong, while those which obey their conscience are right. Many words and deeds can satisfy your desires and claims. But your conscience tells you that you cannot do that. In such case, if one goes against his conscience to satisfy his/her own desires, he/she will feel uneasy and condemned by his conscience.

Where does the conscience that affects one so much come from? Currently it cannot be explained with human technology. But with human intuition, we can perceive that conscience is like the "law" from an unknown field, which tells you what is right, what you can do, and what you can't. One will make people

记"就是人们常说的良心。良心会很直接地让一个人明白自己的言行是否正确，简单的讲，就是违背良心的是错的，顺从良心的才是正确。很多言行能够满足你的欲望要求，但良心告诉你不可以那样做，此时如果一个人违背良心去满足私欲，那么他（她）就会感到不安和来自良心的谴责。

对于一个人影响如此之大的良心究竟是从哪里来的？目前的人类科技还无法解释。但是凭借人的直觉，我们可以感知到，良心就像是来自某个未知领域的"律法"，这部"律法"告诉你什么是对的，可以去做，什么不可以。顺服遵从自己的良心，会让人最终获得正能量，觉得积极向上充满力量，会有

gain positive energy eventually, feel positive and full of strength and feel love if he/she obeys and follows his/her conscience. Conversely, if you violate your conscience, the positive energy will leave you. Negative energy will take advantage of the emptiness to make you gradually ignore your conscience, discard the moral rules, and do whatever you want. As a result, your desires are unrestrainedly satisfied, but you can't feel happy at all. Because positive energy that can make people feel love quietly leaves due to violation of your conscience, and only love can make people happy. Betrayal to conscience can only make people often fall into deep fear because of wrong doings. Such fear is that he/she feels fearful and worried about his/her future due to failure to obtain the happiness needed for human nature as a consequence of clear perception of absence of love, and it is also an effect caused to humans by negative energy in

爱的感觉。相反，如若违背良心，正能量便会离你而去，另外一种负向的能量会乘虚而入，慢慢让你漠视良心，丢弃道义规则，为所欲为。这样做的结果是你的欲望被无节制地满足，却丝毫感觉不到幸福，因为违背良心使得能让人感到爱的正能量悄然离开，而只有爱才能让人们幸福。对良心的背弃只能让人常常因为做错事的缘故陷入深深地恐惧当中，这种恐惧是因为一个人明确感知到因为没有爱，而无法获得人性必需的幸福，进而对自己的未来感到害怕担忧，这也是这个时空当中负向能量给人类带来的作用和影响——让人恐惧。

the space-time --- making people fearful

Loveless People Often Have Hatred

Loveless people are not only accessible to happiness, but will also be full of hostility and blasphemy towards people and things around them due to their inner fear. They simply think that their fears, unhappiness, and pain are from others and what are happening around them. Such thought and concept will cause them to generate hatred. The specific manifestation of hatred is wanting to destroy and hurt, and to make those they hate destroyed or painful. Only in this way can people who hate others get balanced in their hearts. It's only slightly better than nowhere to vent hatred. They still have no chance to be happy. People full of hatred will fall deeply into pain, and the deeper they infringe and hurt others, the deeper and longer

无爱的人常有仇恨

无爱的人不仅无缘幸福快乐，而且由于内在的恐惧，会使得他们对于自己周围的人和事充满了敌意和亵渎。他们会简单地认为自己的恐惧、不快乐和痛苦，正是来自他人和身边发生的事。这样的想法和观念，会让他们出现仇恨的念头，仇恨的具体表现就是想要破坏和伤害，要让他们仇恨的目标对象被摧毁或是痛苦难受。只有这样，仇恨他人的人心里才能得到平衡，但仅仅是平衡，只比仇恨无法宣泄时稍稍好受些，仍然无缘快乐幸福，充满仇恨的人会深深地陷入痛苦当中，并且侵犯伤害他人的程度越深，他们的痛苦也会越深越持久。

their pain will be.

What caused this? Tit-for-tat seems fair in terms of the form. But why are they still painful after retaliation? It is the strong belief in hatred and harm that causes positive energy featuring with love leaves people, and which is the source of human pan. When positive energy leaves a person, he/she will usually not feel something. But those around him/her can feel the obvious change before and after positive energy leaves. The departure of positive energy means the entry of negative energy. Because human life needs such energy to subsist, or we can vividly say that an angel and a devil both can provide humans with energy. If you don't believe in positive energy, or if you don't believe in love, love will leave you and be replaced by negative energy representing the devils. Hatred and hurt are their main features and functioning ways. If love and happiness are feelings brought by positive energy to

这是什么原因造成的呢？以血还血，以牙还牙，从形式上看公平了，可为什么报仇雪恨之后，仍然很痛苦呢。是因为仇恨和伤害的强烈信念，使得以爱为特征的正向能量离开了人们，正能量的离去，才是人类痛苦的根源。当正能量离开一个人的时候，通常不会有太大的自我感受，但这个人身边的人却能感觉到他（她）在正能量离开前后的明显变化。正能量的离开意味着负能量的进驻，因为人的生命需要这样的能量维持，或者我们可以形象的说，天使和魔鬼都可以给人类提供能量。假如你不相信正能量，或者说你不相信爱，爱便会离你而去，取而代之的就是代表魔鬼的负能量，仇恨和伤害是他们的主要特征和作为方式。如果说爱和幸福快乐是正能量带给人们的感觉，那么仇恨和伤害便是负能量施加给人类的最大作用力。如何留住正能量，避免负能量的侵袭，对于所有信奉爱与正能量的人们十分重要。只有心中相信爱，顺从正

people, hatred and hurt are the greatest acting force imposed on humans by negative energy. How to keep positive energy and avoid the invasion of negative energy is very important for all people who believe in love and positive energy. Only by believing in love in the heart, following the implication and guidance given by positive energy via conscience, and always guarding the conscience can one protect the positive energy in his/her body, continuously improve his/her energy level, and then dispel the interference and invasion of negative energy, and help others to drive away the negative energy in their body even when the positive energy in a person is strong enough. Otherwise, once one loses belief in love and hence ignores his/her conscience, positive energy will leave. In such case, negative energy will take advantage of the emptiness to come in. As a result, various changes will happen in them. Emotional changes will

能量透过良心给人的默示指引，并时刻坚守自己的良心，才能保护身上的正能量，不断提高自己的能量等级，进而驱散负能量的干扰侵袭，甚至于在一个人身上的正能量足够强大时，去帮助别人赶走身上的负能量。否则，一旦一个人失去对爱的信仰，进而漠视自己的良心，正能量就会离开，这时负能量很快趁虚而入，各种变化也会出现在他们的身上，情绪方面的变化会较早出现，而后随着负能量对一个人影响程度的加强，仇恨、伤害、破坏、暴力攻击便会在他（她）的身上接连发生，直至这个人最后被负能量完全控制（意味着这个人身上的正能量全部离开）。这时负能量会极力通过仇恨、伤害或破坏来扩大其影响力，并试图动摇身边人对爱的信仰，以求赶走他们身上的正能量，让更多的人和他们一样去仇恨身边的人和这个世界。

come first, and then, as negative energy affects a person more, hatred, hurt, destruction, and violent attacks will happen one after another on him/her, until he/she is finally totally controlled by negative energy (it implies that all the positive energy in the person has left). In such case, the negative energy will try to expand its influence through hatred, harm or destruction, and try to shake the belief in love of the people around them so as to expel the positive energy in them, making more people hate the people around them and this world like them.

Loveless People Often Hurt and Destroy

When one's heart is full of hatred, he/she has been affected or even completely controlled by negative energy. The mark left by positive energy on his/her body --- conscience no longer works. Such person will not feel guilty because his words and deeds violate his/her

无爱的人常常伤害和破坏

当一个人心中充满仇恨的时候，这个人已经被负能量影响甚至是完全控制了。正能量在他（她）身上留下的印记——良心已经不起作用，这样的人不会因为言行违背自己的良心而愧疚，因为受到负能量的影响，他（她）不再相信正能量，

conscience. Due to the influence of negative energy, he/she no longer believes in positive energy, no longer follow the guidance of love and the restraint of conscience, he/she no longer judges what he/she has done according to the law from positive energy - conscience. Because of the control of negative energy, only by continuing to do evil can he/she temporarily numb the pain in his heart, and only by deceiving himself/herself can he/she forget his/her desire for human happiness.

Why only by doing evil can people who are controlled by negative energy temporarily feel less painful. The root cause should come from human defects --- jealousy. The first murder in human history recorded in the Bible --- Cain killed his younger brother --- is the best interpretation of the ugliness of human nature. Jealousy is a mentality and habit of "Don't expect to get what I cannot get". Loving people, or people who are full of positive energy

不再遵循爱的指引和良心的约束，他（她）不再依照来自正能量的律法——良心，去对自己的所作所为进行评判。因为受到负能量的控制，他（她）唯有继续作恶，才能暂时麻痹心中的痛苦，靠欺骗自己才能淡忘对人类幸福快乐的渴望。

为什么只有作恶，才能使受负能量控制的人们暂时感到不那么痛苦和难过。其根源应是来自人类的缺陷——嫉妒，圣经中记载人类历史上的第一桩谋杀案——该隐诛弟，便是对人性这一丑陋的最好诠释，嫉妒就是一种我得不到的，你也别想得到的心态和习惯。有爱的人，或者叫充满正能量的人们，可以凭借正能量之爱，去努力克服自身这种自私恐怖的缺陷，进而知足常乐，益己益人。但受到负能量影响控制的

can try hard to overcome their own selfish and terrifying defects relying on the love of positive energy so as to be happy due to contentment and benefit both themselves and others. But those who are affected and controlled by negative energy will not be able to face the torture of human defect. They will have no chance to be happy due to lack of nourishment of love. Because only love can make people happy, and positive energy is love. And the departure of positive energy can only make humans who yearn for happiness in their hearts become painful and desperate. Because they can't get the happiness that humans want most and can't see hope, their jealousy will soon sprout, subsequently they will commit harms and destructions --- negative energy makes them feel that no one can get what they cannot get. Harm and destruction allow them to numb and deceive themselves. Negative energy makes them mistakenly believe that there is

人们，会无法面对人性缺陷的折磨，他们由于缺乏爱的滋养，而无缘幸福快乐。因为唯有爱才能使人幸福，正能量就是爱，正能量的离开，只能使骨子里渴慕幸福的人类变得痛苦和绝望。由于得不到人类最想要的幸福快乐，并且也看不到希望，他们的嫉妒之心很快萌生，伤害和破坏会紧随其后——负能量使他们觉得，他们得不到的，没有人可以得到。伤害和破坏使他们可以麻痹和欺骗自己，负能量使他们错误地以为，这个世界上原本就没有幸福快乐，没有真诚，也没有善良，每个人都和他们一样充满邪恶的负能量。负能量会使受其控制的人们，用粗鲁和暴力狠狠地伤害那些真诚善良之人，破坏他们的心爱之物或正当财产，用肉体或是短暂的心灵痛苦迫使相信正能量的人们就范，逼迫他们放弃对自己良心的遵从和爱的信仰，折磨他们，并企图让相信正能量的人们最终变得和他们一样残忍暴力。

no happiness, no sincerity, and no kindness in this world originally. Everyone is full of evil negative energy, just like they are. Negative energy will make those under its control rudely and violently hurt those who are sincere and kind, destroy their beloved things or legitimate properties, and force those who believe in positive energy into submission with body or temporary mental pain. Forcing them to give up their obeyance to their conscience and their belief in love. Tormenting them and trying to make those who believe in positive energy finally become as brutal and violent as they are.

Only through continual harm and destruction can the scene expected by people affected and controlled by negative energy appear for a short time, but it cannot last for a long time. Because happiness is taken as the ultimate goal of the pursuit in spite of defects in human nature. In other words, human nature is inherently evil, but it is beautiful

负能量影响控制的人们所期望发生的景象，只有通过他们不断地伤害破坏才会短时间出现，但却不能长久存在下去。因为人性虽有缺陷，但却以追求幸福快乐为终极目标，换句话说，人性本恶，却以向善为美，向善即是遵守良心，顺从爱的指引。即便一个人一时会被蒙蔽，但人性的终极需求（对幸福快乐的需求）会最终迫使

to be good. To be good is to obey conscience and follow the guidance of love. Although one may be blinded for some time, the ultimate needs in human nature (the need for happiness) will eventually force him/her to wake up and return to the embrace of positive energy under the inspiration of love.

Positive Energy That Can't "Defeat" Negative Energy

Positive energy that can bring people love can make people feel happy --- an unchanging pursuit of mankind for thousands of years. Human nature determines that we will suffer pain if we cannot be happy. Pain will make people become hateful. And hatred will cause harm and destruction, and then cause more people to fall into pain. As a result, there will be continual hatred, killings, harms and destructions, and people will fall into a vicious circle of revenge

其惊醒，并在爱的感召下重回正能量的怀抱。

无法"战胜"负能量的正能量

能够给人爱的正能量，可以让人们感受到幸福快乐——一种人类几千年来亘古不变的追求。人类的本性决定，如果我们不能幸福快乐，就会痛苦难受。痛苦会让人心生仇恨，仇恨会带来伤害和破坏，进而让更多的人陷入痛苦，仇恨、杀戮和伤害破坏会因此连绵不断，冤冤相报无了时。并且最可怕的结局是，杀戮和破坏会让越来越多的人失去对正能量的信心，不再信守来自正能量的律法——良心，不再听从爱的感

for grievance. And, the most terrible ending is that, killings and destructions will make more and more people lose faith in positive energy. They will no longer obey the law from positive energy --- conscience, no longer obey the inspiration and guidance of love, finally forcing positive energy to leave from more and more people who violate their conscience.

Something truly terrifying to a person will happen after positive energy has completely left. He/she will soon be affected and controlled by negative energy. Because human life needs energy from the unknown world to subsist. And such energy can be divided into positive and negative, yin and yang (note: the two opposing principles in nature in Chinese philosophy, the former feminine and negative, the latter masculine and positive), or Satan and angel. Such energy is the source power to maintain human life. And the lives controlled by negative energy, as described

召和指引，最终迫使正能量离开越来越多的违背良心的人。

对于一个人真正恐怖的事情，会发生在正能量完全离开之后。他（她）会很快被负能量影响控制，因为人的生命需要来自未知世界的能量维持，而这些能量可以区分标记分为正负、阴阳或是撒旦和天使。这些能量是维系人类生命的源动力，负能量控制的生命，如上面所述带有恐惧、仇恨、伤害破坏的特征，且只能通过连续不断地伤害破坏，才能麻痹缓解其内在的痛苦。一个人的生命完全陷入负能量的控制，也就意味着陷入了万劫不复的境地，被负能量控制的人们，除了仇恨伤害、暴力破坏之外，没有其他的方式可以减轻他们的痛

above, have the features e.g. fear, hatred, harm and destruction. And, only through continual harms and destructions can their inner pain be numbed and relieved. If one's life is completely controlled by negative energy, it implies that he/she has fallen into a situation of everlasting perdition. People controlled by negative energy have no other means to alleviate their pains except hatred and violent destruction. Because the departure of positive energy makes them unable to obtain happiness. The defects in human nature and the despair in their heart determine that only by continual hurt and destructions can their pain be relieved.

When positive energy encounters negative energy, that is, after a person controlled by positive energy interacts with another person full of negative energy, generally, due to the features of negative energy e.g. hatred, harm, destruction, violence, etc., people who

苦。因为正能量的离开使得他们无法得到幸福快乐，人性的缺陷和内心的绝望决定他们只能不断地伤害破坏才能缓解自己的痛苦。

当正能量遭遇负能量之后，也就是被正能量控制的人与充满负能量的人交往之后，通常情况下，由于负能量的仇恨、伤害破坏、暴力等特征，使得原本拥有正能量的人会无法承受抵御来自负能量的攻击。这个时候，不再遵守良心的约束指引，以牙还牙式的反击会是多数人的

originally owned positive energy will be unable to withstand attacks from negative energy. In such case, no longer obeying the restraints of conscience and tit-for-tat counterattack will be the choice of most people. Because they believe that only in this way can they effectively protect their legitimate rights and interests. But the problem is that, after a person with positive energy does so, positive energy will leave him/her due to violation to his/her conscience. So, the momentary pleasure brought by their violation of conscience is also likely to cause to themselves regret and hopelessness to happiness. From then on, they will be destined to become people the same as those who hated and hurt them as they also violated the law from positive energy --- conscience, just like those ones did. The biggest purpose of negative energy is to expel positive energy of human beliefs. The way is quite simple, that is, to irritate humans by

选择，因为他们认为只有这样，才可以有效地保护他们的正当权益。但问题是，当拥有正能量的人这样做之后，由于违背了良心，正能量却会离他（她）而去。因此他们违背良心所带来的一时痛快，也很有可能给自己带来悔恨和对幸福的无望。从那一刻起，便注定了他们最终要变成和仇恨伤害他们的那些人一样的人，因为他们同那些人一样违背了来自正能量的律法——良心。负能量最大的目的，就是赶走人类信仰的正能量，方法很简单，那就是通过伤害破坏来激怒人类，让他们失去理智，漠视良心，嫉妒仇恨，为所欲为。当一个人违背良心且不知悔改，或者根本不认同良心的时候，正能量在人的身上便无法驻留，只能选择离开。

hurting and destroying them to make them lose their senses, ignore their conscience, be jealous and hateful, and do whatever they want. When one violates his/her conscience and does not repent, or does not agree with his/her conscience at all, positive energy cannot stay in him/her and has to leave.

Only some people who are completely controlled by positive energy can resist the provocations and attacks from negative energy. The reason for this is not that such people are more vicious than those who are full of negative energy, but that they can tolerate and forgive appropriately. They are able to counterattack and refuse properly, neither violating their conscience nor allowing negative energy to succeed. However, due to the defects in human nature, the mankind is easily to fall into hatred and violence. Almost all humans will easily lose their minds, and counterattack opponents with anger, hatred and the same

只有一些完全被正能量控制的人,才可以抵御来自负能量的挑衅和攻击。之所以会这样,并不是由于这样的人比充满负能量之人更加狠毒,而是他们可以恰到好处地忍让包容,做到适当地反击和拒绝,既不违背良心,也不让负能量得逞。不过由于人性的缺陷,人类会很容易陷入仇恨和暴力之中,几乎所有的人类在受到伤害攻击或是深爱之人受到伤害的时候,都会轻易失去理智,并采取愤怒、仇恨和同样的暴力去反击对手。如果这个时候,一个人没有把握好反击的尺度,就很容易违背自己的良心。一旦最后他(她)由于仇恨抛弃了自己的良心,那么负能量就会宣

violence when they or their loved ones are hurt or attacked. In such case, if one does not well control his/her counterattack, he/she will easily violate his/her conscience. Once he/she abandons his/her conscience in the end due to hatred, negative energy will declare "victory". Because from then on positive energy will be forced to leave him/her as he/she chooses to believe in hatred and harm and abandon his/her conscience.

A War Similar to "Resident Evil"

There is a saying in the Bible: "and if you do wrong, sin is waiting at the door." (Genesis 4:7) [1] It means that believers should always keep vigilant and sober, and don't fall into the trap of tricks of the devil, Satan, because of being deceived. The contest

告 "得胜"，因为从那时起，由于这样的人选择了相信仇恨和伤害，选择了抛弃良心，就会迫使正能量离开他们。

一场类似 "生化危机" 的战争

圣经中有这样一句话：你若行得不好，罪就伏在门前。意思是让信徒们要时刻保持警惕和清醒，不要因为受迷惑而跌入魔鬼撒旦的诡计陷阱之中。上帝与魔鬼之间的较量，是一场无声但却会改变一切的战争，是决定人类命运和未来的战争，

---

[1] *Bible*, National Committee of Three-Self Patriotic Movement of the Protestant Churches in China (National TSPM), China Christian Council (CCC), 2009 edition, (Genesis 4:7), p.4.

《圣经》，中国基督教三自爱国运动委员会、中国基督教协会 2009 年版，（创 4：7）第 4 页。

between God and the devil is a war that is silent but will change everything, a war that determines the fate and future of mankind, and a war similar to "Resident Evil" (or "Biohazard"). "Resident Evil" is a product of human intelligence, it's a computer game. In the scenario of this game, humans have to fight against terrifying and powerful monsters. What's the most terrifying about these monsters is not that their vitality is so powerful that human weapons cannot eliminate them easily, but that humans cannot withstand their attacks, even if a tap. In that scenario, whoever of the humans injured or even just tapped by a monster will immediately become a monster too, and accordingly become an enemy of the mankind --- this is an awfully terrifying consequence. If humans want to keep themselves safe, there is only one way --- to keep distance from the monsters and eliminate them with a weapon before they touch us.

A game scenario originally simulated by humans can

也是一场类似"生化危机"的战争。"生化危机"是人类智能的产物，是一个电脑游戏。在这个游戏场景之中，人类要同恐怖强大的怪物搏斗。这些怪物最恐怖之处，并不是它们的生命力强大，人类的武器不能轻易将其消灭，而是人类无法承受它们的攻击，哪怕是轻轻一击。在那个场景当中，凡是有人类被怪物击伤，甚至是轻轻碰触到，可怕的结果就会发生——这个被怪物伤害或碰触过的人就会立即变成怪物，变成人类的敌人。人类如果想要保护自己的安全，方法只有一个，那就是和怪物保持距离，并在它碰触自己之前就用武器将其消灭。

人类原本无心模拟出的一个游戏场景，却可以用来形象

inadvertently be used to vividly describe the relationship between humans and unknown forces. We still adopt the what-if analysis, assuming that those who are controlled by positive energy are humans, while those who are instigated and commanded by negative energy have become "monsters". In other words, those who believe in God, Allah, Buddha, etc. and take love as their mission and pursuit are humans, while those who believe in the devil Satan[1] featuring with hatred and violence are "monsters". When the two forces conflict, as described in the previous section, not only can positive energy not directly make negative energy yield, but also cause those who originally believed in the positive energy to be hurt, and then make hatred ignited in their hearts for

地描述人与未知力量之间的关系。我们还是使用假设分析的方法，假定受正能量控制的是人类，而被负能量唆使指挥的人已变成"怪物"。或者说相信上帝、真主、佛祖等以爱为使命和追求的是人类，而相信魔鬼撒但以仇恨暴力伤害为特征的是"怪物"。当这两方的力量发生冲突时，正如上节所描述的那样，正能量不仅无法直接让负能量屈服，还可能由于和负能量靠的太近，使得原本相信正能量的人们受到伤害，进而使他们的心灵因被蛊惑而燃起仇恨，并最终选择和对手一样去伤害杀戮。这时他们的对手很有可能被仇恨的力量摧毁，但结果却仍然是负能量获得了胜利。因为在一个人相信仇恨和暴力可以保护自己的时候，正能量也会无法再和他（她）相处。当正能量完全离开以后，这样的人就成了"怪物"，因为他们

---

[1] Bible, National Committee of Three-Self Patriotic Movement of the Protestant Churches in China (National TSPM), China Christian Council (CCC), 2009 edition, (Revelation 12:9) p.284.

《圣经》，中国基督教三自爱国运动委员会、中国基督教协会 2009 年版，（启 12：9）第 284 页。

being bewitched, and finally choose to hurt and kill like their opponents do as a consequence of being too close to negative energy. In such case, their opponents are likely to be destroyed by the force of hatred. But the result is still that negative energy wins. Because when one believes that hatred and violence can protect himself/herself, positive energy can no longer get along with him/her. When positive energy has completely left, such people will become "monsters" because their hearts will be full of hatred, and they will relieve their pain by hurting and destroying. As demonstrated in the game, one should not get too close to a "monster" controlled by negative energy; otherwise he/she will become hateful in the heart when being attacked, ignore conscience, and gradually lose belief in positive energy. After positive energy leaves, he/she will soon mutate into a "monster".

According to the above

的心中会充满仇恨, 并且他们还会通过伤害破坏来减轻自己的痛苦。正如游戏中演示的那样, 人不应和受负能量控制的"怪物"靠的太近, 否则他 (她) 就会因为受到攻击而心生仇恨, 漠视良心, 并逐渐失去对正能量的信仰, 正能量离开以后, 这个人便会很快变异为"怪物"。

依据上面的假定分析, 我

what-if analysis, only by keeping distance from negative energy with the belief of love --- we would rather suffer its harm than be infected with the fire of hatred --- can we humans retain the positive energy in ourselves, can we become a loving person, and a person who can be happy. As for how to avoid the invasion of negative energy, positive energy will send guidance and revelation to people somewhere far away from negative energy. We only need to often ask the conscience that is imprinted in our bodies by positive energy. So, people do not need to be afraid of powerful and terrifying negative energy and the "monsters" controlled by it. To be happy and not hurt, we only need to believe in positive energy and persistently guard our conscience.

Remain Conscientious & Believe in Love

Loving people all regard positive energy as their authority.

们人类唯有用爱的信仰保持同负能量的距离，宁可承受其伤害，也不要沾染仇恨之火，这样才能留得住自己身上的正能量。我们才可能成为一个有爱的人，一个可以幸福快乐的人。至于如何避开负能量的侵袭，正能量会在距离负能量很远的地方，就向人们发出引导和启示，我们只需要常常问一问正能量印记在我们身上的良心就可以。因此，对于强大恐怖的负能量和受其控制的"怪物"，人们并不用感到恐惧害怕，想要幸福不受伤害，我们只要相信正能量，坚守良心就够了。

守护良心 相信爱

有爱的人们都把正能量视为自己的权威，他们心甘情愿地

They willingly surrender their unreasonable original rights to their authority. And then get close to the positive energy through the implication and guidance of their conscience to gain the feeling of happiness. Whereas people who believe in hatred, harm and violence consider negative energy that turns them into "monsters" as their authority, or more appropriately, authoritarian (authority that makes people feel fearful). They let the hatred in their hearts guide their words and deeds, relieving the pain in their hearts by hurting and destroying.

We assume that positive energy and negative energy both are existences similar to "God particles" in the universe where humans live. People on Earth often describe positive energy using "God", "Allah", "Buddha" and love, while define negative energy using "devil", "Satan", hatred and harm. Both positive energy and negative energy are objective existences. Although

把自己不合理的原始权利交给自己的权威，然后通过良心的默示和指引去亲近正能量，获得幸福快乐的感觉。而相信仇恨、伤害和暴力的人们，却把让他们变成"怪物"的负能量作为自己的权威，或者叫威权（让人心生恐惧的权威）更合适一些。他们任凭心中的仇恨引领自己的言行，通过伤害破坏来减轻内心的痛苦。

我们假定，正能量和负能量是人类所处的宇宙空间之中，类似"上帝粒子"一样的存在。世人常用上帝、真主、佛祖和爱，来描绘形容正能量，也常用魔鬼、撒但和仇恨伤害来定义负能量。正能量和负能量都是一种客观存在，尽管目前凭借人类掌握的科学技术还无法证实这个假设和相关推理得出的结论，但"上帝粒子"的发现，预示着人类的科技已经朝着这

currently such hypothesis and related conclusions drawn by reasoning cannot be verified by the science and technologies mastered by humans, the discovery of "God particle" indicates that human science and technology have stepped towards such direction. Positive energy is featuring with love, while negative energy is featuring with hatred, harm and destruction. Humans will behave differently when being affected and controlled by positive or negative energy. Also, one may be affected by both positive energy and negative energy at the same time. Sometimes he/he will be controlled by positive energy, but sometimes it is negative energy that dominates to determine his/her words and deeds. As long as one bears in mind and sticks to the imprint of positive energy in his/her life --- conscience, positive energy will not leave. He/she will eventually get happiness that all humans yearn for. But if one falls into the "trap", falls into

个方向迈出了步伐。正能量以爱为特征，负能量以仇恨、伤害破坏为特征，人类会因为受到正负能量的影响控制而有不同的表现，一个人也可能同时受正负两种能量的影响，有时他（她）会被正能量控制，但有时却是负能量占据主导地位来决定他（她）的言行。只要一个人牢记坚守正能量印在他（她）生命中的印记——良心，正能量便不会离开，这个人最终也一定可以得到，所有人类都向往渴慕的幸福快乐。但一个人如果因为不够警醒和智慧，而中了"圈套"，陷入负能量的诡计之中，或者说没有经得住魔鬼的迷惑——他（她）就会漠视淡忘良心，直至正能量无法与其共存的时候，便是负能量宣告得胜之时。如何摆脱负能量的控制，守护良心，让自己能够时时处处接受正能量的指引，就成为我们人类的一件极其重要的事情。

the tricks of negative energy, or fails to withstand the delusion of devil as he is not vigilant and wise enough, he/she will ignore and forget his/her conscience. Till positive energy cannot coexist with him/her, it is when negative energy declares victory. How to get rid of the control of negative energy, to protect our conscience, and enable ourselves to accept the guidance of positive energy anytime anywhere has become an extremely important thing for us humans.

Although negative energy is very powerful and full of power of conquest and destruction, but it cannot become the authority of those who pursue happiness. Because negative energy is not the ultimate goal of humans -- necessary for happiness. Although negative energy may play an important role when humans are faced with an existential crisis, in most cases, human needs for nourishment and love of positive energy are far above

负能量虽然十分强大，充满了征服和破坏的力量，但由于负能量不是人类的终极目标——幸福快乐所必需的，所以无法成为追求幸福快乐的人们的权威。尽管负能量可能会在人类面临生存危机之时发挥重要作用，但绝大多数情况下，人类关于正能量滋养爱护的需要，远远超过对负能量的需求，因此负能量只有位居正能量之下，人类社会的秩序平衡才能维系。对于负能量，人类无需恐惧，只要我们始终坚守良心，听从

the needs for negative energy. So, only when negative energy is below positive energy can the order of human society remain balanced. As for negative energy, humans do not need to be afraid of it. As long as we persistently guard our conscience and obey the inspiration of love, linking ourselves to positive energy via belief in love, and respect it as our authority, obey our conscience and surrender our illegitimate rights, positive energy will direct and lead us to peace and happiness.

(II)Order under Authority

"Republic"

In the process of the development and change of human society, many people have ever explored such a wonderful vision that makes people sigh and yearn for infinitely at the same time --- the Republic of human social order. As early as thousands of years ago, someone once sketched

爱的召唤，通过对爱的信仰把自己连接至正能量那里，并尊崇其为我们的权威，顺从良心交出自己不正当的权利，正能量就会指引带领我们得到平安和幸福。

（二）权威下的秩序

"理想国"

在人类社会的发展变迁进程中，曾经有不少人探索过这样一个既让人们叹息，又让人无限向往的美好愿景——人类社会秩序的理想状态。早在数千年前，曾经有人勾勒描绘出一幅人间景象，他把这样的景象做为人类的"理想国"。

a picture of man's world, and he regarded such a scene as the "Republic" of mankind.

In the Republic depicted by him, there are three classes. The first is the rulers of the state (this class also includes legislators and intellectuals). He believes that the king of such state should be a wise philosopher, who is a wise men and able to take on the important responsibility of governing human society with rich knowledge and experience, highly rational minds, and a discernment of beauty and kindness different from that of ordinary people. The second is the guardians of the state and its rules. They are mainly responsible for safeguarding the state, and bravery is their distinctive feature. The third is the producer class that undertakes economic functions, and who are divided into peasants/ farmers, craftsmen, shepherds, merchants, etc. Their responsibility is to satisfy various needs of human society. In such Republic, he believed that as long as people

在他的理想国之中，有这样三个阶层，一是国家的统治者（这一阶层还包括立法者、知识分子），他认为这个国家的君王应该由富有智慧的哲学家来担任，这里的哲学家是具有丰富知识和经验的智者，有着高度理性的头脑，对美和善良有着不同于普通人的辨识力，能够担当起治理人类社会的重任；二是国家和规则的守卫者，他们主要肩负着保卫国家安全的职责，勇敢是他们的显著特征；三是承担着经济职能的生产者阶层，他们又分为农民、工匠、牧者、商人等，他们的职责是满足人类社会各种各样的需求。在这个理想国中，他认为只要各个阶层的人员各司其职，各尽其责，分工协作，人类社会就能实现正义（自然分工，各行其事，秩序和谐）。他认为这样的国度是完美的，是充满智慧的、勇敢的、有节制和正义的，并且不同的道德品格也会明显地体现在不同的阶层那里，

of all classes perform their own duties, fulfill their responsibilities respectively, and collaborate on the basis of division of labor, human society can achieve justice (natural division of labor, each does his/her own thing, and with harmonious order). He believes that such a state is perfect, full of wisdom, bravery, abstinence and justice and different moral characters will be clearly reflected in different classes. For example, wisdom belongs more to the ruling class, bravery is mainly the feature of the state guardians. But the character of abstinence doesn't exclusively belong to any class and should apply to all citizens. Whichever class is required to know how to be abstinent. He believes that only in this way can human social order be harmonious and achieve justice.[1]

比如智慧更多归属于统治阶层，勇敢主要是国家守卫者的特征，节制的品格则不专属于任何一个阶层，节制应该作用于全体国民，无论哪个阶层都需要懂得如何节制。他认为只有这样，人类社会才能秩序和谐，实现正义。

---

[1] *Republic (or Πολιτεία)*, by Plato [Ancient Greece], translated by Chang Weifu, Xiyuan Publishing House, 2009 edition, p. 131-153, 171-179.

[古希腊] 柏拉图:《理想国》，常维夫译，西苑出版社 2009 年版，第 131-153 页、第 171-179 页。

Regardless of whether the vision outlined by this sage is reasonable and legitimate or not, and whether it can truly bring happiness to humans, his yearning for, and pursuit of a better order in human society has indeed brought people dream and hope.

Another "Castle"

If the Lord, God, Allah, etc. that have been verified by modern science and technology to possibly exist and have been depicted in many scriptures of mankind are in a dimension that we cannot directly perceive, there is likely to be another "castle" similar to human society. Simply such castle we cannot directly see with our eyes but hear with our ears. But it cannot be ruled out that we humans can travel there via dreams, where there are a "heaven" for holiness and a "hell" for sin.

A saint once described the scene there to people, "We have

不论这位先哲勾勒出的景象是否合理正当，是否真的能给人类带来幸福快乐，但他对人类社会美好秩序的向往追求，的确给人们带来了憧憬与希望。

另一个"城堡"

如果被现代科学技术证实可能存在的，且在人类诸多经典之中被描述过的神、上帝、真主等，是在某个我们不能直接感知的领域之内，那么在那里就很可能还有一个类似人类社会的"城堡"，只不过这样的城堡，我们无法直接用眼睛去看，用耳朵去听。但不能排除我们人类可以通过梦境游历其中，那里有为圣洁准备的"天堂"，也有为罪恶预备的"地狱"。

曾经有一位圣徒给人们描绘过那里的景象，"我们知道有

learned that there is a city of God, and its Founder has inspired us with a love which makes us covet its citizenship." "To this Founder of the holy city the citizens of the earthly city prefer their own gods, not knowing that He is the God of gods," "The two cities are in this world commingled and implicated with one another." "There is great need of God's mercy to preserve us from making friends of demons in disguise, while we fancy we have good angels for our friends; for the astuteness and deceitfulness of these wicked spirits is equaled by their hurtfulness." [1]

The two "castles" depicted by this saint had provided important guidance and revelation for modern humans to reinterpret human society using science and scriptures as early as thousands of years ago.

一座上帝之城，由于她的创建者用爱激励我们，所以我们希望成为她的公民。""属地之城的公民喜爱他们自己的神灵甚于喜爱这座圣城的创建者，因为他们不知道他是万神之神。""这两座城在这个世界上是相互纠缠和混杂的。""因为从这第一个人那里衍生出来的所有人，有些受到奖赏而与善良的天使联合在一起，有些受到惩罚而与邪恶的天使联合在一起。"

这位圣徒描绘的两个"城堡"，早在数千年前，就为现代人类运用科学和经典记载，重新诠释人类社会，提供了重要的指引和启示。

[1] *The City of God (or De civitate Dei),* by Augustine of Hippo or Saint Augustine [Ancient Rome], translated by Wang Xiaochao, People's Publishing House, 2006 edition, p.444, p.442, p.536.

[古罗马] 奥古斯丁：《上帝之城》，王晓朝译，人民出版社 2006 年版，第 444 页、第 442 页、第 536 页。

Pain in the Human World

It's very easy for everyone to be happy when they come to this world at the beginning. Tasty food, fun stuffs, and nice things . . . can all make us feel happy and satisfied from our heart. But with the growth of life, it gets difficult for people to satisfy their desires and claims, and many people become unhappy as they cannot satisfy themselves. They gradually believe that their happiness comes from something outside themselves, money, power and status become indispensable things in their eyes, and believing in them becomes the living standards of such people. Their belief in money, power, and status links their lives to certain kinds of negative energy in the unknown field of mankind. What such energy causes to us is first unhappiness, and then the desires of greed, deceit, brutality, and fighting. Their purpose is to

人类世界的痛苦

每个人来到这个世界之初，都是很容易快乐的。好吃的，好玩的，好看的…都可以让我们感到发自内心的高兴和满足。但是随着生命的成长，人们的欲望和要求开始变得难以满足，由于不能满足自己，很多人开始变得不快乐。他们慢慢地相信自己的幸福快乐是来自身外的某些物品，金钱、权力和地位成为他们眼中不可或缺的东西，信奉它们成为这些人的生活准则。他们信奉金钱、权力和地位的信念，使他们的生命连接到了人类生存空间未知领域的某些负向能量，这些能量给人带来的感觉首先是不快乐，而后就是贪婪、欺骗、残暴和争斗的欲望，目的是要争夺侵占更多的物质财富和权力地位等人类的身外之物。

scramble more outer things e.g. material wealth and power, status, etc.

The human world begins to suffer pains because of people who are linked to negative energy. People controlled by negative energy can become deceitful, greedy and brutal, and can also harm other compatriots anytime. And more unacceptably, many people who originally did not believe in those external things will also change their beliefs and hence are linked to negative energy if they are with those with negative energy for a long time. Likewise, they will also become unhappy, greedy and cruel, fighting with their compatriots and making both themselves and others painful. If this trend continues, this world will eventually become a "sea of pain" due to the effect and control of negative energy over humans. Because for us humans, negative energy is like a plague, which will soon affect and control those with infirm and unsteady

人类世界因为连接负能量的人们，开始出现痛苦。负能量影响控制的人们会变得欺诈、贪婪和残暴，也会随时伤害其他同胞。并且更让人难以接受的一件事情是，很多原本不信奉那些身外之物的人，如果和拥有负能量的人在一起交往时间久了，也会变得和他们一样，改变自己的信念进而连接到负能量那里。同样地，他们也会变得不快乐，变得贪婪残暴，与同胞争斗，让自己和他人感到痛苦。按照这样的趋势发展下去，这个世界终将会因为负能量对人类的影响控制，而成为一片"痛苦的汪洋"，因为对于我们人类，负能量就像瘟疫，会很快影响控制信念不坚定且与其有接触的人们。

beliefs and are in contact with it.

Pain in the human world can mainly be divided into two categories: physiological pain and spiritual pain. The former includes human pain, hunger, cold, etc.; while the latter includes inequality, discrimination, coercion, and failure to satisfy desires, etc. Most physiological pains can be solved by people's economic activities and value creation and exchange. Such pains will also be relieved when one's physiological needs are satisfied. But spiritual pain is not that easy to heal. The root cause of such pain lies in people's beliefs --- what you believe in, and whether the energy to which such beliefs is linked is positive or negative. In case of negative energy that makes people greedy, deceitful and cruel, the pain cannot be eliminated unless people change their beliefs and gradually get rid of the effect and control of negative energy on them. The biggest feature of such kinds of negative energy is that they make the believers unhappy,

人类世界的痛苦，主要可以分为生理性痛苦和心灵痛苦两大类，前者比如人的疼痛、饥饿、寒冷等，后者比如不平等、受歧视、受胁迫、欲望无法满足等。大部分生理性痛苦可以通过人们的经济活动和价值的创造交换来解决，一个人的生理需求得到满足后，这种类型的痛苦也会随之解除。但心灵上的痛苦，就不是那么容易能够平复，这种痛苦的根源在于人们的信念——也就是你相信什么，以及这些信念背后连接到的能量是正向的还是负向的。如果是负向的——一种让人贪婪、欺诈、残暴的能量，那么痛苦就会无法消除，除非人们改变自己的信念，逐步摆脱负向能量对人的影响控制。这些负向能量的最大特征，就是让相信的人变得不快乐，进而痛苦并且无法自拔。除非人们破坏掉与这些能量相通的连接点——信念，一种让人相信自己可以通过某些方式实现目标的认知和感受。比如一个人认为当他(她)拥有很多金钱以后，就会快乐

and then painful and inextricable. Unless people destroy the linking point to such kinds of energy --- belief, a cognition and feeling which make people believe that they can attain their goals in some way. For example, one thinks that when he/she owns a lot of money, he/she will be happy, or that he/she will be satisfied only when he/she owns a very high social status. Such beliefs make people linked to the unknown kinds of energy. People who hold such beliefs are usually unhappy --- happiness is a common and pleasant psychological feeling for all humans. Such kind of energy is called negative energy as they make people feel unhappy. If one wants to get rid of unhappiness and the pain caused by unhappiness, only by changing and abandoning the beliefs that will be linked to negative energy and make himself/herself believe in something that belongs to positive energy, and re-establish the belief of life to be linked to positive energy can he/she reap

幸福，或者获得很高的社会地位后才能满足。这样的信念会让人连接到未知的能量那里，通常持有这些信念的人们都是不快乐的——快乐是一种人类共通的、愉悦的心理感受。因为给人的感觉不快乐，所以这些能量就被称作是负向的能量。一个人如果想要摆脱不快乐，以及不快乐导致的痛苦，就只有改变丢弃会连接负能量的信念，让自己相信属于正能量的东西，重新确立人生信念连接正能量，这样才能够凭借正能量带给我们的爱，去收获真正的幸福快乐。

true happiness relying on the love brought by positive energy to us.

"Good People" & "Bad People"

There is originally no difference of "good" or "bad" among people. Everyone wants to have happiness and has the freedom to pursue it. But humans also have the right to change their beliefs. And the energy to which beliefs are linked can determine whether one can get happiness or not. The differences among beliefs are the root cause of many issues in the human world. One doesn't believe what you believe, and one will unnecessarily agree with what you agree with. Everyone has their own beliefs (the cognitions and conclusions that people believe in). But such a wrong thought in passing may cause huge differences.

Those who believe in money, those who believe in power, and people who believe in love will certainly show big differences in

"好人"和"坏人"

人本来没有好坏之分，每个人都想拥有幸福快乐，都有追求它们的自由，但人类也有改变自己信仰的权利，而信仰连接到的能量可以决定一个人能否幸福快乐，信仰差异是人类世界很多问题的根源。你相信的他不相信，我认同的你未必认同，人人都会有自己的信念（人们信守的认知和结论），但这里的一念之差，却可以差出天地之别。

信奉金钱的人，信奉权力的人，信奉爱的人，其所作所为必将出现很大的不同。人之所以信奉金钱，是因为人们觉得，

what they do. The reason why people believe in money is that people think that they can't buy what they want without enough money, so they can't be happy, and then they will be painful too. As a result, their lives show a strong attitude --- to grab. They want to get as much wealth as possible. They are also likely to violate the law in their hearts ---- conscience --- to get wealth, as money dominates their mind. Those who believe in power will also commit bloody massacres and repressions regardless of the condemnation of conscience in order to realize their desire to rule others. What such people do is rooted in the belief in their hearts that only when they get the wealth or power they want can their lives be satisfied and uniquely happy. But in fact, as such people violate their conscience or do not agree with the existence of conscience at all, they are unable to be linked to positive energy that can make people happy. Due to their betrayal

钱不够多就无法买到自己想要的物品，就不可能快乐，也会很痛苦，于是他们的生命就显现出一种强烈的姿态——攫取，他们想要获取尽可能多的财富，因为奉金钱为大，他们也很有可能不惜违背心中的律法——良心，去得到财富。信奉权力的人，为了实现统治他人的欲望，也会不惜承受良心的谴责，去血腥屠杀和镇压。这些人的所作所为，其根源皆出自他们内心深处的信念，他们认为只有得到了自己想要的财富或是权力，他们的生命才能得到满足，才会与众不同地快乐。但事实上，由于这些人违背了良心或者说根本不认同良心的存在，使得他们无法连接到能让人幸福快乐的正能量，这些人的生命就会因为不讲良心而无法真正地快乐幸福。并且由于不讲良心，他们也会常常伤害同胞的正当权益，让别人也感受痛苦，甚至是用他们的信念感染他人也变得和他们一样，使更多的人通过信念连接到给人痛苦的负能量。这样的人在不知不觉中，就会成为多数人眼中的"坏人"，

to conscience, their lives would not be truly happy, and they will often harm the legitimate rights and interests of their compatriots, cause others to feel pain, and even infect others with their own beliefs to make them become people like themselves, causing more people be linked to negative energy that makes people painful. Such people will unconsciously become "bad people" in most people's eyes, or people who can make others become "bad".

People who believe in love are those who persistently guard their conscience. The reason why they believe in love is that the beliefs in their hearts allow them to experience happiness often. And such beliefs make them be linked to certain energy in the unknown space of mankind, which is featuring with love --- caring, tolerant, inclusive, harmless, and provide people with what they need. Love is the fundamental reason for human happiness. What gives people love is energy. Such

或者能够让人变"坏"的人。

相信爱的人，也就是坚守良心的人。他们之所以相信爱，是因为心中的信念让他们可以常常体会到幸福快乐，这些信念使他们连接到人类未知空间的某种能量，这种能量以爱为特征——关怀、包容、不伤害、给人所需。爱是人类快乐幸福的根本原因，给人爱的是一种能量，因为能够给人幸福，所以这种能量就被人们称作正能量。曾经有一位了不起的科学家，他的理论被用来制造令人恐惧的武器，一种可以摧毁人类的武器——核武器。核武器

energy is called "positive energy" as it can give people happiness. There was once a preeminent scientist whose theories were used to create a terrifying weapon, a weapon that could destroy the mankind --- nuclear weapon. [1] The energy of nuclear weapon is so enormous that it can destroy the mankind. People affected and controlled by negative energy may detonate such destructive weapon in the future. How to avoid humans to be destroyed by the weapons invented by themselves? Only by trying to be linked to the more powerful positive energy --- love. By detonating the "bomb of love" [2] to spread positive energy rapidly in the human world so as to make more and more people believe in positive energy. Who can shoulder such an important

的能量非常巨大，已经达到了足以摧毁人类的程度。被负能量影响控制的人们可能在未来引爆这种毁灭性的武器，如何避免人类被自己发明的武器毁灭，只有设法连接到更加强大的正能量——爱，通过引爆"爱的炸弹"，在人类世界迅速传播正能量，让越来越多的人相信正能量才可以。谁可以肩负如此重要的责任？只能是相信爱，拥有正能量的人们，如何辨识这些人，只需要看其是否相信良心就行了。良心是爱留在人生命中的印记，或者说是正能量印在人心中的律法，良心会告诉一个人该相信什么，该怎么说、怎么做，良心中蕴含的信念使人们可以连接到正能量。坚守良心的人,是被爱（正能量）充盈的人，是能让自己和他人快乐幸福的人，也是人们眼中的"好人"。

[1] *Encyclopedia Britannica* (international Chinese edition), China Encyclopedia Publishing House, 1999 edition, p. 549.
《不列颠百科全书》（国际中文版），中国大百科全书出版社 1999 年版，第 549 页。
[2] Sue Dreamwalker, A Letter Under Question?:about The Universal Force Which is Love, Dreamwalker's Sanctury, https://suedreamwalker.wordpress.com/2015/04/15/a-letter-from-albert-einstein-to-his-daughter-about-the-universal-force-which-is-love/.

responsibility? Only those who believe in love and own positive energy. How to identify such people? Just need to identify whether they believe in conscience or not. Conscience is the imprint of love in people's life, or the law that positive energy imprints in people's hearts. Conscience tells one what to believe, how to say, and how to do. The beliefs contained in conscience allow people to be linked to positive energy. People who persistently guard their conscience are those who are filled with love (positive energy), those who can make both themselves and others happy, as well as those who are called "good people" in people's eyes.

We Are "Good People" Or Not?

Are we "good people"? It's a tough question to answer, but many people consider themselves "good people." No one wants to be a "bad person", but there are also

我们是不是"好人"

我们是"好人"吗？这是一个很难回答的问题，不过有很多人都认为自己是"好人"。没有人想成为"坏人"，却也有不少人坦然承认自己就是"坏人"。

many people who admit that they are "bad people".

What should "good people" be like? Good people are compassionate, do not scramble with others, avoid conflict with others, do not willfully hurt others, are self-disciplined but generous to others, do something without expecting anything in return, always think of others in their hearts, not selfish, share benefits with others, and are never insatiably greedy. And what are "bad people" like? Bad people are tricky, always frame others, scramble interest with others, deceive and hurt others, are jealous and hateful, instigate conflicts, cannot see that others are happy, destroy others' achievements, and never believe that there are love and happiness in the human world.

These are the rough standards for identifying "good people" and "bad people". But they are not absolute standards and just some "some differences between goodness and badness" that

"好人"应该是什么样子的？好人心怀慈悲，不与人争，避免与人冲突，不去故意伤害别人，自律节制却对人慷慨，做事不计回报，心中常想他人，不自私自利，有好处会与他人分享，从不贪得无厌。"坏人"是什么样子？坏人心怀诡异，处处陷害他人，与人争利，欺骗伤害他人，嫉妒仇恨，煽风点火挑唆矛盾，见不得别人快乐幸福，破坏他人成就，从不相信世间有爱和幸福。

这些是"好人"和"坏人"的大致标准，但不是绝对的，只是多数人较为认同的一些"好坏之别"，以供人们对"好人"和"坏人"做出最基本的辨别。按照上述特征，做为一个人，我们

most people agree with so that people can make the most basic discernment between "good people" and "bad people". According to the above features, as a person, we can ask ourselves "Am I such a person?" We are neither "good people" nor "bad people". Many people would say that we are neither good nor bad; we are just "mortals". The reason why we feel that we are not "good people" is that we know that we have too many unsatisfiable selfish desires, many of which are extremely unreasonable. Only when they are restrained by human conscience and rationality can we show a status of life similar to "good people"; although we are not "good people", we also hate ourselves to be bad people deep in our heart. Although we are full of various desires, we strive to free ourselves from ignorance, rudeness and evil through learning and indoctrination. We consider personality qualities e.g. kindness, honesty and bravery nice.

可以扪心自问，我们是这样的人吗，"好人"或者"坏人"我们都不是。应该会有不少人说，我们不好也不坏，我们只是"凡人"。之所以感觉到我们不是"好人"，是因为我们深知自己有太多难以满足的私欲，这些欲望很多都是极不合理的，只有在它们被人类的良心理性抑制后，我们才能表现出一种近似"好人"的生命状态；尽管我们不是"好人"，但我们的骨子里也极度厌恶自己成为坏人，虽然我们充满了各式各样的欲望，但我们努力通过学习和教化来使自己摆脱愚昧、粗暴和邪恶，我们会以善良、诚实和勇敢等人格品质为美。

Strictly speaking, we are neither good nor bad. We are mortals full of desires. If we satisfy our reasonable desires, we will not become bad people, we will get close to or become "good people" when we satisfy our desires while always thinking of the interests of others. There are defect in human nature. And it is precisely due to such defects that we humans have become a "problematic" creature with high-level intelligence. It is also recorded in the Bible that, "And the Lord saw that the sin of man was great on the earth, and that all the thoughts of his heart were evil." [1] What referred to here should be the defects in human nature or the original sin of mankind.

严格来讲，我们既不是好人，也不是坏人，我们是充满欲望的凡人，满足自己合理的欲望我们就不会成为坏人，满足自己欲望的同时总是惦记他人的利益我们就会接近成为好人。人性是有缺陷的，我们人类正是因着这些缺陷，而成为有"问题"的一种具备高等智能的生物，圣经中也有这样的记载，"人在地上罪恶很大，终日所思想的尽都是恶。"[2]这里指的应该就是，人性的缺陷或者说人类的原罪。

① *Bible*, National Committee of Three-Self Patriotic Movement of the Protestant Churches in China (National TSPM), China Christian Council (CCC), 2009 edition, (Genesis 6:5) p.5.

②《圣经》，中国基督教三自爱国运动委员会、中国基督教协会 2009 年版，（创 6：5）第 5 页。

Where Human Sin Comes From?

We are full of desires and often have many ideas and claims, some of which are reasonable, while some are unreasonable or even evil. Satisfying our desires is sometimes beneficial to both others and ourselves, but is sometimes harmful to both others and ourselves. When we can't control our unreasonable or evil ideas, sin will sprout. In the words of the scriptures, "sin is waiting at the door", which can make people fall at any time. Because in such case only a little irritation is sufficient to make human sin completely become hatred and hurt. And in turn the hurt will breed new hatred. When hatred cannot be suppressed, there will be continual negative energy in this process linked to human spirit to affect and control people's words and deeds.

A policeman seizes a vehicle

人的罪恶从哪里来

我们充满了欲望，常常会有很多的念头和要求，其中有些是合理的，有些是不合理的，甚至是邪恶的。满足我们的欲望，有时于人于己都有益处，但有时却会害人又害己。当我们无法控制自己不合理或是邪恶的念头时，罪恶就会开始萌生，用经典之中的话来讲，就是"罪就伏在门前"，随时可以让人跌倒。因为这时只需要一点点刺激，人的罪恶就会变成赤裸裸的仇恨和伤害，而伤害又会滋生新的仇恨，当仇恨无法被抑制时，就会有源源不断的负能量在这个过程中连接至人的灵魂，进而影响控制人们的言行。

一位警察扣留了一个违章

violating the rules, and the driver of this vehicle feels angry and hates the law enforcement policeman as he/she could not accept the behavior of the policeman. Hatred makes him lose himself. And, an unreasonable desire --- retaliation and hurt forms in his heart very soon. He could have report and reveal the traffic policeman's violations and unjust law enforcement in a rational way, although doing so may encounter lots of resistances and obstacles, or even be totally ineffective. But no matter whether it works or not, most social members agree with such a remedy. Because only by safeguarding rights and interests as per the established rules can form an order in human society, and can the safety of every social member be secured. But such person who loses himself because of hatred is at this moment completely controlled by negative energy and can no longer restrain his impulse, he takes a sharp knife and stabs the policeman to death.

车辆，驾驶这辆车的人不能接受警察的行为，心中感到愤怒，并对执法警察充满仇恨。仇恨让他迷失了自己，不合理的欲望——报复伤害，很快在他的心中形成。他原本可以通过理性的方式，来检举揭发交警的违规行为和不当执法，尽管这样做可能会遇到层层阻力和障碍，甚至毫无效果。但无论行不行得通，绝大多数社会成员都认同这样的救济办法，因为只有依照既定规则来维护权益，人类的社会才有可能形成秩序，每一位社会成员的安全才会有保障。但这个因仇恨迷失自我，在那一刻完全被负能量控制的人，已经无法抑制自己的冲动，拿起了尖刀，狠狠地刺死了那位警察。这样的行为，就是由不合理的欲望发酵而成，交警扣车的代价，变成了付出生命。绝大多数人都不会选择用杀人的方法来解决问题，只有被罪恶绊倒的人，无法抑制不合理欲望的人才可能做得出来。他是充满欲望的凡人，但也是无法阻挡邪恶的罪人。

Such behavior is a consequence of unreasonable desires. The price of the traffic policeman's seizing the vehicle becomes sacrifice of life. Most people will not choose to solve problems by killing people. Only those who are tripped up by sin and those who cannot restrain unreasonable desires can commit that. He is a mortal full of desires. But he is also a sinner who cannot stop evil.

So, it can also be said that human sin comes from ourselves and from our defects --- unreasonable or evil desires, which we are born with and cannot be eliminated.

因此，也可以说，人类的罪来自我们自身，来自我们的缺陷——不合理或邪恶的欲望，这些欲望我们人类与生俱来，无法消除。

"Desires" --- A Prerequisite for Human Happiness

"欲望"是人类幸福的前提条件

Human desires are the source of sin. But can we restrain all human desires in order to suppress sin? Because by reasoning in terms of the form, there will be no possibility for people to crime

人的欲望是罪恶之源，但我们能不能为了抑制罪恶，而禁锢人类所有的欲望呢，因为从形式上来推理，没有了欲望，人便没有了犯罪的可能性。

without desires.

We are mortals full of desires, we are neither good nor bad. Most of our life is spent satisfying our own desires, and among which only a few are reasonable and beneficial to both ourselves and others. Most of one's desires are to satisfy himself/herself, "I want the most, I want the best, I want to win, I want to beat everyone..." These seemingly normal human desires are all self-centered. They take satisfying their own claims as the starting point. As a result, it is easy to cause harm to others, whether intentionally or unintentionally. When one's desires are satisfied, he/she will feel happy. But such kind of happiness will not necessarily lead to happiness (a deep and long, sweet and pleasant feeling). In other words, such kind of happiness may be extremely transient, emptiness, loneliness, and even pain will follow. As when satisfaction of our selfish desires usually does not mean that

我们是充满欲望的凡人，我们既不是好人，也不是坏人。我们的生命绝大部分时间都是在满足自己的欲望，这些欲望当中，合理的、于己于人都有益处的只占很少一部分。一个人大部分的欲望都是在满足自己，"我的要最多，我的要最好，我要赢，我要打败所有人…"，这些看似很正常的人类欲望，都是以自我为中心，把满足自己的要求作为出发点，这样做的结果，就是很容易给他人带来有意无意的伤害。当人的这些欲望被满足时，他（她）会感到快乐，不过这种快乐却不一定会带来幸福（一种深沉长久、甜蜜愉快的感觉）。换句话说，这种快乐有可能极其短暂，而后是空虚、寂寞，甚至是痛苦。因为很多时候，我们的私欲得到满足，并不代表我们真正地得到爱，连接到可以让我们幸福的正能量。对充满爱的正能量的渴慕，才是人类最重要、最理性的欲望要求，离开了这种最基本的欲望，人类会对爱失去兴趣，不相信爱，更

we have truly obtained love and linked to positive energy that can make us happy. Only the yearning for positive energy full of love is the most important and rational human desire. Without such most basic desire, humans will lose interest in love, not believe in love, let alone to be linked to positive energy that can make us happy relying on their own belief in love.

Although desire is the source of evil, if one had no desires, he/she would not be a real human. Such people might become even more terrifying. If one has no desires, it means that he/she has lost the pursuit of love. Whereas one without love may hurt others at any time. Although most of one's desires are selfish, normal people all have a desire for love. Love can make human society harmonious and orderly, and it will make up for the conflicts, combats and traumas caused to humans by selfishness. Being full of selfish desires is a natural

无法凭借自己对爱的信仰，去连接能让我们幸福的正能量。

欲望虽是罪恶之源，但一个人如果没有了欲望，便不是真正的人类了，这样的人有可能变得更加恐怖可怕。因为一个人没有了欲望，也就意味着没有了对爱的追求，无爱的人是随时可能伤害他人的。尽管一个人的多数欲望都是自私的，但正常的人都有对爱的欲望，爱可以让人类社会变得和谐有秩序，会弥补人的自私给人类带来的冲突争斗与创伤。充满私欲是人与生俱来的天然属性，但人的欲望当中也包含对爱的渴慕，一个人有了对爱的追求和信仰，才可以连接到让人幸福的正能量。因此，对爱的欲

attribute of humans. But desire for love is also among human desires. Only when one has the pursuit of, and belief in love can he/she be linked to positive energy that can make people happy. The desire for love thus becomes a precondition for human happiness.

"Unreal" Good People Are the Hope of Mankind

People are all full of desires. And, a considerable part of one's desires are unreasonable and selfish. Satisfying such desires will only cause harm and pain to others. But if one does not satisfy his/her desires, whether reasonable or selfish, the human nature determines that he/she will feel unhappy or even painful. So, people spend most of their lives gaming with their own desires. Legitimate desires shall be satisfied by all means, while illegitimate desires shall be restrained, or for which the

望便成为我们人类幸福的前提条件。

"不真实"的好人是人类的希望

人都是充满欲望的，并且在一个人的欲望当中，有相当一部分都是不合理和自私的，满足这样的欲望，只会给他人带来伤害和痛苦。可是当一个人不满足自己欲望的时候，不管这些欲望是合理正当的还是自私自利的，人的天性决定了他（她）都会感到不快，甚至是痛苦。因此人的一生，大多时候都是在和自己的欲望博弈，正当合理的欲望想尽一切办法去努力实现，不合理的欲望就要想办法抑制或是转移目标。我们也几乎没有可能性，在自己的生命之初就有机会选择做一

target shall be diverted. There is hardly possibility for us to have opportunity to choose to be a good person at the beginning of our lives. We are just mortals full of desires. When we are not vigilant for a little while and can't restrain our selfish but inborn desires, we will soon become bad people in others' eyes. For example, we like to possess others' things, we want to steal public wealth that belongs to everyone, and we want to have affairs with others' beautiful wives...etc. These are all desires that are only good for ourselves, but can harm others and disrupt the order. We can only restrain or divert our attention. Otherwise, when such desire goals are attained, we will become thoroughly bad people.

Though it is hard for us to be good people easily due to our inherent defects --- selfish and unreasonable desires, There are still many good people in this world, regardless of whether they admit that they are good people or

个好人。我们只是充满欲望的凡人，一不留神，当我们不能抑制自己自私却又与生俱来的欲望时，我们很快就会变成别人眼中的坏人。比如，我们很喜欢占有别人的东西，很想窃取属于大家的公共财富，贪恋别人美貌的伴侣…等等。这些都是只对自己有利，却会伤害别人、破坏秩序的欲望，我们只能抑制或是转移自己的注意力，不然当满足这些欲望目标的时候，我们就会成为不折不扣的坏人。

虽然，因着与生俱来的缺陷——自私自利的不合理欲望，我们很难轻松地做一个好人。但仍然有很多的好人在这个世界上，不管他们是否承认自己是好人。在多数人的眼中，他们是好人，他们的言行也称的

not. In most people's eyes, they are good people, and their words and deeds can also be just. Such people did not affect the legitimate interests of others when satisfying their own desires. And they often help others and benefit others. Although good people are mortals full of desires, good people can well restrain their unreasonable desires, or good people can smoothly surmount their selfishness, always thinking of the interests of others. Certain beliefs in the hearts of good people make them linked to a very powerful energy, which not only makes good people feel happy, but also enables them to pass such feeling to more people around them. In other word, due to the beliefs of good people, such energy enables mortals full of desires to become rational, so that they can easily game with their own desires, and ultimately rein human nature and surmount human defects.

But from another perspective, it can also be said that good

上是公义。这些人在满足自己欲望的时候，没有影响到他人的正当利益。并且这些人也经常帮助他人，使他人受益。尽管好人也是充满欲望的凡人，但好人能够很好地抑制自己的不合理欲望，或者说好人可以很顺畅地克服自己的自私自利，总是惦记他人的利益。好人心中的某些信念，使他们连接到了很强大的能量，这种能量不仅使好人自己感到快乐，也让好人将这种感觉传递给身边更多的人。也可以说，由于好人的信念，使得这种能量将充满欲望的凡人变得理性，使他们可以轻松地同自己的欲望博弈，并最终驾驭人性，战胜人类的缺陷。

但从另外一个角度，我们也可以说好人是隐藏了不良欲望

people are mortals who hide bad desires. They are hypocritical and unreal --- they do have certain ideas in their mind, but deliberately conceal or divert their goals without revealing their evil selfish side in human nature. There is nothing wrong to say so. Because human nature is generic. Everyone has evil ideas and cannot be eliminated. All we can do is to hide them or divert our attention. Good people are those who try hard to be such people through belief. Though we can say that good people are unreal and hypocritical, we humans cannot live without good people. If there were no good people, no one was willing to conceal their selfishness and evil, and everyone continued to live as they are, the place where we humans live would become a chaotic and peaceless world where we fight, hurt and kill forever.

So, though good people are "hypocritical", they are the hope of human social order.

的凡人，他们是虚伪和不真实的——心中明明有那样的想法念头，却刻意掩饰或转移目标，不显露出自己人性当中邪恶自私的一面。这样说并没有错误之处，因为人性是相通的，每个人都有邪恶的念头，并且无法消除。我们能做的只是隐藏或转移注意力，而好人就是通过信仰努力去这样做的人。虽然我们可以说好人是不真实的、是虚伪的，但我们人类却不能没有好人。如果没有好人，没有人愿意掩饰隐藏自己的自私邪恶，所有人都按照自己的本来面目去继续生命，那么我们人类居住的地方将会变成互相争斗、伤害杀戮、永无宁日的混乱世界。

所以，好人虽然"虚伪"，但却是人类社会秩序的希望。

Why A Person Should Be Good?

If we all acted as mortals according to our own human nature, allowed our desires to dominate our words and actions, and then turned the place where we human live into a "metropolis" full of desires. There would not be any good people in this world. There would only be more and more bad people who were selfish, cruel and tyrannical and only cared about satisfying themselves but didn't care about whether hurting others or not. Because many of human desires are unreasonable or even evil. But it is also undesirable to completely confine people's desires. As it would deprive people of their right to happiness. Satisfying the desire for love is a necessary condition for humans to obtain happiness. If you didn't believe in love, have no desire for love, you couldn't be linked to positive energy that can

为什么要做好人

如果我们都按着自己的本性去做凡人，任凭我们的欲望去主导自己的言语和行为，进而把我们人类居住的地方变成一个又一个的欲望都市。那么这个世界上便不会有什么好人，只会出现越来越多的，只顾满足自己却不管是否伤害他人，自私自利、残忍暴虐的坏人。因为人的欲望有很多都是不合理的，甚至是邪恶的。不过完全禁锢人的欲望也是不可取的，那样会剥夺人们幸福快乐的权利，满足对爱的欲望是人类获得幸福的必要条件，不相信爱，没有了对爱的欲望，就无法连接到可以让人幸福快乐的正能量。

make people happy.

So, in order to prevent the human world from falling into chaos, our best choice is to be a good person. While not confining all our desires, we must manage to surmount the selfish, unreasonable, and harmful desires in human nature. Doing so can make us become good people who are beneficial to others and the society. It's not easy to be a good person. What's tough is to restrain and surmount the unreasonable desires. It's easy to be a mortal. We just need to obey our desires. But indulging own desires can easily make one degenerate into a bad person harmful to others. According to human nature, everyone likes the new and dislikes the old and is not willing to pay but likes enjoying possession. If to indulge our desires and bodies following human nature, human society would be more terrifying than the snakes and beasts in the jungle. Because lower-level creatures

所以，为了不让人类世界陷入混乱，我们最好的选择就是做好人。不去禁锢自己所有欲望的同时，也要想办法克服人性当中自私、不合理、对他人有害的欲望，这样做可以让我们成为对他人和社会有益的人——好人。做好人不容易，难就难在要抑制克服自己的不合理欲望，做凡人容易，只需要顺从欲望就可以了，但放纵自己的欲望，却很容易让人沦落为对他人有害的坏人。人的本性都是喜新厌旧、不愿付出却喜欢享受占有的，顺着人的本性去放纵我们的欲望和身体，人类社会会比丛林里的毒蛇猛兽更加可怕。因为低等生物虽然凶残，但却没有过度的欲望要求，只要维持自己的生存就够了，不会过多索取，它们的世界可以很自然地形成生态链，生生不息。但人类一旦完全顺从自己的本能欲望，就会成为自私的破坏掠夺者。

don't have excessive desires though they are cruel. They don't ask for too much as long as they can survive. An ecological chain can form in their world naturally, which makes them thrive. But once humans completely followed their own instinctive desires, they would become selfish destroyers and predators.

A man and a woman love each other and give birth to family offspring. In such case, they should also bear the subsequent responsibility and obligation. Such responsibility is that they need to work hard to support and maintain their home. But those who completely follow their instinctive desires can easily become roles that evade responsibilities: those who like the new and dislike the old can easily betray marriage and breed extramarital affairs if they don't know how to bridle themselves; those who are unwilling to work will evade the burden of earning money to support their families, making

男人和女人相爱，孕育家庭后代，这时的他们也应该承担随之而来的责任和义务。这份责任义务就是他们需要用辛勤付出来支撑维系自己的家，但完全顺从本能欲望的人，却很容易成为逃避责任的角色：喜新厌旧的人不懂得收敛就很容易背叛婚姻，滋生出婚外情感；不愿付出劳动的就会躲避赚钱养家的重担，让家庭生活无法继续…像这样由于顺从自己的本性和欲望而导致的人间悲剧还有很多。家是人类社会的基本组成单元，家庭无法维系，婚姻破裂的多了，社会秩序也会出现裂痕和动荡，最终受害的还是我们人类自身。为了我们的家，为了人类社会不失去稳

family life fail to continue... There are still lots of such tragedies in the world caused by following own human nature and desires. Family is the basic unit of human society. More broken marriages due to failure to maintain the family will result in cracks and turbulence of social order. Ultimately, we humans will suffer. For our homes, and, in order for the human society not to lose its stable order, we need to try hard to be good people, to be rational people that can bridle ourselves and are "hypocritical". To keep those benign desires that are beneficial to ourselves and others, and to manage to surmount those selfish, unreasonable and harmful appeals. Only in this way can we jointly maintain the order between people and of human society. In this process, how many social members are willing to try hard to be good people will be crucial to the harmony and stability of human social order.

定秩序，我们需要努力做好人，做收敛自己、"虚伪"的理性人，留下对自己和他人都有益处的良性欲望，然后想办法克服那些自私不合理、对他人有害的诉求，这样大家才能共同维护人与人之间以及人类社会的秩序。在这个过程中，究竟有多少社会成员愿意努力做好人，便会对人类社会秩序的和谐稳定起到至关重要的作用。

Being Good Implies "Lifetime Fight"

It's tough to be a good person as good people are "hypocritical". The hypocrisy of a good person is that he/she hides his/her true desires and claims following human nature for a certain goal. One does want to possess a lot of wealth, but chooses to actively give up such desires for harmony and not to conflict with others; One does like a beautiful girl or woman, but stays away from the temptation of beauty in order not to hurt his spouse; One does want to be overweening, but chooses to carefully listen to the opinions and appeals of others for the interests of more compatriots... Such situations always happen everywhere. Their existence shows a truth, that is, it is not easy to be a good person, a person beneficial to oneself and others.

To be a good person is not only to restrain and hold back own

做好人意味着选择了 "终生战斗"

好人很难做，因为好人是"虚伪"的。好人的虚伪在于他（她）为了某个目标，掩藏了自己发自本性的真实欲望要求。明明想占有很多财富，却为了和谐不与他人发生冲突，而选择主动舍弃；明明很喜欢漂亮的异性，却为了不伤害自己的伴侣，而远离美貌的诱惑；明明很想唯我独尊，却为了更多同胞的利益，选择谨慎听取他人的意见诉求…这样的境况无时无处不在发生，它们的存在都说明了一个道理，那就是想要做一个好人，一个对己对人都有益处的人，不是一件容易的事情。

做好人不仅要压抑忍耐自己的欲望，还要做好承受伤害

desires, but also to be prepared to get hurt. You are giving your income of work to the elderly, the weak, the sick, and the disabled in an unrequited manner as they have no way to get a source of livelihood and they need help from others. But meanwhile, you also need to be prepared to suffer unprovoked harm. Because some people will snoop your wealth and look for opportunities to grab it. Killings for money happen almost every day in the human world. The victims do not deserve punishment. Many of them are people trying to be good.

If a mortal full of desires does something that infringes the interests of others due to failure to confine his/her own bad desires occasionally, such person cannot yet be considered a bad person. What they do is just a mistake in thought and a momentary mistake. After being punished as per the rules of human society, if he/she does not pay the price of life, he/she still has the opportunity to

的准备。你在把自己的劳动所得无偿赠与老弱病残的人，因为他们没有办法获取生活来源，他们需要别人的帮助。可与此同时，你也需要准备好承受无端的伤害，因为有些人会在暗中窥视你的财富，并伺机豪取强夺。图财害命的事在人类世界几乎每天都有发生，受害者并不是罪有应得，他们当中有很多都是在努力做好人的人。

如果一个充满欲望的凡人，因为偶尔无法禁锢自己的不良欲望，而做出了伤害他人利益的事，那么这样的人还算不上坏人，他们所做的只是一念之差、一时之错，在按照人类社会的规则接受惩罚之后，如果没有付出生命的代价，他（她）仍有机会去好好做人，甚至是努力做好人。可是当一个人看到有人努力做好人，就会心里难过，进而想要伤害做好人的

well behave, or even try hard to be a good person. But the case will be quite different when one feels painful and then wants to hurt such good person when seeing someone trying hard to be a good person. Such people are very dangerous. The reason why they are dangerous is not because of themselves, but because of their certain beliefs (not believing that humans can own positive energy and love), which make them linked to negative energy. It is precisely certain beliefs that make people who try hard to be good linked to positive energy. Mortals can either follow good people to become good or follow bad people to become dangerous. Bad people make good people lose their minds making use of human nature and desires, thus make them discard their beliefs that can make them linked to positive energy and turn back to mortals or even become people as dangerous as their opponents in an instant, just like the scene in the game "Resident

人时，情况就大不一样了。这样的人是很危险的，他们的危险之处不是因为他们自身，而是因为他们的某些信念（不相信人类可以拥有正能量和爱），使得他们连接到负向能量那里。而努力做好人的人，也正是因为某些信念使得自己连接到了正能量，凡人可以跟着好人变好，也可以跟着坏人变得危险。坏人会利用人的本性和欲望，让好人失去理智，从而丢弃可以连接正能量的信念，变回凡人，甚至是转瞬成为和对手一样的危险之人，就像在我们人类设计发明的游戏"生化危机"里看到的那样。

Evil" designed and invented by humans.

So, choosing to be a good person implies choosing to be a fighter, a brave warrior who constantly fights with negative energy.

所以，选择做好人，就意味着选择成为一名斗士，一名同负能量不断争斗的勇敢战士。

When One Can't Get What He/She Wants

想要的得不到时

Everyone has their own desires, whether ordinary people, good people or extremely dangerous people, they all have what they like and want. But there are seldom opportunities and occasions for our human desires to be fully satisfied. In addition to basic needs e.g. food, clothing, etc., which are easy to satisfy, people often face desire goals that are hard to satisfy, or even impossible to attain.

每一个人都有自己的欲望，不论是凡人、好人还是极度危险之人，都有自己喜欢的和想要的。但我们人类的欲望能够被充分满足的机会和场合却不多，除了吃饭穿衣等基本需求比较容易满足，人们也常常面临难以满足，甚至是不可能实现的欲望目标。

Most of people's basic physiological needs are easy to satisfy. It does not require too much time and energy to obtain three meals a day, warm clothes,

人的基本生理需求，大多比较容易满足。一日三餐、取暖衣物等等，获取这些并不需要耗费人们太多的时间和精力。可是当一个人不仅想吃饱肚子，

etc. But when one wants not only to get full, but also to taste delicacies of every kind, cubilose and shark fin, not only to dress warmly, but also to wear gold and silver jewelries. One wants to find a most beautiful spouse to satisfy his own emotional desire and multiplication of offspring. . . It becomes tough for people to satisfy such desires.

We usually have no chance to get what we want, or even can never have them. Our desires cannot be fully satisfied. When one cannot get what he/she wants and his/her desires cannot be satisfied, the attitude and practice differ depending on the person. Most mortals will feel unhappy and a little grieving in their hearts when they cannot get the people or things they want. But they will still actively strive for them. If it is not possible to get them at all, they will get angry or vent their bad emotions. But they will not hurt the innocent. A few dangerous people will become even more

还想要山珍海味、燕窝鱼翅，不光穿的暖和，还需佩戴金银，为了自己的情感欲望和繁衍后代，都想找到最漂亮的异性伴侣⋯人们满足这类欲望时就会变得十分困难。

很多时候我们想要的，我们并没有机会去得到，甚至永远不可能拥有，我们的欲望也无法全部被满足。当一个人得不到自己想要的，欲望不能被满足的时候，不同的人会有不同的态度和做法。绝大多数凡人得不到自己想要的人或物时，心中会有不快和些许怨气，但仍会积极努力地去争取。如果根本不可能得到，他们会发怒，宣泄不良情绪，但不会伤害无辜。少数危险之人，如果不能满足欲望，得不到自己想要的，会变得更加危险。他们的信念使得负能量在这个时候，可以控制他们的言行，不仅让他们抱怨发怒，还会伤害他人。所以，

dangerous, their desires cannot be satisfied and what they want cannot be obtained. In such case, their beliefs allow negative energy to control their words and deeds, making them not only complain and get anger, but also hurt others. So, when such people's desires cannot be satisfied, the people around them will be in danger and will be easily hurt by them or by negative energy.

Good people's reaction is different from the situation described above when their desires cannot be satisfied. First, good people will rationally discern whether their desires are legitimate or not, that is, whether they will affect the interests of others. Then, they will make a trade-off between their own interests and others' interests, neither causing harms to others nor making themselves hard. Make good trade-offs so as to get their own desires appropriately satisfied, while taking into account the reasonable needs of others. If the desires of a good person

当这些人的欲望不能被满足时，他们身边的人就会身处危险之中，会很容易受到他们的伤害，或者说是受到来自负能量的伤害。

当好人的欲望不能被满足时，他们的反应不同于上面讲述的情形。首先，好人们会理性辨别自己的欲望是否合理正当，也就是是否会影响他人的利益。然后，他们会在自己和他人的利益之间做出权衡，既不坑害别人，也不为难自己。做好取舍，使自己的欲望得到适当满足，并兼顾他人的合理需求。如果好人的欲望已经无法满足，比如他喜欢的人已为人妇，那么他便会遵循正能量的指引，转移自己的注意力，并以爱的名义，祝福喜欢的人和她喜欢的人幸福快乐，以此缓解并最终消除，因为欲望无法满足而给自己带

cannot be satisfied, for example, the one he likes is already another person's wife, he will follow the guidance of positive energy, divert his attention, and bless the one he likes and the one she likes happiness in the name of love to alleviate and finally eliminate the unhappiness caused to himself because of the unsatisfied desire.

Good people will not vent their anger at will when they can't get what they want, let alone hurting the innocent. They will, relying on positive energy, divert their attention and continue to pursue their own happiness.

When Being Criticized or Blamed

Due to the inherent defects in human nature, it is inevitable for everyone to indulge their own unreasonable desires and needs in the process of their own growth, and intentionally or unintentionally affect or infringe the legitimate rights and interests

来的不快。

当得不到自己想要的，好人不会肆意发怒宣泄，更不会去伤害无辜，他们会依靠正能量转移自己的注意力，进而继续追寻真正属于自己的幸福。

被批评指责时

由于人性方面存在的先天缺陷，每个人在各自的成长过程中，难免会放纵自己的不合理欲望和需求，会有意无意地影响侵害他人的正当权益，也就是说我们人类随时都有可能说错话、做错事。这里的错误是相对于他人的正当权益而言的，

of others, that is, we humans may say wrong words and do wrong things at any time. The mistakes here are mentioned relative to the legitimate rights and interests of others. Wrong words and deeds may well satisfy a perpetrator's own desires but will cause harm to others.

So, when our words and deeds intentionally or unintentionally harm the interests of others, we may be criticized and blamed by others. Human criticisms and blames, as described in the previous chapter, are sometimes influenced by positive energy, but may also be controlled by negative energy. The human nature of loving freedom determines that no one likes to be criticized and blamed, whether such criticism comes from the kind guidance of positive energy or the groundless demand of negative energy. Criticism can make people feel uncomfortable as it conflicts with the human nature of loving freedom. When being criticized and blamed, most people

错误的言行可能很好地满足了行为人自己的欲望，但却会给他人带来伤害。

因此，当我们的言行有意或是无意伤害到他人的利益时，我们就可能被别人批评指责。人类的批评指责如前面的篇章所述，有时是在正能量的影响作用下所为，但有时也可能是受负能量所控制。人类爱好自由的本性，决定了没有人会喜欢批评指责，不管这种批评是来自正能量的善意指引，还是负能量的无端要求。批评指责由于和人的自由天性相冲突，会让人感到不舒服。在被批评指责的时候，大多数人都会失去平和理性，表现出情绪低落甚至是愤怒，这些都是人的本性使然，是在受到批评指责蕴含的能量干扰之后，人类的正常反应。

will lose peace and mind and show depression or even anger. These are all due to human nature, and are normal human reactions after being disturbed by the energy contained in criticism and blame.

So, in most cases, in order not to cause others to lose peace and sense and then conflict with themselves, except for issues involving bottom line and principle, people will try their best to avoid seriously criticizing and blaming others. Because doing so will cause unpleasantness and embarrassment, or even hatred and violence among people from time to time.

Those who are linked to negative energy may react very dangerously when they are criticized due to their beliefs. Mortals will also have irrational reactions when being criticized and blamed. But their reactions will be within the acceptable range of most people. For example, counter-criticism and counter-blame, mild verbal and physical

所以在多数情况下，为了不致他人失去平和理性，继而与自己发生矛盾冲突，除非是遇到底线和原则性问题，人们都会尽力避免严肃认真地批评指责别人，因为那样做会使人与人之间出现不愉快和尴尬，甚至是仇恨和暴力。

由于自己的信念而连接负能量的人们，在受到批评指责时，他们的反应可能会非常的危险。凡人在被批评指责时，也会有不理性的反应，但他们的反应会在多数人可以接受的范围程度之内，比如反过来指责批评者，出现轻度的语言和肢体暴力，或者短暂的仇恨等等。可是一旦连接负能量的人受到了批评指责，那么仇恨的怒火，

violence, or temporary hatred, etc. Once those who are linked to negative energy are criticized and blamed, however, they may do something driven by hatred and anger that most people cannot accept. For example, because of a well-intentioned criticism, negative energy will drive the criticized to attack the critic severely, getting the critic physically harmed and fearful therewith; even someone people get killed because of a frank and straightforward blame. These are all because of the huge hatred and destructive force in those who are controlled by negative energy.

But the case will be quite different when a similar situation happens to people who are linked to positive energy. First, they will surmount their negative emotions caused by criticism relying on the guidance of positive energy. The rationality from positive energy will tell them whether such criticisms and blames are correct and appropriate or not.

可能驱使这些人做出多数人无法接受的事情。比如，因为一句善意的批评，负能量会驱使被批评者狠狠地攻击批评者，让批评者受到肉体伤害，从而心生恐惧；甚至于有人会因为一次直率坦白的指责，而召来杀身之祸。这些都是因为在负能量影响控制的人身上，蕴藏着巨大的仇恨和破坏力。

当相似的情况，发生在连接正能量的人们这里时，情况就大不一样了。首先，他们会依靠正能量的指引疏导，克服掉因受到批评而产生的不良情绪，来自正能量的理性会告诉他们，这样的批评指责是否正确适当。如果是对的，理性会让他们虚心接受这样的批评，进一步克服自己的私欲，改正自己身上被指责的缺点和问题。如果经

If they are right, rationality will allow them to humbly accept such criticisms, further surmount their own selfish desires, and correct the shortcomings and problems against which they have been criticized. If the critics' blames are considered to be wrong after rational thinking, positive energy will also guide them to deal with them in an appropriate way. For example, identify whether the opponent's criticism comes from negative energy, whether they need to respond frontally or avoid the temptation and invasion of negative energy.

When Being Misunderstood or Not Understood

One is doing things seriously, using his/her hard work and sweat in exchange for the fruits of labor so as to attain his/her goals to satisfy his/her own desires and needs in his/her life in most cases. This is a very meaningful process.

过理性的思考，认为批评者的指责是错误的时候，正能量也会引导他们采用适当的方式去应对处理。比如辨识对方的批评是否来自负能量，是否需要正面回应，或是避开负能量的试探和侵袭。

被误会和不理解时

一个人的生命历程中，有很多时候他（她）都是在认真努力地做事，在用自己的付出和汗水，换取劳动果实，进而实现目标，满足自己的欲望需求。这是个很有意义的过程，辛勤耕耘过后，自己的欲望需求

After hard work, one's own desires and needs are satisfied, value in human society is created and the economy gets prosperous therewith. Getting happy due to contentment in the heart, while feeling no pain when enduring fatigue as fatigue is rewarded, and the rewards of labor will make people wealthy and contented.

But people often suffer in their life from hard work or fatigue. Fatigue beyond their tolerance or, all their efforts not understood by others at all both make people afraid of hard work and fatigue. Normally, the more efforts one makes, the more tired he/she will be, and the more rewards he/she will get. But one's labor may become worthless and meaningless when his/her hard work is not understood by others. Only when one's labor can satisfy the legitimate needs of others or the society can his/her labor create value. When one's contribution is not understood or misunderstood, even if his/her labor can satisfy the

得到满足，人类社会的价值因此被创造，经济也因此而繁荣。内心满足而快乐，忍受劳累却丝毫不痛苦，因为劳累是有回报的，劳动的回报会让人富裕知足。

但人生的很多时候，也经常因为辛勤付出或劳累而痛苦，或是劳累超出了自己的承受范围，或是所有的付出丝毫不被别人理解，都会让人们惧怕付出和劳累。正常情况下，越是付出的多，越是劳累，得到的回报也会越多。但是当一个人的劳累付出不被别人理解时，他（她）的劳动就可能变得没有价值，没有意义。一个人的劳动只有在满足他人或社会的正当需求时，才能创造价值。当一个人的付出不被理解或是误会时，即便他（她）的劳动能够满足他人和社会的正当需求，由于误会和不理解，这样的劳动成果也没有机会去满足需求，价值不能实现，酬劳或回报也

legitimate needs of others and the society, as being misunderstood or not understood, such fruits of labor have no chance to satisfy the needs, and the value cannot be realized, and hence there will also be no rewards generated. This is the reason for the pain of giving. People are not afraid of being tired but afraid of not being recognized and rewarded after being tired.

Many people choose to give up when what they do is not understood. They cannot get rewards in the foreseeable future --- this is a justification for their choice to give up. For example, a great navigator completed his voyage around the world, but many navigators before him chose to give up as they didn't know that the earth was round. And such abandonment seemed to be a normal choice at that time. Almost all people out of the ordinary in history were not understood or misunderstood. What on earth made them choose to persevere? --- It's not simple and incidental.

会无从产生。因付出而感到痛苦的原因就在于此，人们不怕劳累，怕的是付出劳累之后得不到认同和回报。

有不少人在做事不被理解时，会选择放弃，在可以预见的未来无法得到回报，是他们选择放弃的正当理由。就像了不起的航海家完成了环球航行，可是由于不知道地球是圆的，让在他之前的很多人都选择了放弃，并且这样的放弃在当时看来也是很正常的选择。历史上那些与众不同的人，几乎都曾经不被理解和误会过，究竟是什么让他们选择坚持下去，并不是件简单偶然的事情，很多人没有选择坚持，是因为当时有足够的理由让他们相信自己是正确的，但那些与众不同的人会不会是某种特别的能量让他们做出了那样的选择呢？

Many people did not choose to persevere as there were enough reasons to make them believe that they are right. But did those quite different people make such a choice due to certain special energy?

Perhaps it is negative energy that makes such people become the ones who initiate a world war; it may also be positive energy that makes them become the ones who are able to make a "bomb of love".

When Conflicting with Others

We humans are full of desires, and it is possible for all of us to get into conflict with others. Because usually our desires and needs are almost exactly the same --- need to eat when hungry, need to drink when thirsty, need to keep warm when cold and with erotic desires and selfish ideas. When such desires and needs collide between people, disputes and conflicts will occur. Food and

或许是负向的能量，让这个人成为了掀起世界大战的人；也可能是正向的能量，让他们成为能够制造"爱的炸弹"之人。

与他人发生冲突时

我们人类是充满欲望的，每个人之间都有发生矛盾冲突的可能。因为我们的欲望需求在很多时候，几乎一模一样，饿了要吃，喝了要喝，冷了要保暖，有情欲，有自私的念头…当这些欲望需求在不同的人之间发生碰撞时，争执和冲突便会发生。食物和饮水不够充足，但是大家都需要，冬天很冷，可能够保暖的衣物却不足以人人都有，多人喜欢上同一个异性

drinkable water are insufficient but everyone needs it; it is very cold in winter, but there are not enough warm clothes for everyone. Several people like the same girl/woman or boy/man, etc. --- These are all causes for conflicts and fights in human society.

For the above issues, we humans can do nothing due to defects in human nature. There is no direct evidence for such facts, but it is not difficult to find them when everyone asks themselves. In other words, there is no possibility for us to eliminate conflicts and fights in human society from the source. As everyone needs to eat when hungry and drink when thirsty. Conflicts will be inevitable when all want to satisfy the same desire. So, it can also be said that "war" is the natural state of human society while "peace" is the result of deliberate pursuit of humans for their own interests.

With such a viewpoint, when we conflict with others for various reasons, don't believe selfishness

等等，这些都是人类社会冲突和争斗的原因。

上面所述的问题我们人类自身无法改变，因为人的天性是有缺陷的，尽管没有直接的证据，但每个人扪心自问时，这样的事实不难发现。换句话说，我们没有从根源上消除人类社会冲突争斗的可能性。因为饿了必须要吃，渴了必须要喝，都要满足相同欲望的时候，矛盾冲突就会不可避免。因此也可以说，"战争"是人类社会的自然状态，而"和平"是人类为了自身利益刻意追求的结果。

带着这样的观点，当我们因为种种原因与他人发生冲突时，请不要相信私欲和仇恨能

and hatred can help you attain your goals. If they work, negative energy will affect and control your words and deeds through your false beliefs. Although sometimes hatred and violence are very effective and will allow you to get what you want very soon. The belief that hatred and violence can solve problems can cause negative energy to come and thus intensify conflicts and fights between people. This is what people often say --- "people will fall into a vicious circle of revenge for grievance", "If you are patient in one moment of anger, you will escape a hundred days of sorrow". But how to be patient and to what extent you should be patient in case of conflicts between people is a difficult question. If what you are facing are the legitimate appeals of others, negotiation, communication and mutual concessions will be the best outcome. Because each of us is aware of our own defects and bottom lines, and we will seek

让你达到目地，如果那样的话，负能量就会通过你的错误信念影响控制你的言行。虽然有时候仇恨和暴力很有效，会让你很快得到你想要的，但相信仇恨暴力可以解决问题的信念，却会引来负能量，进而加剧人与人之间的冲突和争斗。这也就是人们常说的冤冤相报无了时，退一步才能海阔天空，可是人与人发生冲突之时如何退，退多少，是个很难的问题。如果你面临的是他人正当的诉求，协商沟通和共同让步会是最好的结局，因为我们每个人都清楚自己的缺陷和底线，会寻求合理的节点来约束自己的不当诉求，或者自觉遏制超过合理限度的欲望需求，这个合理的标准就是不阻碍他人的正当诉求。虽然很难用语言准确描述，但凭着良心人们会很快明白问题所在并达成妥协，比如食物问题，合理的度或节点，应该是让每个人都吃饱，如果不能让每个人都吃饱，那么按数量来平均分配也是多数人能够接受的。至于由谁来分，仍然有合理的标准可以遵循——大家

reasonable nodes to restrain our improper appeals, or consciously curb the desires and needs exceeding the reasonable limit. And the standard for "reasonable" here is not to hinder the legitimate appeals of others. It is difficult to describe accurately in words, but with conscience, people will soon understand what the problem is and reach a compromise, e.g. the issue of food, the reasonable degree or node should be to get everyone full; and if cannot get everyone full, even distribution based on quantity will be acceptable to most people. As for to be distributed by whom, there are still reasonable standards to follow --- anyone who everyone can trust will do.

If you encounter someone who does not consider the interests of others at all, that is, a person who is unwilling to concede to the legitimate appeals of others, such people only considers their own benefits, and their selfish beliefs will make them linked to negative

都信得过的人就行。

　　如果你遇到了完全不考虑他人利益的人，也就是对于他人的正当诉求也不肯让步的人，这样的人只考虑自己的好处，自私自利的信念会让他们连接至负能量。要当心控制他们的负能量，不要与其正面冲突或直接对抗，因为只要人们相信负

energy. Be careful to control their negative energy, and don't directly conflict or confront with them. As negative energy can make them never surrender as long as people believe in it. In such case, only by letting more human compatriots know what they have done and affecting and guiding them to change their wrong beliefs through the common belief that most people believe in love and positive energy will negative energy fail to control them and can it possible for people to live in harmony.

Exposing the causes and details of conflicts to the media for dissemination or submitting to the judiciary for ruling is usually the best way to make the common beliefs of mankind work and game with negative energy.

When Being Deceived and Hurt

Deceit and harm, if are not due to kindness, will be true deceit and hurt, and which will have a

能量，负能量可以让他们永不屈服。这个时候只有将他们的所作所为，让更多的人类同胞知道，通过多数人相信爱与正能量的共同信念，来影响引导他们改变自己错误的信念，这样负能量就无法控制他们，大家才有可能和睦共处。

把冲突的缘由和经过，诉诸媒体传播或交给司法机构裁判，通常是让人类共同信念发挥作用，同负能量博弈的最佳方式。

受到欺骗伤害时

欺骗和伤害如果不是因着善良所为，那便是真正的欺骗和伤害，它们会对所有的人产生

great negative effect on all people. Such acting force not only makes people feel painful, but also makes people believe in the temptation of deceit and hurt, making people feel that the goals can be attained sooner through deceit and that it's easy to make people yield by means that hurt. When one has such belief, he/she will be soon linked to negative energy. His/her words and deeds will soon have the features of negative energy. Such people's desires will be satisfied under the guidance of negative energy. But negative energy will also cause them to drift away from the happiness that mankind pursues and eventually have to numb themselves by deceiving and hurting others and deceiving themselves that they don't need happiness. But those who believe in deceit will end up in vain no matter how hard they try. Because people controlled by negative energy cannot get rid of pain.

When we encounter real

很大的负面作用。这种作用力不仅让人感到痛苦，还会使人相信欺骗和伤害的诱惑，让人觉得通过欺骗能更快地实现目标，使用伤害的手段会很轻易地令人屈服。当一个人有了这样的信念，便会很快连接至负能量，他（她）的言行将迅速具备负能量的特征，这些人的欲望会因为负能量的指引得到满足，但负能量也会让他们与人类追求的幸福快乐渐行渐远，而最终不得不通过不断地欺骗伤害他人来麻痹自己，欺骗自己不需要幸福快乐。不过相信欺骗伤害的人无论再怎么努力，最终都会是徒劳，因为受负能量控制的人是无法摆脱痛苦的。

当我们遭遇真正的欺骗和

deceit and hurt, we should not treat others with their own way. As we need to protect the positive energy in us. We humans cannot eliminate the negative energy. But we can affect and control negative energy in the human world under the guidance of positive energy. Blindly fighting against those who are controlled by negative energy, tit-for-tat can only cause us to be caught in the trap of negative energy and eventually become the captive of negative energy, just like the opponent. The defects in human nature determine that no one can resist the temptation of hatred, with which there will be negative energy, in the process of fights among humans. So, we should not directly conflict with them frontally, and also deal with our compatriots by means of deceit and harm --- doing so will only increase the sphere of influence of negative energy. What we need to do is to let more people know what have happened to keep more people away from

伤害时，不要用其人之道去还治其人之身。因为我们要保守我们身上的正能量，我们人类无法消除负能量，但我们可以在正能量的指引帮助下，影响控制人类世界的负能量。一味地同受负能量控制的人们争斗，以血还血，以牙还牙，只能中了负能量的圈套，最终变得和对手一样，成为负能量的俘虏。人性的缺陷决定了，在人类争斗的过程中，没有人能抵得住仇恨的诱惑，有了仇恨，就有了负能量。所以，我们不要与其正面冲突，也去使用欺骗伤害的手段对付同胞，那样做只会让负能量的势力范围越来越大。我们要做的是，让更多的人知道所发生的一切，让更多的人远离这些人，用不了多久，被负能量迷惑的同胞便会清醒，会主动丢弃原本的信念，到那时负能量就无法继续控制他们了。

them. It will not be long before the compatriots deceived by negative energy will wake up and will actively discard their original beliefs. Then negative energy can no longer control them.

In the human world, there are still some other deceits and harms which are not real deceit and hurt from negative energy. The feeling they give people is that you feel love from them in the end in spite of deceit and harm --- a feeling that only positive energy can give you. Like deceit and harm of negative energy, they also use the means of "deceit" and "harm", e.g. deceiving the patients, concealing the conditions from them, weakening the bad belief in the patients' heart, and gradually expelling the negative energy from them, helping them recover and heal; parents scold and punish their children in order to correct their wrong beliefs and curb the affect and control of negative energy on them lest they make greater mistakes in the future.

在人类世界还有一些欺骗和伤害，不是真正的欺骗伤害，或者说不是来自负能量的欺骗伤害。它们给人的感觉，尽管也是被骗和被伤害，但最终你却从中感受到了爱——一种正能量才能给你的感觉。和负能量的欺骗伤害一样，它们也采用"欺骗"和"伤害"的手段，比如欺骗病人，对他（她）隐瞒病情，削弱病人心中的不良信念，慢慢驱赶他们身上的负能量，帮助其健康痊愈；父母为了子女将来不犯更大的错误，责骂体罚他们，为的是纠正他们的错误信念，遏制负能量对他们的影响和控制。这些都是来自正能量的"欺骗和伤害"，是善意的"谎言和暴力"，是对人类有益的。

These are all "deceits and harms" from positive energy, which are white "lies and violence" beneficial to mankind.

When encountering real deceits and harms, what we need to do is to keep away from them. Record them and how they make us feel, and disclose them as appropriate. We can win if we no longer get close to them. As long as we humans do not believe in negative energy and don't directly fight against those who are controlled by different kinds of negative energy unless we are forced to do so, negative energy will have no chance to affect and control us, and hence their sphere of influence will get smaller and smaller, until ultimately they succumb to positive energy.

When Being A Power Controller

Power, as described in previous chapters, is transfer of rights from social members. The

当遭遇真正的欺骗和伤害时，我们要做的是远离它们，记录下它们以及它们给我们的感觉，并适时予以公布，不再接近它们，我们就能得胜。只要我们人类不相信且不到迫不得已不同负能量控制的人们直接争斗，负能量便没有机会影响控制我们，其势力范围会越来越小，直至最后臣服于正能量。

成为权力掌控者时

权力如前面篇章中所述，是来自社会成员自身权利的让渡。这里的权利让渡，尽管没有直

transfer of rights mentioned here, it cannot be ruled out that the process is an invisible energy transfer although there is no direct evidence. The method may be that people transfer some energy to those who they think deserve such energy via their own belief. Whether a hereditary king or a democratically elected leader (organization) cannot control and master the power of human society --- a unilateral dominance for which the consent from the counterparty is not required and which can restrain and control the rights (freedoms) of social members --- for long without the recognition and support (transfer of rights) of social members (the public).

The decision-making power of power controllers ultimately depends on the recognition and support of other social members whether in a human society governed through the rules formulated by most people upon negotiation or in a human society

接证据，但也无法排除其过程是一种无形的能量转接或传递，方法可能是人们通过自己的信念，将某些能量转接或传递给了他们认为应该得到这些能量的人。无论是世袭的王，还是民主选举的领袖（机构），离开了社会成员（公众）的认可和拥护（权利让渡），都不可能长久掌控管理人类社会的权力——一种不需要对方同意的单向支配力，它可以约束控制社会成员的权利（自由）。

人类社会不管是让多数人协商制定规则来治理，还是实行集权独裁，由一个人或者少数人去统治，掌控权力者手中的决定权，最终都依赖于其他社会成员的认可和拥护。只要一个国家（一种人类社会组织形态）的多数人拥护他们的领袖（机

with centralized dictatorship which is ruled by one or a few people. As long as most people in a country (a form of organization of human society) support their leader (organization) or king, it will be legitimate for such leader (organization) or king to control the power of such country. As the beliefs of social members differ, however, the energy they give to the power controller through recognition and support is not necessarily positive energy that makes people happy, it may also be negative energy that makes people nervous, angry and painful. But even negative energy itself can still serve as the "authority" of human society within a certain period and scope (it is also called "authoritarian" as it is not the most powerful positive energy) and can lead the formation of certain rules of form and content to bring a country order and stability within certain period of time and range. When one day the public no longer believes that leader (organization)

构）或是王，那么这个领袖（机构）或是王，就具有正当性（合理性）来掌控管理国家的权力。不过由于社会成员的信仰不同，他们通过认可拥护交给权力掌控者的能量，不一定都是让人快乐幸福的正能量，也可能是使人紧张、愤怒、痛苦的负能量。但即便是负能量，仍然可以在一定时期和范围内，作为人类社会的"权威"（因为不是最强大的正能量，也叫做"威权"），并主导形成一定形式和内容的规则，给国家带来秩序和稳定。当有一天公众不再相信领袖（机构）或是王可以引领保护他们时，这些人（或机构）掌控的权力便会很快失去正当性，曾经掌控权力的人此时也会变得十分危险。公众随时会以各种理由来认定他们掌控的权力伤害了自己的正当权益，而把他们置于任人宰割的境地——被公众收回权利后（失去认可拥护，无法获取所需能量），他们就会失去权力，变成普通的社会成员，他们也可能因为之前的所作所为而受到惩罚，甚至付出生命的代价。

or the king can lead and protect them, the power controlled by such people (or organization) will quickly lose its legitimacy. In such case, those who once controlled power will also become very dangerous. The public will at any time believe that the power controlled by them has infringed their legitimate rights and interests with various reasons, and thus put them in a situation where they can be treated in any way --- after the public takes back the rights (losing recognition and support, and consequently unable to obtain the energy needed), they will lose the power and become ordinary social members. They may also be punished for what they have done before, or even pay the price with their lives.

So, for the power controllers of human society, what we should be wary of is that the recognition and support (society members make power controllers obtain the energy needed using their own beliefs, which is also called

因此，对于人类社会的权力掌控者，应当警惕的事情是，不能失去多数社会成员的认可拥护（社会成员用各自的信念让权力掌控者获取所需的能量，形式上也叫做"权利让渡"或者"能量传递"）。不管是正能量，

"transfer of rights" or "transfer of energy" in form) of most social members cannot be lost. For whether positive energy or negative energy, the recognition and support of the public are necessary means for power controllers to get more energy. The more people who recognize and support, the greater the power and the greater the acting force that can affect others will be. And in the long run, only when power controllers gain strong positive energy can their reign be truly safe and stable. How the power controllers obtain the positive energy needed mainly depends on the beliefs of most social members, that is, it depends on what most social members believe in. If everyone is pursuing happiness and upholding love and justice, such public will let their leader (king) obtain strong positive energy; conversely, social members who do not believe in love, positive energy and justice but only believe in loyalty, power,

还是负能量，公众的认可拥护都是权力掌控者得到更多能量的必需手段。认可拥护的人越多，权力就越大，可以影响他人的作用力也就越大，并且长远来看，权力掌控者只有获取强大的正能量，才是真正安全和稳固的。权力掌控者如何获取所需的正能量，主要取决于这个社会多数成员的信仰，也就是要看多数社会成员相信什么。如果大家都在追求幸福快乐，崇尚爱和公义，那么这样的公众就会让他们的领袖（王），得到强大的正能量；相反，不相信爱和正能量，不讲公义却只相信忠诚、权力、仇恨和暴力征服的社会成员，就只能转接或传递负能量。负能量的控制最终会让人痛苦，并且随着事实真相的不断曝光，公众会改变信念，收回权利，瓦解领袖（王）所掌控的权力。

hatred and conquest by violence can only transfer negative energy. The control of negative energy will ultimately make them painful, and with the continuous exposure of the truth, the public will change their beliefs, take back their rights, and disintegrate the power controlled by the leader (king).

When Being A Celebrity

People who are followed by many people are called celebrities, whose words and deeds will draw the attention from many people. Their appearances and deportments, the objects they use... all people and things related to celebrities will be the focus of their followers to imitate and talk about.

How a person becomes a celebrity has anything to do with positive energy or negative energy? Before answering this question, we can first understand generally how one becomes a celebrity. In human society, except

成为名人时

被很多人关注的人是名人，他们的言行举动会牵动很多人的注意力。他们的仪态外表，他们所用的物品…所有与名人有关联的人和物，都会是关注者们效仿、谈论的焦点。

一个人是怎样成为名人的，和正能量或是负能量有关系吗？在回答这个问题之前，我们可以先了解通常情况下，一个人的成名之路是怎样的。人类社会除了少数人由于种种原因，从他（她）的出生便会受到一

a minority of people who will draw attention from a country or even the world from his/her birth due to various reasons, most people are ordinary people who don't draw much attention. If one wants to draw attention from others, he/she must be unique and be known by the public. Uniqueness is to be outstanding or special. The more outstanding and special, the easier for one to draw attention from others. The leader (king) of a country is a celebrity. The public often pays attention to his/her words, deeds and decisions. Those who are outstanding in singing and dancing are also celebrities. Those who have made great achievements in a certain industry are also celebrities. As long as one's unique enough to draw attention from others he/she can become a celebrity. Such uniqueness can be acquired through hard work, or it can be inherent. As long as one is unique, and it is difficult for others to be achieve same,

国甚至是世界范围内的关注外，绝大多数人都是平凡普通不会有太多关注的人。一个人如果想要得到别人的关注，必须要有与众不同之处，且让公众知晓。与众不同就是出众或特别，越是出众、特别，越容易被人关注。一个国家的领袖（王）是名人，公众很多时候都在关注他（她）的言行和决策，唱歌跳舞出众的也是名人，在某个行业领域作出丰功伟绩的也是名人，只要他（她）的特别之处足够吸引别人的关注，他（她）就可以成为名人。这种特别之处，可以是后天努力得来，也可以是先天自然而来，只要与众不同，其他人难以做到，他（她）就会成为别人关注的对象，进而成为名人。并且获得公众持续关注的时间多少，会直接决定着他们做名人的时间长短，人们不再关注他（她）了，他（她）就会失去举手投足间影响牵动他人的能力，会变成普通人。

he/she will become the target of others' attention and then become a celebrity. And the length of time they draw continuous attention from the public directly determines the length of time of their identity as celebrities. If people no longer follow them, they will lose their abilities to influence others through their behaviors and become ordinary people.

Although public attention is drawn, celebrities can also, in terms of their influences and roles, be divided into two groups: one group is those of hope and power, what they bring us is plenty of sunshine and affection; the other group is those of disappointment or fear, what they cause to us is negative and pessimistic mood. Yet, we can make such a hypothesis: what the two different groups of celebrities convey to us is positive energy and negative energy respectively, the former makes us happy while the latter makes us sorrowful. Celebrities are linked to these kinds of energy

尽管被公众所关注，名人也因着影响作用不同而分为两大类：一类会给人希望和力量，让人觉得他们充满阳光和友爱；一类则会让人失望或恐惧，给人消极悲观的情绪。我们仍然可以做这样的假设，不同类型的名人给人们传递的，分别是让人幸福快乐的正能量，和最终使人痛苦的负能量，名人们因着自己的信念和他人的关注，而连接到了这些能量，进而又让这样的能量来影响自己和关注者们的言行。如果这样的假设推理能够成立，那么当一个人想得到公众的持续关注，长久地成为名人，他（她）通过自己的信念和他人的关注，去

via their own beliefs and attention from others, and which will in turn affect the behaviors of themselves and their followers. Given that such what-if reasoning holds, then, if a person wants to become a long-standing celebrity with ongoing attention from the public, the best way is to enable himself/herself and his or her followers to harvest happiness from positive energy at the same time by linking and spreading love and positive energy via his or her own beliefs and attention from others.

Only If Family Is Maintained Can Love Remain

Love will produced if a man and a woman who like each other get along for a long time. They will set up a family. That is how humans multiply and thrive. Human love is a feeling which can make people reap happiness and sweetness. People who own love are linked to positive energy

连接传播爱与正能量，使自己和关注者都能获得来自正能量的快乐幸福，将会是最好的办法。

守得住家才留得住爱

互相喜欢的异性在一起时间长了，便会生出爱情，并孕育出家庭，人类也因此而繁衍不息。人类的爱情是一种感觉，爱情能让人收获幸福甜蜜，拥有爱情的人们，通过自己相信爱的信念连接到了使人幸福的正能量。

that makes people happy via their belief in love.

After a man and a woman set up a family, many responsibilities and burdens will be added to themselves respectively, e.g. miscellaneous housework, child rearing and education, the hardship of earning money to support the family and the obligation to support the elderly, etc. All these will bring different feelings to family members --- it turned out that believing in love requires so much hard work, and needs to endure such deep hurt and misunderstanding in order to retain the feeling of love and find the final peace and happiness. Why work hard and endurance are needed? Is it not OK to live selfishly and willfully and only ask for something? Of course it is OK, as this is everyone's right --- the freedom of a person to behave at will. If one chooses to live this way, however, there must be someone who loves him/her and pay for him/her; otherwise, he/

男人和女人组建家庭后，就会给各自增添很多责任和负担，繁杂的家务，孩子的抚养教育，还有赚钱养家的艰辛和赡养老人的义务等等。这些都给家庭成员带来了不一样的感受——原来相信爱，需要付出这么多的辛苦，需要忍耐这么深的伤害和误会，才能留得住爱的感觉，才能找到最后的平安和幸福。为什么要辛苦和忍耐，一味索取、自私任性地生活不行吗？当然可以，因为这是每个人的权利——按照自己意愿去做的自由。不过一个人如果选择这样的生活，必须有爱他（她）的人为之付出才行，要不然他们便无法持续获取生活所需的资源和财富。为之付出的人，只能选择辛苦忍耐，用自己的劳动果实去不断填满所爱之人的欲望沟壑，这样的人通常只会是他（她）的家人或愿意与其组建家庭的人。直到有一天他们幡然醒悟时，会明白他们给深爱自己的人带来了多大的痛苦，他们会从被爱中学会爱，

she cannot obtain the resources and wealth needed for life on an ongoing basis. Those who pay for him/her can only choose to hard work and tolerate, continuously fill the desire gap of the loved one with their fruits of labor. Typically, such people are only his/her family members or people who are willing to set up a family with them. Until one day when they come to realize their errors, they will understand how much pain they have caused to those who love them deeply. They will learn to love from being loved, and then burst out the powerful energy of love in form of gratitude, and to influence people around them to let them also obtain the feeling of love --- happiness and sweetness. Here, the hard work of the one who loves you is actually to keep the fortress of love --- the family. Because every family member needs to obtain material and spiritual food from the family to feed their body and spirit. Family is the fortress of love. When a

进而用感恩回报的方式迸发出爱的强大能量，去感染身边的人，让他们也得到爱的感觉——幸福甜蜜。在这里，爱人之人的辛苦付出，其实是为了守住爱的堡垒——家，因为每一个家庭成员都需要从家中获取物质和精神食粮，来供养自己的肉体和灵魂。家是爱的堡垒，家庭破碎了，人们便不能从中获取生命之所需，无法再在家中找到爱的感觉。在人类社会当中，没有比家更能让人感受到爱的地方了，家是人类社会的基本单元，家庭的成员也只有在家中，才能收获真正的幸福和快乐。

family is broken, people can no longer get what they need for life and find the feeling of love in the family. In human society, there is no place where people can feel love more than family, which is the basic unit of human society. Only when family members are at home can they reap real happiness.

It can also be said that only by maintaining home can love and positive energy that give people happiness remain.

Family Members Should Be Considerate to One Another

The defects in us humans, as well as the inherent selfishness (people can feel satisfied when they are selfish --- a feeling similar to happiness) determine that it is impossible for conflicts not to happen among people. Conflicts among social members are the norm, while harmonious coexistence is just the result of the joint efforts and compromises of

也可以说，守得住家，我们才能留得住给人幸福快乐的爱与正能量。

家庭成员应互相体谅

我们人类的自身缺陷，和与生俱来的自私自利（人在自私自利时会获得满足感——一种类似幸福快乐的感觉），决定了人与人之间不可能没有矛盾，人类社会成员之间的冲突会是常态，而和谐相处只是大家共同努力，妥协让步的结果。

everyone.

In a family, as the smallest unit of human society, quarrels, conflicts and estrangements among members are also inevitable. We can say that these are due to human nature and are thus all normal. Conflict or even break-off among family members is a thing that makes people very sad. But we are all mortals with unreasonable desires and needs called "selfishness". According to human nature, every morning we want to sleep until we wake up naturally. But who will be the right one to prepare breakfast? A man in love says to a woman, "I will satisfy all your needs, as long as you can marry me". But we are all mortals with selfishness. Can you guarantee to prepare breakfast for her for a lifetime? Presumably no one will be able to do it. It's not because you don't love her, but because you ignore the defects in human nature and consequently make an unfulfilled promise so as to get her love. To set up a family

家庭作为人类社会的最小组成单元，也无法避免成员之间的争吵冲突和隔阂。我们可以说，这些是人类的本性使然，都是正常的，尽管家庭成员的冲突甚至决裂，是一件很让人伤心难过的事情。但我们都是凡人，都有被称作是"私心"的不合理欲望和需求。每天早晨依着我们的本性，都想要睡到自然醒，早饭谁来准备合适呢？恋爱中的男人对女人说，我会满足你所有的要求，只要你能嫁给我。可是我们都是凡人，都有私心，你能保证一辈子都给她做早餐吗？应该没有人能够做到，不是不爱她，而是为了得到她的爱，忽略了人性的缺陷，做出了无法兑现的承诺。组建家庭是为了得到爱，但有些感觉不是真正的爱，什么样的是真爱呢？下面这句话是值得考虑信赖的——"我一定会用心呵护你，不让你受伤害。"人类的本性决定了，与人冲突、伤害他人是很容易发生的事情，自己能够做到一直呵护，不去伤害心爱的人，就已经难能可

is to get love. But some feelings are not true love. Then, what is true love like? The following words is worthy of consideration and trust --- "I will definitely take care of you and protect you against harms." Human nature determines that it is very easy to conflict with and hurt others. It is already commendable that one can always take care of the one he/she loves and doesn't hurt him/her. One doesn't have to expect to satisfy all her claims.

As a family member, how to get with the spouse, the children or the elderly? After admitting the defects in human nature, in order to safeguard the family --- to be precise, to safeguard the state of mutual care among family members, what we need to do is to be patient and considerate of the defects of family members as sometimes they are unable to surmount their own problems. If to choose to be patient and considerate, of course, you'll first feel you are "hurt". But such hurt

贵了，不必奢望可以满足她所有的要求。

作为一个家庭的成员，爱人、孩子或者老人，该怎样和他们和睦相处？在承认人性的缺陷之后，为了守住家庭——准确地说，是守住家庭成员之间互相关心呵护的状态，我们需要做的就是，忍耐体谅家庭成员的缺陷和不足，因为有时他们无法克服自己的问题。当然选择忍耐体谅，首先给人的感觉就是受到"伤害"，但这种伤害是可以修复补偿的。修补的方法就是，我们忍耐体谅的家庭成员，慢慢地明白或者突然顿悟爱与被爱的道理，开始用

is repairable and compensable. The way to repair it is that our family members to whom we are patient and considerate will gradually understand or suddenly realize the truth of loving and being loved, and thus begin to reward our common family heartedly -- to satisfy the needs of the family with his/her efforts.

Once those to whom family members are patient and considerate understand the truth about love (positive energy), the joint efforts of family members will protect the family as a solid fortress. Family members will be linked to powerful positive energy via their beliefs in love to nourish and guide every family member. Thereby the feeling of happiness will always be with everyone.

When Being Seriously Hurt by Him/her

Family is the fortress of love, and the source and harbor of happiness for every family

心回报我们共同的家——用他（她）的努力去满足家人的需求。

被家庭成员忍耐体谅的人，一旦明白了关于爱（正能量）的道理时，家庭成员的共同努力会把家守护的像一个坚固的堡垒，家人们会通过对爱的信仰，连接到强大的正能量，来滋养引领每一位家庭成员，幸福快乐的感觉便会常常萦绕在大家的身边。

当被他（她）深深伤害时

家是爱的堡垒，是每一位家庭成员获取幸福快乐的源泉和港湾。家庭成员的共同信念——

member. Common beliefs of family members --- belief in love --- make family the best place for family members to be linked to positive energy. Returning to a loving family will make people calm down naturally, whether loving or being loved will both make people reap happiness --- a feeling given to people by positive energy.

But often, family can also be a place where people get hurt and feel painful. When one is painful, one thing is certain, that is, positive energy is leaving or has left you, and is replaced by negative energy that makes you painful. Why does the positive energy leave? Your belief in love sways, you no longer believe in love, and finally totally deny love. All these will cause positive energy no longer be with you.

When people won't believe in love? Only when their spirit (or one's soul) is seriously hurt, people will easily feel that the reason why they are hurt is

相信爱，使得家是一个让家庭成员能够连接正能量的最佳场所，回到一个有爱的家中，会让人很自然地平静下来，无论是爱或是被爱，都会让人收获幸福快乐——一种正能量给人的感觉。

但在很多时候，家也会成为一个让人受伤害、感到痛苦的地方。一个人痛苦难受的时候，有一件事是可以确定的，那就是正能量正在或者已经离你而去，取而代之的是让你痛苦的负能量。为什么正能量会离去，你对爱的信念动摇了，不再相信爱，直至最后完全否定爱，都会导致正能量无法继续存留在你的身上。

人在什么时候会不相信爱，只有在自己的灵魂（或者说是一个人的心灵）深深地被伤害时，会很容易让人觉得受伤害是自己太相信爱、太善良的缘

because they believe in love too much and are too kind. What is such hurt of spirit on earth? Looking back each experience when our soul is hurt, we will find that the hurt is actually disappointment --- our own desires were not satisfied. Some desires and claims are legitimate, and some not. People will be disappointed if their legitimate claims cannot be satisfied, and such disappointment is hurt. Whilst those unreasonable desires that cannot be satisfied will also make people disappointed. But this is not real hurt. Because most people agree that human irrational desires should not be satisfied. The common feelings of most people determine the standard for psychic hurt (disappointment) of human society. Little kids need to be cared for. If their parents do not satisfy their indispensable needs, they will get hurt or even lose precious lives. But when one grows up, if he/she has the ability to work but still only asks for something

故。这种灵魂的伤害究竟是什么呢，回想一下每次心灵受伤害的经历，我们会发现其实伤害就是失望——自己的欲望要求没能得到想要的满足。有的欲望要求是正当合理的，有些不是，正当合理的要求不能被满足，会让人失望，这种失望就是伤害。而那些不合理的欲望不能被满足也会让人失望，但却不是真正的伤害，因为多数人都认同不应该满足人类不合理的欲望，多数人的共同感受决定了人类社会心灵伤害（失望）的标准。一个孩子在年幼时，需要关心照顾，大人不满足他（她）必需的要求，他们就会受到伤害，甚至失去宝贵的生命。但当一个人成年以后，有劳动能力却仍然一味索取不知回报，不满足他（她）的欲望要求，就不算真正的伤害，正当合理的欲望要求不能被满足，才是伤害。一个人一心一意为了自己的伴侣和孩子，在外面辛苦打拼，流汗流泪，而他（她）的伴侣却不知珍惜，肆意挥霍家庭财富，甚至出轨、发生婚外情。绝大多数人类都会认为这

instead of rewarding in return. Non-satisfaction of his/her desires cannot really hurt. Only non-satisfaction of legitimate desires is hurt. One is wholeheartedly devoted to his/her spouse and children, working hard somewhere away from home, sweating and crying. But his/her spouse doesn't cherish it, squandering family wealth, even cheating and having extramarital affairs. Most humans would consider this serious psychic hurt because in such case most humans have the legitimate needs --- loyalty to marriage and understanding to the spouse. Your child grows up after about two decades of hard work to raise him/her, but he/she doesn't make efforts, keeps asking you for something and doesn't cherish, or even speaks harshly to you and punches you --- these are all hurt that makes you very painful.

How should we address such hurt? Treating others with their own way is a way to temporarily relieve one's hatred. You cheat and

是一种很深的心灵伤害，因为绝大多数人类在这个时候的正当需求都是一致的——需要一份对婚姻的忠诚和对伴侣的理解。当你含辛茹苦把孩子抚养成人，他（她）却不知付出努力，仍然向你索取且不知珍惜，甚至对你冷言恶语、拳脚相加，这些都是让人非常痛苦的伤害。

遇到这些伤害时，我们该怎样去面对呢？以其人之道还治其人之身，是一种暂时让人痛快解恨的方法。你出轨背叛，

have extramarital affairs, so will I; you hurt me, so I will hurt you too. Human nature determines that those who hurt others also have their own legitimate needs, and if which cannot be satisfied, they will also get hurt. So, retaliating against those who hurt you in a tit-for-tat way will have an effect, which is that he/she will also feel painful due to disappointment. But the biggest downside of doing so is destruction of good and bad alike. Because you are with the belief of hatred when retaliating others. You believe that only hatred can solve your pain. So you no longer believe in love. And you cannot be linked to positive energy --- the energy that makes you happy. As a result, usually those who hurt you also get hurt, and often more seriously than you do (you don't satisfy their legitimate needs). But in such case the problem is that you are still in pain. Because your belief in hatred prevents you from being linked to positive energy that makes you happy.

我也出轨背叛，你伤害我，我也伤害你。人类的天性决定了伤害别人的人，自己也会有正当需求，如果不被满足，他们同样会受到伤害。所以，用同样的手段去报复回应伤害你的人，是会有效果的，效果就是他（她）也会因为失望而感到痛苦。但这样做最大的坏处就是——玉石俱焚，因为当你在报复别人的时候，会带着仇恨的信念，会相信恨才能解决你的痛苦，这样你便不再相信爱，你会无法连接正能量——让你幸福快乐的能量。结果常常是，伤害你的人也受到伤害了，往往比你伤的还重（你不去满足他们更多的合理需求）。可这时的问题是，你依然在痛苦，因为你相信仇恨的信念，使你无法连接到让你快乐的正能量。

Any better ways to deal with pain (psychic hurt)? Yes. That is to forgive those who hurt you (no more hurt --- continue to satisfy their legitimate needs e.g. the right to equality at the level of personality, their need of not being treated as a lower-level creature), offer them opportunities to satisfy your legitimate needs. Their efforts may make up for the hurt that has caused to you, or even completely repair your pain. But sometimes the hurt may be severe (those who hurt you have no possibility or opportunity to satisfy your reasonable needs). You'll get painful every time you see them, interact with them. In such case, you can choose to leave so as to alleviate the hurt caused by unfulfilled reasonable needs. Continuing to be together will not only be painful, but may also make your belief in love sway, or even deepen your hatred and incur negative energy.

In such case, the best way is to endure your pain, and keep

有没有更好的解决痛苦（心灵伤害）的办法呢？有，那就是原谅伤害你的人（不再伤害——继续满足其合理需求，比如人格层面的平等权、不被当做低等生物对待的需求），给他们满足你合理需求的机会，他们的努力付出，可能会弥补曾经给你带来的伤害，甚至完全修复你的痛苦。但有时，会出现伤害太深的状况（伤害你的人已经没有可能、没有机会来满足你的合理需求），每次看到他（她）、接触他（她），都会让你觉得痛苦。这时的你可以选择离开，来缓解合理需求不能被满足而给自己带来的伤害，继续在一起不仅痛苦，还可能动摇你对爱的信念，甚至加深仇恨，引来负能量。

此时，最好的办法，就是忍着你的痛，带着你对爱的信念

away from those who hurt you taking your belief in love and positive energy. In the near future, the positive energy in you will once again bring you happiness (your legitimate needs are satisfied in unexpected ways somewhere sometime). As for those who hurt you, just let them be punished by the social contract rules; or perhaps they won't be punished at all. But you still need to leave them to keep away from the negative energy in them that makes you painful. Only when you can endure the pain for a while and do not waver in your belief in love can you have the hope to be linked to more positive energy and obtain happiness at last.

State/Country/Nation

Humans are full of desires. Everyone's growth is a process of constantly satisfying their own needs. In the course of human life, it's the common choice for most people to set up a family.

与正能量，远离伤害你的人们。在不久的将来，你身上的正能量会重新让你获取快乐和幸福（某时某地你的合理需求会被意料之外的方式满足）。至于伤害你的人，就让他们承受社会契约规则的约束惩罚吧，或许他们根本不会受到惩罚，但仍然要离开他们，远离他们身上让人痛苦的负能量。忍得一时之痛，不动摇对爱的信念，才有希望连接更多的正能量，得着最后的幸福。

国　家

人类是充满欲望的，每个人的成长都是不断满足自我需求的过程，在人类的生命历程中，组建家庭会是多数人的共同选择，因为通常只有在家中，人们最基本的需求才能得到保

Because usually only with family can people's most basic needs be secured. With family, people are no longer so afraid of hunger and cold. With the fortress of family, people are no longer afraid of invasion of poisonous insects and beasts. Family has become the main way for human society to multiply and thrive for thousands of years.

We solve the most basic human desires and needs by setting up a family, or it can be said that we resist the threat from the natural environment in which we live relying on family. For example, damages from lower-level creatures e.g. Jackals, wolves, tigers and leopards, shortage of food, etc. But family cannot defend against the threat from us humans. The defects in human nature determine that it is possible for humans to hurt each other, and it is easy to happen. Family is not enough to resist harms and killings among humans caused by negative energy e.g. jealousy, greed, hatred,

障。有了家，人们便不再那么惧怕饥饿和寒冷，有了家的壁垒，人们也不再害怕毒虫野兽的侵袭，家庭成为人类社会几千年来，繁衍生息的主要方式。

我们用组建家庭的方式解决了人类最基本的欲望需求，或者也可以说，我们用家抵御了来自我们所生存的自然环境的威胁。比如，豺狼虎豹等低等生物的伤害、食物的匮乏等。但家却无法防御来自我们人类自身的威胁，人性的缺陷决定了人类有互相伤害的可能，并且很容易发生。因为嫉妒、贪婪、仇恨等负面能量导致的人类之间的伤害和杀戮，家是不足以抵御的。为了防止遭遇来自人类自身的伤害，同时也为了能够联合更多的力量，去抵御较大的自然灾害，人类社会先后出现了氏族、部落、国家等组织形态。

etc. To prevent damage from us humans, and to unite more forces to resist major natural disasters, human society has successively experienced the organizational forms e.g. Clan, tribe, state, etc.

The existence of such human organizational forms, whether clan, tribe or state, is to solve the issue of humans themselves, as well as the most fundamental issue --- the right to life --- for people to live without being hurt, to get their reasonable desires satisfied, and to pursue the happiness that belongs to humans. Otherwise, what for humans choose to live with others and set up families and states? So, it can be said that a state (clan, tribe) is a "big family" formed by people to defend themselves and their own small families. Different "family members" (people who form the common contract) lead to different "big families" formed (different states).

To protect people's homes, lives and properties, such a "big family" needs to erect the army,

无论是氏族部落还是国家，这些人类组织形态的存在，都是为了解决人类自身的问题，并且是最根本的问题——生命权，是为了人们能够活着，不被伤害，能够满足自己的合理欲望，去追求属于人类的幸福快乐。要不然，人类为什么要选择与他人共处，组建家庭和国家。因此可以这样说，国家(氏族部落)是人们为了保卫自己和自己的小家而组建起的一个"大家"，"家人"(形成共同契约的人)不一样，他们组建出的"大家"也会不一样(不同的国家)。

为了保卫人们的家和生命财产安全，这个"大家"需要组建军队、警察和司法部门，用

police and judicial departments to guard the state and address the domestic conflicts among social members. In modern society, such a "big family" also needs public organizations --- public organizations at all levels that can run normally and serve social members (the government and its working departments). Besides, for the long-term stability of social order, it also needs representative organizations that can express their opinions on behalf of social members and legislature authorities that formulate rules on behalf of social members. Such above-mentioned organizations and authorities and the social members who are responsible for their operation and control relevant power jointly constitute the whole of a state. The existence of a state is mainly to defend the fundamental interests of the people in it (including but not limited to: the right to life, liberty, property, etc.). The fundamental interests can be interpreted in

来守护国家和处理内部社会成员之间的矛盾冲突。在现代社会，这个"大家"还要有公共组织机构——能够正常运转、服务社会成员的各级公共机构（政府及其工作部门），另外为了社会秩序的长久安定，还要有能代表社会成员发表意见的代议机构和代表社会成员制定规则的立法机关。上面这些部门机构和负责其运转并掌控相关权力的社会成员，共同组成了国家的全部。国家的存在主要是为了捍卫该国民众的根本利益（包括但不限于人的生命权、自由权、财产权等），根本利益可以有很多种解释，但无论如何解释，非常核心的一点是，国家必须是为了保卫国民而被组建的，否则它就会失去正义性（绝大多数社会成员的认可）。只有保护国民，捍卫每一位国民的正当权利（自由），努力保障他们获取幸福快乐，这样的国家才是真正被人们接受的国家。人类爱好自由的天性，决定了人类也有不参加任何组织的自由，之所以会选择组建家庭、部族和国家，正是由于多数人类社

many ways. But whatever the interpretation is, the core is that the state must be formed to guard its citizens, otherwise it will lose its justice (recognition by most social members). Only by protecting its citizens, defending the legitimate rights (freedoms) of every citizen, and striving to ensure their happiness can such a state be truly accepted by people. The human nature of uphold freedom determines that humans also have the freedom not to participate in any organization. The reason why they choose to set up families, tribes and states is precisely because most social members believe that this is the best way to satisfy their legitimate needs.

War vs. People's Livelihood

What corresponds to war should be peace, which is a distinction made by the operating status of human society. In terms

会成员都认为，这样是满足他们正当合理需求的最佳方式。

战争和民生

和战争对应的应该是和平，这是从人类社会的运行状态上来做的区分。如果从国家的职能来看，国家可以主要用来关

of the functions of state, state can mainly be used to focus on improving the livelihood of the domestic people, and can also be used to organize military forces to wage wars, or resist aggression to protect the safety of people's lives and properties.

Then, what should be the primary function and role of a state? Force is sometimes necessary to solve the threat from mankind itself. Because of the defects in human nature, many dehumanizing deeds in human history have committed by humans themselves. It's just to avoid the continuation of tragedy to suppress violence with violence. Armed force is an effective means of stopping human violence. Both the armed force and the police force are authorities that can legally carry out violence. Because they are authorized by the state and the people (a transfer of rights, the rights of most people condense into power --- a unilateral power of dominance and control, when it is accompanied

注改善国内民众的生活状况，也可以用来组织军事力量发动战争，或是抵抗侵略保卫民众的生命财产安全。

那么对于一个国家来说，首要的功能和作用应该是什么呢？武力对于解决来自人类自身的威胁有时是必要的，因为人性的缺陷，在人类历史上有不少灭绝人性的事情都是人类自身所为，以暴制暴，只是为了避免悲剧的继续发生。武装力量是制止人类暴力行为的有效手段，军队和警察部队都是可以合法实施暴力的机关，因为他们得到了国家和民众的授权（一种权利的让渡，多数人的权利凝结成权力——一种单向的支配控制力，当它伴随着暴力时就成为了军队或是警察的权力。）对于国家，合法的暴力行为是必须的，要么用来对付侵略者，要么用来惩罚违反规则的少数社会成员以维护秩序。不过即便是这样，这些合法的暴力也

by violence. It becomes the power of the army or the police when it comes with violence.) For a state, legitimate acts of violence are necessary. Either to deal with aggressors or to punish a few social members who violate the rules in order to maintain order. Even so, however, such legitimate violence should not become the norm of a state. Only when the people and their homes are endangered by aggression can war violence be legitimate. Only when social members blatantly trample on the rules recognized by other social members can police violence be supported by most people. The above-mentioned violence represents the common will of social members --- we need to drive out the aggressors, and we need to punish the social members who violate the rules.

The purpose of lawful violence necessary for a state is ultimately not to demonstrate the might of the state, or the level of violence of the army and the

不应该成为一个国家的常态，只有在民众和他们的家园面临侵略危险时，战争暴力才具有正当性，只有在社会成员公然践踏其他社会成员共同认可的规则时，警察暴力才能得到多数人的拥护支持。上述情形下的暴力行为，是代表了社会成员的共同意志——我们需要赶出侵略者，我们需要惩罚破坏规则的社会成员。

一个国家所必须的合法暴力的目的，最终不是为了展示国家的威力，或者军人和警察的暴力程度，而是为了守卫该国的民众能够更好地满足作为

police, but to better serve the legitimate needs of the people who guard the state, so that they can have the right and conditions to pursue their own happiness. It is the whole of our human life to satisfy various self-needs. "To satisfy needs" can also be synonymous with "life". So, in most cases, a state should embody its function in improving people's livelihood, satisfying more of their reasonable needs, and striving to make people live happily. Only in this way will people willingly continue to surrender their rights to maintain the state formed by them, just like they try hard to guard a family that benefits them.

The principle of founding a state and that of setting up a family are the same in essence. First, both are to satisfy human desires and needs, and then defend against dangers from nature or humans themselves. So, for a state, people's livelihood outweighs war.

一个人的正当合理需求，从而让他们有权利和条件去追求自己的幸福快乐。满足各种各样的自身需求，是我们人类生活的全部，满足需求也可以说是生活的同义语。因此，国家在大部分时候，应该把它的功能体现在改善提高民众的生活水平方面，满足他们更多的合理需求，努力让人们生活的幸福。只有这样，大家才会心甘情愿地继续交出权利来维护自己组建的国家，就好像他们努力守护让自己获益的家庭那样。

人类建立国家和组建家庭的道理，实质上是相通的。首先，都是为了满足人类的欲望和需求，而后才是为了抵御防范来自自然界或是人类自身的危险。因此，对于一个国家，民生要比战争更加重要。

A State's Territory

People all need a place for themselves and their families to live after setting up a family. Whether owned by oneself or rented from others, it should be a place that at least can shelter from wind and rain to satisfy the most basic living needs of family members. How big does such place need to be? In terms of satisfying people's physiological needs, one's residence doesn't have to be very large --- place for dinning, clean and hygienic place, place for storage of daily items, place for resting and otherwise, for example, the space cannot be so small that it makes most family members feel depressed. It is difficult to define a clear standard for the size of the residence of a person or a family, but most members of human society can reach a consensus on this issue.

Similar issues arise after people found a state. The territory

国家的疆域

人们组建家庭以后，都需要一个供自己和家人生活的场所。不管是属于自己的，还是租借他人的，至少都应该是能够挡风遮雨的地方，以满足家庭成员最基本的居住需求。这个地方需要多大呢？从满足人的生理需求来说，一个人的居所不需要很大，有提供饮食的地方，清洁卫生的地方，存放生活物品的地方，休息的地方，另外还有其他方面的要求，比如空间不能太过狭小以至于让多数人感到压抑郁闷。对于一个人或是一家人的居所大小问题，虽然很难界定出明晰的标准，但绝大多数人类社会成员就此问题可以达成共识。

当人们建立国家以后，类似于上面的问题也会出现。国

of a state, like the place a family needs, should also guarantee to satisfy the basic living needs of its people. But the needs mentioned here emphasize that all the citizens' needs for resources, transportation, safety, etc. can be satisfied overall. A state needs water, food, and land suitable for people to live in, as well as various resources that can drive social and economic development e.g. oil, coal, rivers, lakes, territorial waters, etc.

But how big a country needs to be before it can be recognized by most social members is a more difficult question to define than how big a home needs to be. Factors e.g. the size of a state's population, historical differences, strength of power, etc. all determine that this issue is not only difficult and complex, but can also cause disputes and hatred in human society extremely easily. Before solving this difficulty, let's first take a look at a phenomenon that easily occurs in modern

家的疆域，就像一个家庭需要的场所一样，同样应保障一国民众基本的生活需求。不过这里的需求强调的是，能够从整体上保障所有国民生活的资源、交通、安全等方面的需求。一个国家要有水、粮食、适宜人们居住的土地，还要有可以驱动社会经济发展的各类资源，比如石油、煤炭、江河、湖泊、海洋等等。

但是一个国家的疆域需要多大，才会被多数人类社会成员所认可，是一个比家需要多大地方更难确定的问题。一国人口的多少、历史状况的差异、力量的强弱等因素，都决定了这个问题不仅困难复杂，而且极其容易引起人类社会的争执与仇恨。在没有解决这个难题之前，我们先来看一个现代人类社会比较容易发生的现象——难民潮。当一个国家因为社会动乱或是自然环境恶化，而失去可以保障其国民生活的秩序和条件时，该国民众的生存权等最基

human society --- refugee tide. When a state loses the order and conditions that can guarantee the life of its citizens due to social turmoil or deterioration of its natural environment, a crisis will arise from the most basic rights of its citizens e.g. the right to subsistence, etc. In such case, in order to subsist, people in this state will choose to get out of the territory of this state to seek an environment that can guarantee the basic life of humans. In this process, people cannot go abroad through normal channels, they often have to take risks, risking their lives to cross the border. What's worse, such unsecured escape is very likely to end those lives pursuing freedom very early, whether adults or children. [①] Will everything get all right

本的权利, 就会出现危机。此时, 这个国家的人们为了能够继续生存下去, 会选择走出这个国家的领域, 去寻找可以保障人类基本生活的环境。在这个过程中, 由于人们不能通过正常渠道走出国门, 往往只能铤而走险, 冒着生命危险去跨越国境线。并且没有安全保障的逃生, 也极有可能早早终结追求自由的生命, 无论是大人还是小孩。当他们历经千辛万苦到达异国疆域时, 一切都会美好起来吗? 并不尽然, 异国的文化和民众的社会契约, 有时会和他们格格不入。为了生存而被迫踏上异国土地的人们, 通常会被称作"难民", 很多难民大量涌入异国的现象, 便是"难民潮"。

---

① *Shocking images of drowned Syrian boy show tragic plight of refugees*, published on Support the Guardian, https://www.theguardian.com/world/2015/sep/02/shocking-image-of-drowned-syrian-boy-shows-tragic-plight-of-refugees 23:55 Mar 7, 2017.

搜狐公众平台:《这张图让无数网友心碎 3 岁小男孩陈尸海滩》, 载搜狐网, http://mt.sohu.com/20150905/n420437297.shtml, 访问时间: 2017 年 3 月 7 日 23: 55。

when they enter the territory of a foreign land after experiencing all the hardships? Not necessarily. The culture and people's social contracts of a foreign country sometimes are not compatible with them at all. Those who are forced to set foot on a foreign land in order to survive are usually called "refugees". The phenomenon that many refugees pour into foreign countries in large numbers is "refugee tide".

Due to the previous environment and experience, many refugees are with negative energy in them. If they cannot change their original beliefs in time and let them understand the truth of self-restraint, they are very likely to take the negative energy of disturbing their motherland into a new country. So, the influx of refugees has become a tough local social problem. The town mayor will bring the refugees that he/she cannot face and manage to the mayor or the president. And, the people will also deal with refugees

由于之前的环境和经历，很多难民的身上都会带有负向的能量，如果不能及时改变他们原有的信念，并让他们明白自我收敛的道理，他们就很有可能将原本作乱其祖国的负能量带入新的国家。于是，难民的涌入就会成为当地的社会难题。镇长会带着无法面对和管理的难民去找市长或是总统，民众也会因为难民对社会契约规则的违犯，而使用极端的手段去对付他们。但无论如何受正能量控制的人类社会成员是不会去真正伤害难民的，因为难民也是人类的同胞，是人类世界

by extreme means due to their violation to the social contract rules. But in no case will members of human society controlled by positive energy truly hurt refugees. Because refugees are also human compatriots as well as members of the human world. The attribute of positive energy --- love --- determines that people under its influence and control will not resort to violence against refugees. People who believe in positive energy will usually choose ways that can guarantee the basic rights of refugees. But how to deal with refugees is still a tough question. Because there is no simple and effective way. Just like when positive energy encounters negative energy, the former can only outsmart the latter instead of forcibly attacking it. Otherwise, the latter will win. Consequently, such state will gradually lose its order because its people are affected and controlled by negative energy.

Evasion is obviously not the

的成员。正能量的属性——爱，决定了受其影响控制的人们，不会去采取暴力手段对付难民，信奉正能量的人们，通常都会选择可以保障难民基本权利的做法来处理。不过如何对待难民，仍然是一个难题，因为没有简便有效的办法，就好像正能量遭遇负能量，只能智取，不能强攻，否则负能量就会得胜，进而这个国家会因为，民众受负能量影响控制，而慢慢失去秩序。

躲避显然不是办法，因为

answer. Because it is refugees who flee from their homeland, and they cannot drive those who accept them out of their own state. A relatively fair way is to make a state's territory large enough to enable its citizens to find an environment for survival without crossing the border of their homeland in whichever crisis they encounter. According to such logic, how big a state's territory should be depends on the specific conditions of the states. It can be either large or small. The ideal status is that each state owns a territory that can ensure that its citizens live and work in peace and contentment and pursue happiness.

Aggression/Invasion

When the coercive power of a state forces their way into the territory of another state without the permission of its people, it will be completely different from the influx of refugees. Refugees are forced to enter another state due

难民才是逃离祖国的人，不能把接纳他们的人赶出原本属于自己的国家。相对公平的办法是，让一国的疆域够用到可以让这个国家的国民无论遇到什么危机，无须踏出祖国边界就能找到继续生存的环境。按照这样的逻辑，一国的疆域该有多大，就取决于国与国的具体情况，可以大，也可以小，比较理想的状态是，每个国家都拥有可以保障其国民安居乐业，追求幸福快乐的疆域。

侵 略

当一国的强制性力量，未经他国民众允许而强行进入该国的疆域，那么这样的进入便完全不同于难民的涌入。难民是迫于无奈和逃生的需要，而上述行为大多是有预谋、有组织的暴力行为（如一国军队进

to helplessness and the need to escape, whilst most of the above-mentioned acts are premeditated and organized violent acts (e.g. the entry of the army of a state into the territory of another state), which are not allowed by most members of human society and are also serious violations to human social contracts. People call such behavior "aggression".

Any aggression or invasion means violence, destruction and harm. Such behavior also indicates that the aggressors are with strong negative energy. It is the negative energy that makes the aggressors fierce and brutal. Army is a coercive power of the country. When the soldiers commit harm and destruction due to their loyalty and obedience to command, they will be unreservedly linked to negative energy. The barracks where such soldiers are located will be full of negative energy that is no different from the negative energy to which people don't believe in love are linked. Both

入他国境内），是不被人类社会多数成员所允许的，也是严重违反人类社会契约的行为，人们会将其称作——侵略。

只要是侵略，就意味着暴力、破坏和伤害。这样的行径，也说明实施侵略的人身上有着很强的负能量，是负能量让侵略者变得凶狠和残暴。军队作为一种国家的强制性力量，当士兵们因为信奉忠诚和服从命令，而去伤害和破坏的时候，他们便毫无保留的将自己连接到了负能量那里。这样的士兵所在的军营就会充满负能量，这种负能量和人们因为不相信爱而连接到的负能量没有区别，都会给人们带来仇恨、破坏和伤害的力量。

will cause to people the force of hatred, destruction, and harm.

But in one case, violence and harm are not caused by negative energy, that is, when people who persistently guard positive energy are attacked by negative energy and have nowhere to hide, positive energy will definitely lead people who believe in it as an authority to resist and counterattack. When resisting the attack of negative energy, positive energy also forces the opponent into submission with violence, and also makes the opponent fearful, so that those who believe in negative energy dare not continue to bully those who persistently guard love and kindness. But unlike violence of negative energy, the violence, destruction and harm of the camp of positive energy only occurs when being attacked by negative energy, that is, it is only used to defend and protect people who believe in positive energy.

It can be said that aggression is caused by those affected and

但在一种情形下，暴力和伤害却不是负能量所为，那就是当坚守正能量的人们受到负能量的侵袭，且无处躲避的时候，正能量必将引领信奉其为权威的人们进行抵抗和反击。在抵抗负能量的侵袭时，正能量也使用暴力强迫对手就范，也通过伤害让对手害怕，使那些信奉负能量的，不敢再继续欺凌坚守爱和善良的人们。但与负能量暴力伤害不同的是，正能量阵营的暴力、破坏和伤害，只发生在被负能量侵袭之时，也就是只会用于防卫保护信奉正能量的人们。

可以这样说，侵略是负能量影响控制的人群所为，而抵

controlled by negative energy, while the strong force of resistance to aggression comes from positive energy. Both use violence and harm, but one symbolizes evil and pain; while the other is just (recognized by the most people), and is a necessary means to freedom and happiness.

Terrorism

What is terror? Terror is a terrifying atmosphere or environment that makes people fearful. You did nothing, let alone hurt anyone. But you'll still be hurt or even lose your life. For the victim, there's absolutely no reason for the harm they're suffering. People or organizations that carry out terrorist acts have their own purposes. They hope to achieve these purposes by means of terrorist acts. The ideology of attaining the goals by carrying out terrorist acts in an organized and targeted manner is terrorism, which is used to guide people and

抗侵略的强大力量则来自正能量。虽然都使用了暴力和伤害，但一个象征着邪恶和痛苦，一个却是正义的（多数人认可），是通往自由幸福的必要手段。

恐怖主义

什么是恐怖，就是令人恐惧害怕的气氛环境。你什么也没做，更别说伤害到谁，但你一样会被伤害，甚至失去生命，对于受害者来说，他们所遭遇的伤害完全没有理由。实施恐怖行为的人或组织，都有自己的目的，他们希望借助恐怖的行径来达成这些目的。以有组织、有目标地实施恐怖行为来达成目的的思想观点体系，就成为恐怖主义。恐怖主义用来指导使用恐怖手段的人和组织，去制造恐怖事件，进而实现自己的目的。

organizations that use terrorist means to create terrorist incidents to attain their own goals.

The biggest feature of terrorist acts is to harm innocent people and people who have no conflict of interest with terrorists. The victims are the elderly, women and children, or unarmed civilians. In short, the more innocent people are, the more seriously they will be harmed, and the more terrifying the atmosphere and environment will appear, and the more people will get fearful, so that terrorists and organizations can attain their goals. Then, what is the root cause of the behaviors that terrify all of us as humans?

Judging from the murderous and violent characteristics of terrorist acts themselves, the energy that controls humans to carry out terrorist acts is undoubtedly negative energy. It is a certain person or group that is linked to a very strong negative energy due to certain beliefs. Such kinds of negative energy cause

恐怖行为最大的特征，就是伤害无辜，伤害和恐怖份子没有利害冲突的人们，受害者或是老人和妇女儿童，或是没有武装的平民百姓。总之越是无辜的人受伤害，就越能显现出恐怖的氛围和环境，让更多的人恐惧，从而达到恐怖份子和组织的目的。那么这些令我们所有人类恐惧不安的行为，其根源究竟是在什么地方呢？

单从恐怖行为本身的凶残和暴力特征来看，控制人类实施恐怖行为的这种能量无疑属于负能量。是某个人或者群体，由于某些信念而连接到了很强的负能量，这些负能量让他们可以视生命如草芥，能够杀人不眨眼，让他们无辜伤害他人而不觉得愧疚。正常人即便是不相信爱的正能量，会连接到

them to view lives as mustards, to kill other without blinking, and to harm others for no reason without feeling guilty. Even if normal people who don't believe in the positive energy of love can be linked to negative energy, they will not be linked to so strong negative energy that can control them to commit terrorist acts which seriously violate human social order.

People or groups that practice terrorism are mostly linked to the strongest negative energy --- terror --- due to their own certain belief after their spirit get seriously hurt. "Terror" is synonymous with damage and destruction. There is nothing that "terror" cares about. "Terror" is the strongest negative energy in the human living space so far. What we can perceive is that it is extremely easy for humans to be linked to such energy and then become a puppet controlled by "terror" once the human spirit is severely hurt. Once one is affected and controlled

负能量，但却不会连接这么强的负能量，让其控制他们作出严重侵害人类社会秩序的恐怖行为。

凡是奉行恐怖主义的人或人群，大多是在灵魂受到严重伤害之后，由于自己的某种信念而连接到最强的负能量——恐怖。"恐怖"的代名词，可以称作是破坏和毁灭，没有什么是"恐怖"所在意的，"恐怖"是人类生存空间迄今为止最强的负能量，我们能够感知的是，一旦人类的灵魂被深深地伤害以后，人类就极其容易连接到这种能量，进而成为"恐怖"所控制的傀儡，一个人一旦被其影响控制，就会很快成为一台不讲人类感情的"杀戮机器"。

by negative energy, he/she will become a "killing machine" that totally ignores human feelings very soon.

So, whether in the East or the West, and regardless of skin color, how to prevent our compatriots from being continually harmed and reduced to "puppets and tools" of "terror" is a difficulty that all of us humans have to face and solve together.

Sum-up to "About Authority"

In ancient China, there is a saying --- "One must first cultivate oneself, then keep the family in order, next govern the country well, and finally bring peace to the world" [1] What does "bring peace to the world" mean? It means to enable human society to have

因此，无论东西方，不管肤色差异，如何不让我们的同胞持续受到伤害，沦为"恐怖"的"木偶和工具"，才是我们所有人类要共同面对解决的难题。

权威篇之结语

在古老的中国流传着这样一句话——修身齐家才能治国平天下。何谓平天下，就是让人类社会能有和谐稳定的秩序，人们安居乐业，不再相互残害，生灵涂炭。何谓齐家，就是使家庭和睦，互敬互爱，家庭成员人人快乐。修身是指要懂得自律，

---

[1] *Great Learning* (Chapter 1), by Zeng Shen, published on gushiwen.cn, http://www.gushice.com/bookview_3043.html, access time 00:01 on Mar 8, 2017.

曾参:《大学》(第1章)，载古诗文网，http://www.gushice.com/bookview_3043.html，访问时间: 2017 年 3 月 8 日 0:01。

a harmonious and stable order, enable people to live and work in peace and contentment and no longer harm each other and ruin lives. What does "keep the family in order" mean? It means to make the family harmonious, to respect and love one another, and to make all family members happy. "Cultivate oneself" means to self-discipline, often bridle one's unreasonable desires and claims, let alone hurting compatriots and relatives. "Govern the country well" means to govern the people's "big family" --- country --- well with correct ideals and beliefs to secure the people's survival and safety.

The logic contained in this sentence is that one shall first know the importance of "self-cultivation", which means to improve one's cultivation. Self-cultivation refers to a status of life in which one is positive for goodness. It is a natural inside-to-outside self-discipline, self-restraining one's unreasonable

常常收敛自己不合理的欲望诉求，更不要去伤害同胞和亲人。治国应带着正确的理想和信念，将民众的大家——国家治理好，让国民有生存和安全的保障。

这句话蕴含的逻辑关系是，一个人首先要知道"修身"的重要性，修身即要提高自身修养。修养是指人积极向善的一种生命状态，它是一种自然的、由内而外的自律，自我约束自己不合理的欲望诉求，为他人着想，包容不伤害他人，与人为善，和他人和睦相处。只有懂得修养，人们才能更快地组

desires and claims, thinking of others, tolerating and not harming others, being kind to others, and getting along with others harmoniously. Only when people learn how to cultivate themselves can they set up a family faster, or can the families they set up make family members harmonious and loving for a longer time. Only when every small family is harmonious and loving can the "big family" founded by people --- the state fundamentally achieve harmony and stability, social and economic prosperity and rich people, and can the state own powerful force to protect its own people and achieve national prosperity. Likewise, if all states achieve harmony, the world --- our world --- will be peaceful; the states will be in good neighborliness and friendliness; and all states will jointly guard the harmony of the human world and provide environment and conditions for real value creation for human society (to satisfy the

建起家庭，或者他（她）组建的家庭才能让家庭成员更加长久的和睦恩爱。每一个小家都和睦恩爱了，由民众组建的大家——国家，才能从根本上实现和谐稳定，社会经济繁荣，民众富裕，国家也会拥有强大的力量来保护自己的民众，实现国泰民安。同样道理，所有的国家都实现了和谐，那么天下——我们的世界，就会太平，国与国之间睦邻友好，所有的国家共同守护人类世界的和谐，给人类社会真正的价值创造（满足同胞的正当合理需求）提供环境和条件，不断致力于人类社会的文明与进步。

legitimate needs of compatriots), and be continuously committed to the civilization and progress of human society.

But in the current human world, from "people", to "home" and then to "the state and the world", disharmony is the main feature. What is harmony in the human world? It means that each is in his/her proper place, not to invade each other, and occasional conflicts can be solved timely, not being so extreme that "terrorist" means are used to vent the hatred and settle issues. Whether for the family, the state or the entire human world, a harmonious order is still our yearning goal. Although most members of human society are striving for order, the harmony of the human world, from families to countries, is still far away from us. Having been enlightened and inspired by the latest discoveries in natural science and the ancient scriptures, we believe our world can achieve an unprecedented status of harmony - one world,

但现在的人类世界，从"人"、"家"再到"国与天下"，不和谐却是主要特征。人类世界的和谐是什么，是各得其所，互不侵犯，偶有冲突也能及时化解，不会极端到要用"恐怖"手段去宣泄仇恨、解决问题。无论对于家庭、国家还是整个人类世界，和谐的秩序仍是我们渴慕向往的目标。尽管多数人类社会成员都在不竭余力的追寻秩序，小到家庭，大到国家，可人类世界的和谐，仍然距离我们很远。当自然科学界的最新发现与古老的经典记载，给我们启示后，相信通过辨识人类未知空间的正能量和负能量，并信奉正能量为我们的权威，守护良心，相信爱，找到人类权利（自由）的边界，我们的世界可以实现前所未有的和谐状态——天下一家。

one family --- by identifying the positive energy and the negative energy in the unknown dimension of mankind, and believing in positive energy as our authority, and remaining conscientious, believing in love, and finding the boundaries of human rights (freedoms). ①

---

① *The Military Prophecies of China,* by Li Chunfeng, Yuan Tiangang [the Tang Dynasty, China], published in Baidu Encyclopedia, http://baike.baidu.com/link?url=iEmu0wYWQOEokQcoPu YCYoBWHiY4iUqv9rfbHZt4GkDnLZqQzF0AZYnJObxonA55yGeXk92mSAFJZs3mMdwc OJvmcC2Sczu_vq4c5PrywhII9FVr3A1zGEyO3MO9RJ9E, access time: 19:03 Mar 7, 2017.

（唐）李淳风、袁天罡:《推背图》, 载百度百科, http://baike.baidu.com/link?url=iEmu0 wYWQOEokQcoPuYCYoBWHiY4iUqv9rfbHZt4GkDnLZqQzF0AZYnJObxonA55yGeXk9 2mSAFJZs3mMdwcOJvmcC2Sczu_vq4c5PrywhII9FVr3A1zGEyO3MO9RJ9E, 访问时间: 2017 年 3 月 7 日 19: 03。

References:

1. *Bible*, National Committee of Three-Self Patriotic Movement of the Protestant Churches in China (National TSPM), China Christian Council (CCC), 2009 edition, , (Exodus 1:22) p. 53.

2. *Leviathan* by Hobbes [Britain], translated by Zhang Yan and Zhao Wendao, Hu'nan Literature and Art Publishing House, 2011 edition, p.72.

3. *Politics by* Aristotle [Ancient Greece], translated by Wu Shoupeng, the Commercial Press, 1965 edition, p. 113.

4. *Das Kapital* by Marx [Germany], translated by Jiang Jinghua and Zhang Mei, Beijing Publishing House, Beijing Publishing Group Co., Ltd, 2012 edition, p.40-41.

5. *The Political Essentials of the Zhenguan Era* by Wu Jing (The Tang Dynasty, China) (Volume 8), translated by Pian Yusai and Pianhua, Zhonghua Book Company 2009 Edition, ("The Criminal Law: Article 31") p.212.

6. *Xi'an Daily* (Xi'an, China): "Around 20,000 police and citizens

参考文献：

1、《圣经》，中国基督教三自爱国运动委员会、中国基督教协会2009年版，（出1：22）第53页。

2、[英]霍布斯:《利维坦》，张妍、赵闻道译，湖南文艺出版社2011年版，第72页。

3、[古希腊]亚里士多德:《政治学》，吴寿彭译，商务印书馆1965年版，第113页。

4、[德]马克思:《资本论》，姜晶花、张梅译，北京出版集团公司北京出版社2012年版，第40-41页。

5、（唐）吴兢:《贞观政要》（第8卷），骈宇骞、骈骅译，中华书局2009年版，（刑法第三十一）第212页。

6、西安日报（西安）:《两万名警民齐聚纽约送别华裔警察》，载网易新

gathered in New York to see off a Chinese police", published in Netease News, http://news.163.com/15/0106/04/AF8HVH4D00014AED.html, access time: 15:46 Mar 7, 2017.

7. *The Criminal of the Case of Car Theft and Infanticide Was Executed on Nov 22nd*, 2013, published in "the Rule of Law" column, Xinhuanet, http://news.xinhuanet.com/legal/2013-11/22/c_118259457.htm, access time: 16:03 Mar 07, 2017.

8. Jessica Simeone，Accused carjacker caught on video after stealing jeep with baby still inside, New York Post, http://nypost.com/?s=Accused+carjacker+caught+on+video+after+stealing+jeep+with+baby+still+inside，March 8,2017 14:23pm.

9. *The History of Chinese Legal System*, by Zeng Daiwei, the Law Press, 2001 Edition, p.150.

10. *The God Particle: If the Universe Is the Answer, What Is the Question?* by Leon Lederman [America]，Dick Teresi, Translated by Mi Xujun, Gu Hongwei, Zhao Jianhui, and Chen Hongwei, Shanghai Science, Technology and Education Press, 2003 edition, p.422.

闻，http://news.163.com/15/0106/04/AF8HVH4D00014AED.html，访问时间：2017 年 3 月 7 日 15：46。

7、新华网:《长春盗车杀婴案罪犯 22 日被执行死刑》，载新华网法治，http://news.xinhuanet.com/legal/2013-11/22/c_118259457.htm，访问时间：2017 年 3 月 7 日 16：03。

9、曾代伟:《中国法制史》，法律出版社 2001 年版，第 150 页。

10、[美] 利昂·莱德曼、迪克·泰雷西:《上帝粒子：假如宇宙是答案，究竟什么是问题》，米绪军、古宏伟、赵建辉、陈宏伟译，上海科技教育出版社 2003 年版，第 422 页。

11. Wikipedia, Isaac Newton, Wikipedia the Free Encyclopedia, https://en.wikipedia.org/wiki/Isaac_Newton#cite_ref-tiner_126-0.

12. Wikipedia, Albert Einstein, Wikipedia the Free Encyclopedia, https://en.wikipedia.org/wiki/Albert_Einstein#Political_and_religious_views.

13. Amanda Gefter, Newton's apple，The real story, NewScientist, https://www.newscientist.com/blogs/culturelab/2010/01/newtons-apple-the-real-story.html.

14. *The Origin of Species,* by Darwin [Britain], translated by Zhou Jianren, Ye Duzhuang, and Fang Zongxi, the Commercial Press, 1997 edition, p.525.

15. *The Grand Design,* by Hawking, Leonard Mlodinow [Britain], translated by Wu Zhongchao, Hu'nan Science and Technology Press, 2011 edition, p.153.

16.*A Brief Analysis of the Nobelists' Beliefs,* by Wen Dao, published in the Chinese Data Journal Database, http://www.cqvip.com/read/read.aspx?id=12312889#, access time: 17：07 Mar 7, 2017.

17. Wikipedia, General Scholium,

14、[英]达尔文:《物种起源》, 周建人、叶笃庄、方宗熙译，商务印书馆 1997 年版，第 525 页。

15、[英]霍金、蒙洛迪诺:《大设计》，吴忠超译，湖南科学技术出版社 2011 年版，第 153 页。

16、文刀:《诺贝尔奖得主信仰小考》，载中文数据期刊数据库，http://www.cqvip.com/read/read.aspx?id=12312889#，访问时间:2017 年 3 月 7 日 17：07。

Wikipedia the Free Encyclopedia, https://en.wikipedia.org/wiki/General_Scholium.

18. *The Collected Papers of Albert Einstein* (Volume 1), the Commercial Press, 1994 Edition, p.283.

19. *Albert Einstein*, Shaanxi Normal University Press, 2010 edition, p.87-88.

20. *The Military Prophecies of China,* by Li Chunfeng, Yuan Tiangang [the Tang Dynasty, China], published in Baidu Encyclopedia, http://baike.baidu.com/link?url=iEmu0wYWQOEokQcoPuYCYoBWHiY4iUqv9rfbHZt4GkDnLZqQzF0AZYnJObxonA55yGeXk92mSAFJZs3mMdwcOJvmcC2Sczu_vq4c5PrywhII9FVr3A1zGEyO3MO9RJ9E, access time: 19:03 Mar 7, 2017

21. *Bible*, National Committee of Three-Self Patriotic Movement, the Protestant Churches in China (National TSPM), China Christian Council (CCC), 2009 edition, (Isaiah 9:6, 9:7, 11, 11:2, 11:3, 11:4, 11:5) p.667, p.669~670.

22. *Sunan of Abu Dawud,* by Mahdi, published in Baidu Encyclopedia, http://baike.baidu.com/link?url=2KeXP2Ul1sLoUmT3e4mU5El2xzsbzdspthoM2MxKIAdqCk0Xp9CjhYUOdBYuB5fCCY

18、《爱因斯坦文集》（第 1 卷），商务印书馆 1994 年版，第 283 页。

19、《爱因斯坦自述》，陕西师大出版社 2010 年版，第 87-88 页。

20、（唐）李淳风、袁天罡：《推背图》，载百度百科，http://baike.baidu.com/link?url=iEmu0wYWQOEokQcoPuYCYoBWHiY4iUqv9rfbHZt4GkDnLZqQzF0AZYnJObxonA55yGeXk92mSAFJZs3mMdwcOJvmcC2Sczu_vq4c5PrywhII9FVr3A1zGEyO3MO9RJ9E，访问时间：2017 年 3 月 7 日 19：03。

21、《圣经》，中国基督教三自爱国运动委员会、中国基督教协会 2009 年版，（赛 9：6、9：7、11、11：2、11：3、11：4、11：5）第 667 页、第 669-670 页。

22、艾布达吾德圣训：马赫迪，载百度百科，http://baike.baidu.com/link?url=2KeXP2Ul1sLoUmT3e4mU5El2xzsbzdspthoM2MxKIAdqCk0Xp9CjhYUOdBYuB5fCCY9O

9OWhd4rpEokQqb9BfrAiZi--WGuRP1idcX0tFfHHIOsftkbUVEEz3ThRQEPNS4, access time: 19:20 Mar 7, 2017

23. *The Transformation from the Pure Land of Maitreya to the Pure Land of Amita",* by Shi Guangming, published in Masters' Lecture on Buddhist Knowledge, edited by editorial department of Knowledge of Literature and History, Zhonghua Book Company, 2016 edition, p.232-233.

24. *Hawking Admits That He Likes betting As He Lost $100 This Year Due to Nobel Prize",* published in International News, China News Network , http://www.chinanews.com/gj/2013/11-13/5496233.shtml, access time: 19:26, Mar 7, 2017.

25. *CERN Announces the Discovery of God Particles, cnBeta,* published in Network CBN News, China Broadcasting, http://www.cnr.cn/gundong/201207/t20120704_510111540.shtml, access time: 19:33 Mar 7, 2017

26. *Nobel Prize Winners in Physics for 2013 Announced,* by Mei Jin and Zhang Xiao, published in Sciencenet

Whd4rpEokQqb9BfrAiZi--WGuRP1idcX0tFfHHIOsftkbUVEEz3ThRQEPNS4, 访问时间：2017 年 3 月 7 日 19：20。

23、施光明："从弥勒净土到阿弥陀净土嬗变"，载《文史知识》编辑部编：《名家讲佛教知识》，中华书局 2016 年版，第 232-233 页。

24、中国新闻网:《霍金承认喜欢打赌 因今年诺贝尔奖输掉100 美元》，载中国新闻网国际新闻，http://www.chinanews.com/gj/2013/11-13/5496233.shtml，访问时间：2017 年 3 月 7 日 19：26。

25、cnBeta:《欧洲核子研究中心宣布发现上帝粒子》，载中国广播网央广快讯，http://www.cnr.cn/gundong/201207/t20120704_510111540.shtml，访问时间：2017 年 3 月 7 日 19：33。

26、梅进、张笑:《2013 年诺贝尔物理学奖揭晓》，载科学网新闻，http://news.sciencenet.

News, http://news.sciencenet.cn/htmlnews/2013/10/283493.shtm?id=283493, access time: 19:40 on Mar 7, 2017.

27. *Bible*, National Committee of Three-Self Patriotic Movement, the Protestant Churches in China (National TSPM), China Christian Council (CCC), 2009 edition, (John 1: 4, 4:2, 4:3, 4:6, 4:13, Revelation 16:14) p.270, p.286.

28. *The Grand Design,* by Hawking, Leonard Mlodinow [Britain], translated by Wu Zhongchao, Hu'nan Science and Technology Press, 2011 edition, p.153.

29.*Bible*, National Committee of Three-Self Patriotic Movement, the Protestant Churches in China (National TSPM), China Christian Council (CCC), 2009 edition, (Genesis 2:7, John 19:30, Acts 7:59, Ecclesiastes 12:7, Matthew 10:28) p.2, p.130, p.142, p.650, p.12.

30.*Quran,* translated by Ma Jian, China Social Sciences Press, Oct 10, 1981 has 1981 edition, p.218-219, p.356-357.

31. A Thin and Weak Mother Removed A Prefabricated Slab Alone to Rescue Her Crushed Son", by Xi Qinling, published in Sohu News, http://

cn/htmlnews/2013/10/283493.shtm?id=283493，访问时间：2017年3月7日19：40。

27、《圣经》，中国基督教三自爱国运动委员会、中国基督教协会2009年版，（约翰一书4、4: 2、4: 3、4: 6、4: 13启示录16: 14）第270页、第286页。

28、[英] 霍金、蒙洛迪诺:《大设计》，吴忠超译，湖南科学技术出版社2011年版，第153页。

29、《圣经》，中国基督教三自爱国运动委员会、中国基督教协会2009年版，（创2:7、约19:30、徒7:59、传12:7、太10:28）第2页、第130页、第142页、第650页、第12页。

30、《古兰经》，马坚译，中国社会科学出版社1981年4月第1版，第218-219、356-357页。

31、席秦岭:《瘦弱母亲独自挪开200多斤预制板 救出被压儿子》，载 搜 狐 新 闻，http://news.sohu.com/20130421/n373420709.shtml，

news.sohu.com/20130421/n373420709. shtml, access time: 20 : 16 Mar 7, 2017.

32. *Someone Abused a Kitten to Death and Then Put It Next to Its Mother and Scolded by Passers-by for His Inhumanity,* published in Highlights, xilu.com, http://shizheng.xilu. com/20140104/1000150000502158. html, access time: 23:08 Mar 7, 2017

33. *A 6-year-old Boy Had His Eyes Gouged out and Were Thrown away at the Scene of Crime,* Shanxi TV, published in Sina News Video, http:// hebei.sina.com.cn/video/news/2013-08-27/15136436.html , access time: 23:13, Mar 7, 2017

34. *A Jiangsu Man Chopped at Little Children with A Knife and Claimed to Be Revenge, with One Killed and One Injured,* by Liu Qingxiang, published in Tencent News, http://news.qq.com/ a/20141105/022017.htm, access time: 23:16 Mar 7, 2017.

35. *Revealed: Dongguan Beggars Cruelly Mutilated Elderly and Children and Forced Them to Beg,* published in Phoenix Satellite TV, Guangzhou, http://gz.ifeng.com/zaobanche/ detail_2014_03/18/1999361_1.shtml,

访问时间: 2017 年 3 月 7 日 20: 16。

32、西陆网:《虐猫后将尸体放回母猫身边 路人怒骂人性何在》，载西陆网要闻，http://shizheng.xilu. com/20140104/1000150000502158. html，访问时间: 2017 年 3 月 7 日 23: 08。

33、山西电视台:《6 岁男孩被挖掉双眼 眼珠被遗弃案发现场》，载新浪网新闻视频，http://hebei. sina.com.cn/video/news/2013-08-27/15136436.html，访问时间: 2017 年 3 月 7 日 23: 13。

34、刘清香:《江苏男子持刀砍伤幼童致一死一伤 自称系报复》，载腾讯新闻，http://news.qq.com/ a/20141105/022017.htm，访问时间: 2017 年 3 月 7 日 23: 16。

35、凤凰卫视:《东莞丐帮揭秘: 东莞丐帮残忍将老人小孩致残 逼其乞讨》，载凤凰广州，http://gz.ifeng.com/zaobanche/ detail_2014_03/18/1999361_1. shtml，访问时间: 2017 年 3 月 7 日

access time: 23:20 Mar 7, 2017

36. *Jordanian Pilot Hostage Burnt Alive by ISIS,* Dailymail.com, published in China.com Http://news.china.com/hd/11127798/20150204/19275718.html, access time: 23:31 Mar 7, 2017.

37. *Declaration of Independence (1776),* by Thomas Jefferson, etc. published in https://billofrightsinstitute.org/primary-sources/declaration-of-independence Access time: 00:12 Mar 8, 2017.

38. *A Sanitation Worker Who Found A Purse Waited for 2 Hours in the Rain and Moved the Owner to Tears,* dzwww.com/-Qilu Evening News, published in Sina News Center, http://news.sina.com.cn/s/2010-05-18/070620293147.shtml , access time: 23:33, Mar 7, 2017

39. *A Crushed Little Girl Was Ignored by 18 passers-by* But Saved by A Scavenger, by Zhang Shuling, published in Tencent News, http://news.qq.com/a/20111017/000066.htm, access time: 23:35 Mar 7, 2017.

40. *Bible*, National Committee of Three-Self Patriotic Movement of the Protestant Churches in China (National

23: 20。

36、每日邮报:《IS 对被俘约旦飞行员人质执行火刑处决》，载 China.com，http://news.china.com/hd/11127798/20150204/19275718.html，访问时间：2017 年 3 月 7 日 23: 31。

37、杰弗逊等:《美国独立宣言全文及译文》，载华中大法律网，http://law.hust.edu.cn/Law2008/ShowArticle.asp?ArticleID=495，访问时间：2017 年 3 月 8 日 0: 12。

38、大众网 - 齐鲁晚报:《环卫工捡钱包雨中苦等两小时 失主感动落泪》，载新浪新闻中心，http://news.sina.com.cn/s/2010-05-18/070620293147.shtml，访问时间：2017 年 3 月 7 日 23: 33。

39、张淑玲:《18 名路人见死不救 拾荒阿姨救起遭碾压女童》，载腾讯新闻，http://news.qq.com/a/20111017/000066.htm，访问时间：2017 年 3 月 7 日 23: 35。

40、《圣经》，中国基督教三自爱国运动委员会、中国基督教协会 2009 年版，(创 4: 14, 4: 16)第 4 页。

TSPM), China Christian Council (CCC), 2009 edition, (Genesis 4:14, 4:16) p.4.

41. *Bible*, National Committee of Three-Self Patriotic Movement of the Protestant Churches in China (National TSPM), China Christian Council (CCC), 2009 edition, (Genesis 4:7), p.4.

42. *Bible*, National Committee of Three-Self Patriotic Movement of the Protestant Churches in China (National TSPM), China Christian Council (CCC), 2009 edition, (Revelation 12:9) p.284.

43. *Republic* (or Πολιτεία), by Plato [Ancient Greece], translated by Chang Weifu, Xiyuan Publishing House, 2009 edition, p. 131-153, 171-179.

44. *The City of God* (or De civitate Dei), by Aurelius Augustine (or Augustine of Hippo or Saint Augustine) [Ancient Rome], translated by Wang Xiaochao, People's Publishing House, 2006 edition, p.444, p.442, p.536.

45. *Encyclopedia Britannica* (international Chinese edition), China Encyclopedia Publishing House, 1999 edition, p. 549.

46. Sue Dreamwalker, A Letter Under Question?:about The Universal Force Which is Love, Dreamwalker's

41、《圣经》，中国基督教三自爱国运动委员会、中国基督教协会2009年版，（创4：7）第4页。

42、《圣经》，中国基督教三自爱国运动委员会、中国基督教协会2009年版，（启12：9）第284页。

43、[古希腊]柏拉图:《理想国》，常维夫译，西苑出版社2009年版，第131-153页、第171-179页。

44、[古罗马]奥古斯丁:《上帝之城》，王晓朝译，人民出版社2006年版，第444页、第442页、第536页。

45、《不列颠百科全书》（国际中文版），中国大百科全书出版社1999年版，第549页。

Sanctury , https://suedreamwalker. wordpress.com/2015/04/15/a-letter-from-albert-einstein-to-his-daughter-about-the-universal-force-which-is-love/.

47. *Bible*, National Committee of Three-Self Patriotic Movement of the Protestant Churches in China (National TSPM), China Christian Council (CCC), 2009 edition, (Genesis 6:5) p.5.

48. *Shocking images of drowned Syrian boy show tragic plight of refugees,* published on Support the Guardian, https://www.theguardian. com/world/2015/sep/02/shocking-image-of-drowned-syrian-boy-shows-tragic-plight-of-refugees 23:55 Mar 7, 2017.

49. *Great Learning* (Chapter 1), by Zeng Shen, published on gushiwen.cn, http://www.gushice.com/bookview_3043.html, access time 00:01 on Mar 8, 2017.

47、《圣经》，中国基督教三自爱国运动委员会、中国基督教协会 2009 年版，（创 6：5）第 5 页。

48、搜狐公众平台：《这张图让无数网友心碎 3 岁小男孩陈尸海滩》，载搜狐网，http://mt.sohu. com/20150905/n420437297.shtml，访问时间：2017 年 3 月 7 日 23：55。

49、曾参：《大学》（第 1 章），载古诗文网，http://www.gushice. com/bookview_3043.html，访问时间：2017 年 3 月 8 日 0：01。

www.ingramcontent.com/pod-product-compliance
Lightning Source LLC
Chambersburg PA
CBHW022042020426
42335CB00012B/504